Fields of Gold

A classical collection of inspirational quotations
from ancient and modern times.

Compiled by

Priscilla Shepard

Designed by Gordon Brown

The C.R.Gibson Company, Norwalk, Connecticut

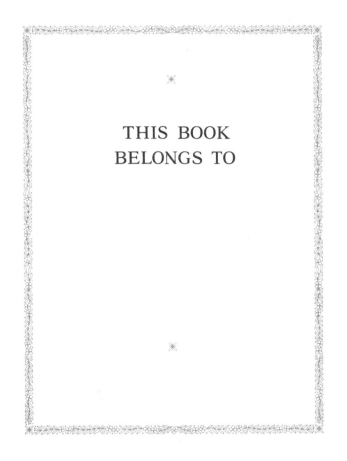

THIS BOOK
BELONGS TO

Contents

Aspiration and Achievement

Opportunity

There is a tide in the affairs of men,
Which, taken at the flood, leads on to fortune;
Omitted, all the voyage of their life
Is bound in shallows and in miseries.
We must take the current when it serves,
Or lose our ventures.

William Shakespeare

The lure of the distant and the difficult is deceptive. The great opportunity is where you are.

John Burroughs

People are always blaming their circumstances for what they are. I don't believe in circumstances. The people who get on in this world are the people who get up and look for the circumstances they want, and if they can't find them, make them.

George Bernard Shaw

Don't refuse to go on an occasional wild-goose chase; that is what wild geese are made for.

Henry S. Haskins

A man in earnest finds means, or if he cannot find, creates them.

William Ellery Channing

Have thy tools ready. God will find thee work.

Charles Kingsley

Do not suppose opportunity will knock twice at your door.

Sebastien R. N. Chamfort

I have never been bored an hour in my life. I get up every morning wondering what new strange glamorous thing is going to happen and it happens at fairly regular intervals. Lady Luck has been good to me and I fancy she has been good to everyone. Only some people are dour, and when she gives them the come-hither with her eyes, they look down or turn away and lift an eyebrow. But me, I give her the wink and away we go.

William Allen White

Not only strike while the iron is hot, but make it hot by striking.

Oliver Cromwell

Everyone has a fair turn to be as great as he pleases.

Jeremy Collier

You will never "find" time for anything. If you want time you must make it.

Charles Buxton

It is no use to wait for your ship to come in, unless you have sent one out.

Belgian Proverb

The commonest form, one most often neglected, and the safest opportunity for the average man to seize, is hard work.

Arthur Brisbane

The world is moving so fast these days that the man who says it can't be done is generally interrupted by someone doing it.

Elbert Hubbard

The reason a lot of people do not recognize an opportunity when they meet it is that it usually goes around wearing overalls and looking like hard work.

Anonymous

To improve the golden moment of opportunity, and catch the good that is within our reach, is the great art of life.

Samuel Johnson

Let not the opportunity that is so fleeting, yet so full, pass neglected away.

O. L. Frothingham

Two roads diverged in a yellow wood,
And sorry I could not travel both
And be one traveler, long I stood
And looked down one as far as I could
To where it bent in the undergrowth;

Then took the other, as just as fair,
And having perhaps the better claim,
Because it was grassy and wanted wear;
Though as for that, the passing there
Had worn them really about the same,

And both that morning equally lay
In leaves no step had trodden black.
Oh, I kept the first for another day!
Yet knowing how way leads on to way,
I doubted if I ever should come back.

I shall be telling this with a sigh
Somewhere ages and ages hence:
Two roads diverged in a wood, and I —
I took the one less traveled by,
And that has made all the difference.

Robert Frost — The Road Not Taken

There is an hour in each man's life
     appointed
To make his happiness, if then he
     seize it.

Francis Beaumont and John Fletcher

A ship in harbour is safe, but that is not what ships are built for.

William Shedd

Great opportunities come to all, but many do not know they have met them.

W. E. Dunning

Every individual has a place to fill in the world, and is important in some respect whether he chooses to be so or not.

Nathaniel Hawthorne

The best men are not those who have waited for chances but who have taken them; besieged the chance; conquered the chance; and made chance the servitor.

Edwin Hubbell Chapin

Some of us miss opportunity because we are too dull to try. Others let opportunity go by, too much startled when they see it to take hold of it.

Arthur Brisbane

The winds and waves are always on the side of the ablest navigators.

Edward Gibbon

One ship drives east and another drives west
     With the selfsame winds that blow.
          'Tis the set of the sails
          And not the gales
     —Which tells us the way to go.

Like the winds of the sea are the ways of fate,
     As we voyage along through life:
          'Tis the set of a soul
          That decides its goal,
     And not the calm or the strife.

Ella Wheeler Wilcox — The Winds of Fate

Today is, for all that we know, the opportunity and occasion of our lives. On what we do or say today may depend the success and completeness of our entire life-struggle. It is for us, therefore, to use every moment of today as if our very eternity were dependent on its words and deeds.

Henry Clay Trumbull

Do you see difficulties in every opportunity or opportunities in every difficulty?

Anonymous

There's place and means for every man alive.

William Shakespeare

I held a moment in my hand,
    Brilliant as a star,
    Fragile as a flower,
    A shiny sliver out of one hour.
I dropped it carelessly.
    O God! I knew not
    I held opportunity.

Hazel Lee — What Might Have Been

Isn't it strange
That princes and kings,
And clowns that caper
In sawdust rings,
And common people
Like you and me
Are builders for eternity?

Each is given a bag of tools,
A shapeless mass,
A book of rules;
And each must make,
Ere life is flown,
A stumbling-block
Or a stepping-stone.

R. L. Sharpe — A Bag of Tools

We must not hope to be mowers,
    and to gather the ripe gold ears,
Unless we have first been sowers
    And watered the furrows with tears.

It is not just as we take it,
    This mystical world of ours,
Life's field will yield as we make it
    A harvest of thorns or of flowers.

Johann Wolfgang von Goethe

We have no wings, we cannot soar;
But we have feet to scale and climb
By slow degrees, and more and more,
The cloudy summits of our time.

Henry Wadsworth Longfellow

There is no future in any job. The future lies
in the man who holds the job.

George W. Crane

Four things come not back:
    The spoken word;
    The sped arrow;
    Time past;
The neglected opportunity.

Omar Ibn, Al Halif

They do me wrong who say I come no more
When once I knock and fail to find you in;
For every day I stand outside your door,
And bid you wake, and rise to fight and win.

Wail not for precious chances passed away!
Weep not for golden ages on the wane.
Each night I burn the records of the day,
At sunrise every soul is born again.

Though deep in mire, wring not your hands and
    weep:
I lend my arm to all who say, "I can!"
No shamefaced outcast ever sank so deep,
But yet might rise and be again a man!

Walter Malone — Opportunity

Lost, yesterday, somewhere between sunrise
and sunset, two golden hours, each set with
sixty diamond minutes. No reward is offered
for they are gone forever.

Horace Mann

Look upon the day-star moving,
Life and tyme are worth improving.
Seize the moments while they stay!
    Seize and use them,
    Lest ye lose them,
And lament the wasted day.

Anonymous

Endeavor

Nothing left loose ever does anything creative.
No horse gets anywhere until he is harnessed.
No steam or gas ever drives anything until
it is confined. No Niagara is ever turned into
light and power until it is funneled. No life
ever grows until it is focused, dedicated,
disciplined.

Harry Emerson Fosdick

The man who does his work, any work, conscientiously, must always be in one sense a great man.

Dinah Maria Mulock Craik

When God wanted sponges and oysters, He made them, and put one on a rock, and the other in the mud. When He made man He did not make him to be a sponge or an oyster; He made him with feet, and hands, and head, and heart, and vital blood, and a place to use them, and said to him, "Go, work!"

Henry Ward Beecher — Go, Work!

Whatever is worth doing at all, is worth doing well.

Lord Chesterfield

The man who rows the boat generally doesn't have time to rock it.

Anonymous

If you do your work with complete faithfulness, ... you are making as genuine a contribution to the substance of the universal good as is the most brilliant worker whom the world contains.

Phillips Brooks

Let me but do my work from day to day,
In field or forest, at the desk or loom.
In roaring market-place or tranquil room;
Let me but find it in my heart to say
When vagrant wishes beckon me astray,
"This is my work; my blessing, not my doom;
Of all who live, I am the one by whom
This work can best be done in the right way."

Then shall I see it not too great, nor small,
To suit my spirit and to prove my powers;
Then shall I cheerful greet the laboring hours,
And cheerful turn when the long shadows fall
At eventide, to play and love and rest,
Because I know for me my work is best.

Henry van Dyke — Let Me Do My Work Today

I like work; it fascinates me. I can sit and look at it for hours. I love to keep it by me: the idea of getting rid of it nearly breaks my heart.

Jerome K. Jerome

No person who is enthusiastic about his work has anything to fear from life.

Samuel Goldwyn

The moment a man can really do his work, he becomes speechless about it; all words are idle to him; all theories. Does a bird need to theorize about building its nest, or boast of it when built? All good work is essentially done that way; without hesitation; without difficulty; without boasting.

John Ruskin

I never did anything worth doing by accident; nor did any of my inventions come by accident; they came by work.

Thomas Edison

The beauty of work depends upon the way we meet it, whether we arm ourselves each morning to attack it as an enemy that must be vanquished before night comes — or whether we open our eyes with the sunrise to welcome it as an approaching friend who will keep us delightful company and who will make us feel at evening that the day was well worth its fatigue.

Lucy Larcom

Do your work — not just your work and no more, but a little more for the lavishing's sake; that little more which is worth all the rest. And if you suffer as you must, and if you doubt as you must, do your work. Put your heart into it and the sky will clear. Then out of your very doubt and suffering will be born the supreme joy of life.

Dean Briggs

Happiness lies not in the mere possession of money; it lies in the joy of achievement, in the thrill of creative effort. The joy and moral stimulation of work no longer must be forgotten in the mad chase of evanescent profits.

Franklin Delano Roosevelt

The greatest calamity is not to have failed; but to have failed to try.

Anonymous

I start where the last man left off.

Thomas A. Edison

I don't pity any man who does hard work worth doing. I admire him. I pity the creature who doesn't work, at whichever end of the social scale he may regard himself as being.

Theodore Roosevelt

Every year I live I am more convinced that the waste of life lies in the love we have not given, the powers we have not used, the selfish prudence that will risk nothing, and which, shirking pain, misses happiness as well. No one ever yet was the poorer in the long run for having once in a lifetime "let out all the length of all the reins."

Mary Cholmondeley

Don't believe the world owes you a living; the world owes you nothing — it was here first.

R. J. Burdette

No one ever gets very far unless he accomplishes the impossible at least once a day.

Elbert Hubbard

If you want knowledge, you must toil for it; if food, you must toil for it; and if pleasure, you must toil for it; toil is the law.

John Ruskin

I don't like work — no man does — but I like what is in work — the chance to find yourself. Your own reality — for yourself, not for others — what no other man can ever know.

Joseph Conrad

So much unhappiness, it seems to me, is due to nerves; and bad nerves are the result of having nothing to do, or doing a thing badly, unsuccessfully or incompetently. Of all the unhappy people in the world, the unhappiest are those who have not found something they want to do. True happiness comes to him who does his work well, followed by a relaxing and refreshing period of rest. True happiness comes from the right amount of work for the day.

Lin Yutang

No man is born into the world whose work Is not born with him; there is always work, And tools to work withal, for those who will; And blessed are the horny hands of toil!

James Russell Lowell

It is impossible to enjoy idling thoroughly unless one has plenty of work to do.

Jerome K. Jerome

One thing I am resolved upon: I will not be a sponge or a parasite. I will give an honest equivalent for what I get. I want no man's money for which I have not rendered a full return. I want no wages that I have not earned. If I work for any man or any company or any institution, I will render a full, ample, generous service. If I work for the city or the state or the nation, I will give my best thought, my best effort, my most conscientious and efficient endeavor. No man, no body of men, shall ever be made poor by their dealings with me. If I can give a little more than I get every time, in that shall be my happiness. The great commonwealth of human society shall not be the loser through me. I will take good care to put into the common fund more than I take out.

Washington Gladden

When a man's pursuit gradually makes his face shine and grow handsome, be sure it is a worthy one.

William James

Labor, if it were not necessary for the existence, would be indispensable for the happiness of man.

Samuel Johnson

Happiness is a rebound from hard work. One of the follies of man is to assume that he can enjoy mere emotion. As well try to eat beauty! Happiness must be tricked. She loves to see men work. She loves sweat, weariness, self-sacrifice. She will not be found in palaces but lurking in cornfields and factories and on over littered desks. She crowns the unconscious head of the busy man.

David Grayson

9

The most unhappy of all men is the man who cannot tell what he is going to do, that has got no work cut out for him in the world, and does not go into any. For work is the grand cure of all the maladies and miseries that ever beset mankind — honest work which you intend getting done.

Thomas Carlyle

In order that people may be happy in their work, these three things are needed: they must be fit for it; they must not do too much of it; and they must have a sense of success in it — not a doubtful sense, such as needs some testimony of other people for its confirmation, but a sure sense, or rather knowledge, that so much work has been done well, and fruitfully done, whatever the world may say or think about it.

John Ruskin

Man must work. He may work grudgingly or he may work gratefully; he may work as a man, or he may work as a machine. There is no work so rude that he may not exalt it; no work so impassive that he may not breathe a soul into it; no work so dull that he may not enliven it.

Henry Giles

There is always somebody or something to work for; and while there is, life must be, and shall become, worth living.

Le Baron Russell Briggs

Work, and thou wilt bless the day
    Ere the toil be done;
They that work not, cannot pray,
    Cannot feel the sun.
God is living, working still,
    All things work and move;
Work, or lose the power to will,
    Lose the power to love.

John Sullivan Dwight

Blessed is the man who has some congenial work, some occupation in which he can put his heart, and which affords a complete outlet to all the forces there are in him.

John Burroughs

Find your place and hold it: find your work and do it. And put everything you've got into it.

Edward William Bok

Thank God every morning when you get up that you have something to do, which must be done, whether you like it or not. Being forced to work and forced to do your best, will breed in you temperance, self-control, diligence, strength of will, content and a hundred other virtues which the idle never know.

Charles Kingsley

A mistake at least proves that somebody stopped talking long enough to do something.

Anonymous

Work thou for pleasure — paint, or
        sing, or carve
The thing thou lovest, though the body
        starve —
Who works for glory misses oft the
        goal;
Who works for money coins his very
        soul.
Work for the work's sake, then, and it
        may be
That these things shall be added unto
        thee.

Kenyon Cox

The handling of tools need not put a gulf between man and God; it does not demean their user, does not cheat life of dignity, does not of itself desert men to the impersonal world of things. To use hammer, plane, chisel, and saw belongs to a tradition which the Son of God himself reverenced. When he used the plumbline, the God-man lost none of his glory. The workshop is a legitimate area for week-long service of God and man. Indeed, the profound hope of the labor world in the twentieth century is the hammer and sickle in the hand of Christ and his servants.

Carl F. H. Henry

Blessed is he who has found his work; let him ask no other blessedness.

Thomas Carlyle

10

Whatever I have tried to do in life, I have tried with all my heart to do well; whatever I have devoted myself to, I have devoted myself to completely.

Charles Dickens

Far better it is to dare mighty things, to win glorious triumphs, even though checkered by failure, than to take rank with those poor spirits who neither enjoy much nor suffer much, because they live in the grey twilight that knows not victory nor defeat.

Theodore Roosevelt

Work is doing what you now enjoy for the sake of a future which you clearly see and desire. Drudgery is doing under strain what you don't now enjoy and for no end that you can now appreciate.

Richard C. Cabot

Perseverence

Our greatest glory is not in never falling but in rising every time we fall.

Confucius

They fail, and they alone, who have not striven.

Thomas Bailey Aldrich

An ounce of performance is worth more than a pound of preachment.

Elbert Hubbard

Life affords no higher pleasure than that of surmounting difficulties, passing from one step of success to another, forming new wishes, and seeing them gratified. He that labors in any great or laudable undertaking has his fatigues first supported by hope, and afterwards rewarded by joy.

Samuel Johnson

Let us, then, be up and doing,
    With a heart for any fate;
Still achieving, still pursuing,
    Learn to labor and to wait.

Henry Wadsworth Longfellow

I studied the lives of great men and famous women; and I found that the men and women who got to the top were those who did the jobs they had in hand, with everything they had of energy and enthusiasm and hard work.

Harry S. Truman

Do what you love. Know your own bone; gnaw at it, bury it, unearth it, and gnaw it still.

Henry David Thoreau

It is not he that enters upon any career, or starts in any race, but he that runs well and perseveringly, that gains the plaudits of others or the approval of his own conscience.

Alexander Campbell

I have learned that success is to be measured not so much by the position that one has reached in life as by the obstacles which he has overcome while trying to succeed.

Booker T. Washington

Diligence is the mother of good luck.

Benjamin Franklin

Perseverance is a great element of success. If you only knock long enough and loud enough at the gate, you are sure to wake up somebody.

Henry Wadsworth Longfellow

Nothing in the world can take the place of persistence. Talent will not; nothing is more common than unsuccessful men with talent. Genius will not; unrewarded genius is almost a proverb. Education will not; the world is full of educated derelicts. Persistence and determination alone are omnipotent. The slogan "press on!" has solved and always will solve the problems of the human race.

Calvin Coolidge

Consider the postage stamp, my son. It secures success through its ability to stick to one thing till it gets there.

Josh Billings

Positive anything is better than negative nothing.

Elbert Hubbard

11

Persistent people begin their success where others end in failures.

Edward Eggleston

The temptation to be discouraged is common to every man. Walt Disney was dismissed from a major newspaper and told that he had no talent as an artist; Richard Byrd, famous pilot, and who was first to reach the South Pole, crash-landed the first two times he soloed in a plane, and the third time he flew head on into another plane; Rod Serling wrote and marketed 40 stories before he sold one; Zane Grey was fired by five newspapers because he couldn't do the job as a reporter.

Anonymous

If we begin with certainties, we shall end in doubts; but if we begin with doubts, and are patient in them, we shall end in certainties.

Francis Bacon

God loves to help him who strives to help himself.

Aeschylus

What on earth would a man do with himself if something did not stand in his way?

H. G. Wells

Don't let life discourage you; everyone who got where he is had to begin where he was.

Richard L. Evans

The difference between perseverance and obstinacy is, that one comes from a strong will, and the other from a strong won't.

Henry Ward Beecher

The real difference between men is energy. A strong will, a settled purpose, an invincible determination can accomplish almost anything; and in this lies the distinction between great men and little men.

Thomas Fuller

Genius is one per cent inspiration and ninety-nine per cent perspiration.

Thomas A. Edison

The conditions of conquest are always easy. We have but to toil awhile, believe always — and never turn back.

W. G. Simms

Nothing will ever be attempted if all possible objections must be first overcome.

Samuel Johnson

When you get into a tight place, and everything goes against you, till it seems as if you could not go on a minute longer, never give up then, for that's just the place and the time that the tide will turn.

Harriet Beecher Stowe

To run well we must run to the end.

M. L. Hagoon

Say not, the struggle nought availeth,
The labor and the wounds are vain,
The enemy faints not, nor faileth,
And as things have been they remain.

If hopes were dupes, fears may be liars;
It may be, in yon smoke concealed,
Your comrades chase e'en now the fliers,
And, but for you, possess the field.

For while the tired waves, vainly breaking,
Seem here no painful inch to gain,
Far back, through creeks and inlets making,
Comes silent, flooding in, the main.

And not by eastern windows only,
When daylight comes, comes in the light;
In front, the sun climbs slow, how slowly!
But westward, look, the land is bright!

Arthur Hugh Clough — Say Not

Training is everything. The peach was once a bitter almond; cauliflower is but cabbage with a college education.

Mark Twain

It is the greatest of all mistakes to do nothing because you can only do a little. Do what you can.

Sydney Smith

Genius, that power which dazzles mortal eyes,
Is often perseverance in disguise.

Henry Willard Austin

Persistency attracts confidence, more than talents and accomplishments.

E. P. Whipple

Doing easily what others find difficult is talent; doing what is impossible for talent is genius.

Henri-Frédéric Amiel

I find the great thing in this world is not so much where we stand, as in what direction we are moving. To reach the port of heaven, we must sail sometimes with the wind, and sometimes against it; but we must sail, and not drift, nor lie at anchor.

Oliver Wendell Holmes

The greater the obstacle the more glory in overcoming it.

Jean Baptiste Molière

That which grows fast withers as rapidly; that which grows slowly endures.

Josiah Gilbert Holland

However things may seem, no evil thing is success, and no good thing is failure.

Samuel Longfellow

One man of tolerable abilities may work great changes, and accomplish great affairs among mankind, if he first forms a good plan, and, cutting off all amusements or other employments that would divert his attention, makes the execution of that same plan his sole study and business.

Benjamin Franklin

One who fears limits his activities. Failure is only the opportunity to more intelligently begin again.

Henry Ford

He who wants to do a great deal at once will never do anything.

Samuel Johnson

The spirit of "Let George do it" will never win in sports or in the game of life.

Fielding H. Yost

'Twixt failure and success the point's so fine
Men sometimes know not when they touch
  the line,
Just when the pearl was waiting one more
  plunge,
How many a struggler has thrown up the
  sponge!
Then take this honey from the bitterest cup:
"There is no failure save in giving up!"

Howard Dillingham — Don't Give Up

Genius is the capacity for taking infinite pains.

Thomas Carlyle

One of the rarest things that man ever does is to do the best he can.

Josh Billings

It takes less time to do a thing right than it does to explain why you did it wrong.

Henry Wadsworth Longfellow

The saints are the sinners who keep trying.

Robert Louis Stevenson

He has half the deed done, who has made a beginning.

Horace

The man who feels certain he will not succeed is seldom mistaken.

Frances Osgood

Perseverance gives power to weakness, and opens to poverty the world's wealth. It spreads fertility over the barren landscape, and bids the choicest flowers and fruits spring up and flourish in the desert abode of thorns and briars.

S. G. Goodrich

The worst bankrupt in the world is the man who has lost his enthusiasm. Let him lose everything but enthusiasm and he will come through again to success.

Anonymous

Attempt the end, and never stand in doubt;
Nothing's so hard but search will find it out.

Robert Herrick

I believe when you are in any contest you
should work like there is, to the very last
minute, a chance to lose it.

Dwight D. Eisenhower

Just a turn in the road,
A turn to the right,
Then, you'll find a pathway—
A beautiful sight.

Your pathway to heaven!
You can't go astray;
You'll see a bright starlet
To light up your way.

All hope will be reborn—
New vistas unfold.
Push on to your mountain—
Push on to your goal.

Just keep right on striving,
Though heavy the load,
And you'll come at last
To the turn in the road.

A turn in the road
Where life starts anew.
A turn in the road
Where dreams will come true.

So, lift up your head
And laugh at your load;
At last you will come
To the turn in the road.

Hilda Gross Feinblum — A Turn In The Road

If seeds in the black earth can turn into such
beautiful roses, what might not the heart of man
become in its long journey toward the stars?

Gilbert Keith Chesterton

Ride on! Rough-shod if need be, smooth-shod
if that will do, but ride on! Ride on over all
obstacles, and win the race!

Charles Dickens

The desire to begin over again is one of those
longings so common and universal that we may
say it is a native instinct . . . that we have
failed, and failed again and again, need not
intimidate us for a new trial. Aspirations,
imperfections, and failures are intimations of
future achievements. Defeats foretell future
successes. The sin to be dreaded is the unlit
lamp and ungirt loin. Our light must be burning
however dimly, and we must keep on the right
road, however often we stumble on the way.
Under no circumstances can it be true that
there is not something to be done, as well as
something to be suffered. Let us sit down before
the Lord and count our resources, and see
what we are not fit for, and give up wishing
for it. Let us decide honestly what we can do,
and then do it with all our might.

Amelia E. Barr

Not perfection as a final goal, but the ever-
enduring process of perfecting, maturing,
refining, is the aim in living. The good man is
the man who, no matter how morally unworthy
he has been, is moving to become better. Such
a conception makes one severe in judging
himself and humane in judging others.

John Dewey

Behold the turtle: He makes progress only
when he sticks his neck out.

James Bryant Conant

Thank God, a man can grow!
He is not bound
With earthward gaze to creep along the
    ground:
Though his beginnings be but poor and low,
Thank God, a man can grow!
The fire upon his altars may burn dim,
The torch he lighted may in darkness fail,
And nothing to rekindle it avail—
Yet high beyond his dull horizon's rim,
Arcturus and the Pleiades beckon him.

Florence Earle Coates — Per Aspera

The highest reward for man's toil is not what
he gets for it but what he becomes by it.

John Ruskin

How does the soul grow? Not all in a minute;
Now it may lose ground, and now it may win it;
Now it resolves, and again the will faileth;
Now it rejoiceth, and now it bewaileth;
Now its hopes fructify, and then they are
    blighted;
Now it walks sullenly, now gropes benighted;
Fed by discouragements, taught by disaster;
So it goes forward, now slower, now faster,
Till all the pain is past, and failure made whole,
It is full grown, and the Lord rules the soul.

Susan Coolidge

A tree that it takes both arms to encircle grew
from a tiny rootlet. A many-storied pagoda is
built by placing one brick upon another brick.
A journey of three thousand miles is begun
by a single step.

Lao-tzu

I do not know what we are here for upon this
wonderful and beautiful earth, this incalculably
interesting earth, unless it is to crowd into a
few short years every possible fine experience
and adventure; unless it is to live our lives to
the uttermost; unless it is to seize upon every
fresh impression, develop every latent capacity;
unless it is to grow as much as ever we have
it in our power to grow.

David Grayson

Nature does not require that we be perfect; it
requires only that we grow, and we can do this
as well from a mistake as from a success.

Rollo May

The urge of growth is the creative urge, the
creative power in the universe. It lures and fires
us in the people we love. It lights enthusiasm
for an adventure, for a college, for a business,
for a child, for a garden, for a home or a family,
for the majesty of a forest after sunset. In such
moments we feel more alive, more genuinely
ourselves than usual. The fire within us is fed
by the life around us and we get into the current
of that life. In such moments we grow in
sympathy, in self-mastery, in honesty, or in
sensitiveness to beauty.

Richard C. Cabot

It is not for man to rest in absolute contentment. He is born to hopes and aspirations as
sparks fly upward unless he has brutified his
nature and quenched the spirit of immortality
which is his portion.

Robert Southey

When I was young I felt so small
And frightened for the world was tall.

And even grasses seemed to me
A forest of immensity.

Until I learned that I could grow,
A glance would leave them far below.

Spanning a tree's height with my eye,
Suddenly I soared as high,

And fixing on a star I grew,
I pushed my head against the blue!

Still, like a singing lark, I find
Rapture to leave the grass behind.

And sometimes standing in a crowd
My lips are cool against a cloud.

Anne Morrow Lindbergh — Height

The strongest principle of growth lies in human
choice.

George Eliot

The measure of success is not whether you
have a tough problem to deal with, but whether
it's the same problem you had last year.

John Foster Dulles

Success

Whatever you are by nature, keep to it; never
desert your line of talent. Be what nature
intended you for, and you will succeed.

Sydney Smith

Just do a thing and don't talk about it. This is
the great secret of success.

Sarah Grand

Nothing great was ever achieved without enthusiasm.

Henry Ford

There was never a person who did anything worth doing that did not receive more than he gave.

Henry Ward Beecher

Success slips away from you like sand through the fingers, like water through a leaky pail, unless success is held tightly by hard work, day by day, night by night, year in and year out. Everyone who is not looking forward to going to seed looks forward to working harder and harder and more fruitfully as long as he lasts.

Stuart Pratt Sherman

Every great and commanding moment in the annals of the world is the triumph of some enthusiasm.

Ralph Waldo Emerson

No man can stand on top because he is put there.

H. H. Vreeland

That man is a success who has lived well, laughed often and loved much; who has gained the respect of intelligent men and the love of children; who has filled his niche and accomplished his task; who leaves the world better than he found it, whether by an improved poppy, a perfect poem or a rescued soul; who never lacked appreciation of earth's beauty or failed to express it; who looked for the best in others and gave the best he had.

Robert Louis Stevenson

There isn't any map on the road to success; you have to find your own way.

Anonymous

If a man write a better book, preach a better sermon, or make a better mousetrap than his neighbor, though he build his house in the woods, the world will make a beaten path to his door.

Ralph Waldo Emerson

The common idea that success spoils people by making them vain, egotistic, and self-complacent is erroneous; on the contrary it makes them, for the most part, humble, tolerant, and kind. Failure makes people bitter and cruel.

W. Somerset Maugham

We have forty million reasons for failure, but not a single excuse.

Rudyard Kipling

Hit the ball over the fence and you can take your time going around the bases.

John W. Raper

Try not to become a man of success but rather try to become a man of value.

Albert Einstein

The secret of success is constancy of purpose.

Benjamin Disraeli

It is not the going out of port, but the coming in, that determines the success of a voyage.

Henry Ward Beecher

To do for the world more than the world does for you — that is success.

Henry Ford

The talent of success is nothing more than doing what you can do well; and doing well whatever you do, without a thought of fame.

Henry Wadsworth Longfellow

The only true measure of success is the ratio between what we might have done on the one hand and the thing we have made of ourselves on the other.

H. G. Wells

If you want to be not only successful, but personally, happily, and permanently successful, then do your job in a way that puts lights in people's faces. Do that job in such a way that, even when you are out of sight, folks will always know which way you went by the lamps left behind.

Kenneth McFarland

Hope and Expectation

Anticipation

The best verse hasn't been rhymed yet,
   The best house hasn't been planned,
The highest peak hasn't been climbed yet,
   The mightiest rivers aren't spanned;
Don't worry and fret, faint-hearted,
   The chances have just begun
For the best jobs haven't been started,
   The best work hasn't been done.

                Berton Braley — No Chance

We must always remember that God has given
to every soul the responsibility of deciding
what its character and destiny shall be.

                Charles E. Jefferson

Almighty God doesn't call any man or woman
to a trivial or unimportant life work. If you
can't see your job as being somehow vital and
meaningful to mankind, change it or get out
of it.

                John Oliver Nelson

God gives every bird his food, but He does
not throw it into the nest.

                Josiah Gilbert Holland

The natural flights of the human mind are not
from pleasure to pleasure, but from hope to
hope.

                Samuel Johnson

All human wisdom is summed up in two
words — wait and hope.

                Alexandre Dumas, père

Happiness depends chiefly on our cheerful
acceptance of routine, on our refusal to assume,
as many do, that daily work and daily duty
are a kind of slavery.

                Le Baron Russell Briggs

Never stand begging for that which you have
the power to earn.

                Miguel de Cervantes

To suffer woes which Hope thinks infinite;
To forgive wrongs darker than death or night;
   To defy Power, which seems omnipotent;
   To love and bear; to hope till Hope creates
From its own wreck the thing it contemplates;
   Neither to change, nor falter, nor repent:
This, like thy glory, Titan, is to be
Good, great and joyous, beautiful and free;
This is alone Life, Joy, Empire, and Victory.

                Percy Bysshe Shelley

Hope is a much better stimulant of life than
any happiness.

                Friedrich Nietzsche

Hope is a thing with feathers
That perches in the soul,
And sings the tune without the words,
And never stops at all.

                Emily Dickinson

God sometimes puts us on our back so that
we may look upward.

                Unknown

Great hopes make great men.

                Thomas Fuller

I know of no more encouraging fact than the unquestionable ability of man to elevate his life by a conscious endeavor.

Henry David Thoreau

Hope is itself a species of happiness, and, perhaps, the chief happiness which this world affords.

Samuel Johnson

The day will bring some lovely thing,
I say it over each new dawn;
"Some gay, adventurous thing to hold
Against my heart, when it is gone."
And so I rise and go to meet
The day with wings upon my feet.

I come upon it unaware—
Some sudden beauty without name;
A snatch of song, a breath of pine;
A poem lit with golden flame;
High tangled bird notes, keenly thinned,
Like flying color on the wing.

No day has ever failed me quite—
Before the grayest day is done,
I come upon some misty bloom
Or a late line of crimson sun.
Each night I pause, remembering
Some gay, adventurous, lovely thing.

Grace Noll Crowell — The Day

There are no hopeless situations; there are only men who have grown hopeless about them.

Clare Boothe Luce

Man is, properly speaking, based on Hope; he has no other possession but Hope.

Thomas Carlyle

Hope and patience are two sovereign remedies for all, the surest reposals, the softest cushions to lean on in adversity.

Robert Burton

Greatly begin! Though thou have time
But for a line, be that sublime—
Not failure, but low aim is crime.

James Russell Lowell

Perhaps the day may come, oh anxious world
When we, with gallant hope, will win life's fame.
Till then, we'll climb the ladder, step by step,
Striving till we've reached our highest aim.

Never give up the hope that we shall win
The temporal joys of love and life unknown.
If we but walk the straight and narrow way,
We'll build ourselves a shining stepping-stone.

Sara Anderson — Reaching Our Goal

When all else is lost, the future still remains.

Christian N. Bovee

The poorest of all men is not the man without a cent; it is the man without a dream.

Anonymous

A handful of pine-seed will cover mountains
with the green majesty of forest.
I too will set my face to the wind
and throw my handful of seed on high.

Fiona Macleod

A man's ambition should be high;
Not scratched in dirt—carved in the sky.

Thomas L. Forest

Make no little plans; they have no magic to stir men's blood and probably themselves will not be realized. Make big plans, aim high in hope and work, remembering that a logical diagram once recorded will be a living thing asserting itself with ever-growing insistency.

Daniel H. Burnham

Let us be of good cheer, remembering that the misfortunes hardest to bear are those which never happen.

James Russell Lowell

Ah, but a man's reach should exceed his grasp,
Or what's a heaven for?

Robert Browning

If a man constantly aspires, is he not elevated? Did ever a man try heroism, magnanimity, truth, sincerity, and find that there was not advantage in them—that it was a vain endeavor?

Henry David Thoreau

To each one is given a marble to carve for the
  wall;
A stone that is needed to heighten the beauty
  of all;
And only his soul has the magic to give it
  grace;
And only his hands have the cunning to put it
  in place.

Yes, the task that is given to each one, no
  other can do;
So the errand is waiting; it has waited through
  ages for you.
And now you appear; and the hushed ones
  are turning their gaze,
To see what you do with your chance in the
  chamber of days.

Edwin Markham — The Task That Is Given to You

Man is preeminently a creative animal, pre-
destined to strive consciously for an object and
to engage in engineering — that is, incessantly
and eternally to make new roads, wherever
they may lead.

Fyodor Dostoyevsky

Be not simply good — be good for something.

Henry David Thoreau

We men of Earth here have the stuff
Of Paradise—we have enough!
We need no other stones to build
The Temple of the Unfulfilled—
No other ivory for the doors—
No other marble for the floors—
No other cedar for the beam
And dome of man's immortal dream.
Here on the paths of every-day—
Here on the common human way
Is all the stuff the gods would take
To build a Heaven, to mold and make
New Edens. Ours the stuff sublime
To build Eternity in time!

Edwin Markham

Too low they build, who build beneath the stars.

Edward Young

Anything that one does, from cooking a dinner
to governing a state, becomes a work of art if
motivated by the passion for excellence and
done as well as it can be. A man who does his
job in that spirit will be the one who gets the
most satisfaction out of life.

L. P. Jacks

If you can't be a pine on the top of the hill,
  Be a scrub in the valley—but be
The best little scrub by the side of the rill;
  Be a bush if you can't be a tree.

If you can't be a bush, be a bit of the grass,
  Some highway happier make;
If you can't be a muskie, then just be a bass—
  But the liveliest bass in the lake!

We can't all be captains, we've got to be crew,
  There's something for all of us here,
There's big work to do, and there's lesser to do,
  And the task we must do is the near.

If you can't be a highway, then just be a trail,
  If you can't be the sun, be a star;
It isn't by size that you win or you fail—
  Be the best of whatever you are!

Douglas Malloch — Be the Best of Whatever You Are

One hour of life, crowded to the full with
glorious action, and filled with noble risk, is
worth whole years of those mean observances
of paltry decorum, in which men steal through
existence, like sluggish waters through a marsh,
without either honour or observation.

Sir Walter Scott

Great minds have purposes, others have wishes.

Washington Irving

It is the stars as not known to science that I
would know, the stars which the lonely traveler
knows.

Henry David Thoreau

The purpose of life is not to be happy — but
to matter, to be productive, to be useful, to
have it make a difference that you lived at all.

Leo Rosten

Let each become all that he was created capable of being, expand, if possible, to his full growth and show himself at length in his own shape and stature be these what they may.

Thomas Carlyle

There is one great and universal wish of mankind expressed in all religions, in all art and philosophy, and in all human life: the wish to pass beyond himself as he now is.

Beatrice Hinkle

The urge to grow; the urge to climb,
  I count the greatest gift of time.
This is the dream that leads us on,
  Always to better what is gone;
To build, to fashion and invent
  Peace at the forge of discontent;
Always to look at life and see
  Glimpses of better days to be;
Ever to walk with restless feet
  A world that never is complete.
What good were Time should dawn the sun
  Upon a day when dreams were done,
When every venture has been tried
  And all mankind were satisfied?
Then we should merely live and browse
  As dumb and placid as are cows.

Edgar A. Guest — Restlessness

Ideals

He who cherishes a beautiful ideal in his heart, will one day realize it. Columbus cherished a vision of another world, and he discovered it; Copernicus fostered the vision of a multiplicity of worlds and a wider universe, and he revealed it; Buddha beheld the vision of a spiritual world of stainless beauty and perfect peace, and he entered into it. Cherish your visions; cherish your ideals; cherish the music that stirs in your heart, the beauty that forms in your mind, the loveliness that drapes your purest thoughts, for out of them will grow all delightful conditions, all heavenly environment; of these, if you but remain true to them, your world will at last be built.

James Allen

Ideals are like stars; you will not succeed in touching them with your hands, but like the seafaring man on the desert of waters, you choose them as your guides, and, following them, you reach your destiny.

Carl Schurz

Hold fast to dreams
For if dreams die
Life is a broken-winged bird
That cannot fly.

Hold fast to dreams
For when dreams go
Life is a barren field
Frozen with snow.

Langston Hughes

The submergence of self in the pursuit of an ideal, the readiness to spend one's self without measure, prodigally, almost ecstatically, for something apprehended as great and noble, spend one's self without knowing why — some of us like to believe that this is what religion means.

Benjamin Cardozo

To accomplish great things, we must not only act but also dream, not only plan but also believe.

Anatole France

The power of ideals is incalculable. We see no power in a drop of water. But let it get into a crack in the rock and be turned to ice, and it splits the rock; turned into steam, it drives the pistons of the most powerful engines. Something has happened to it which makes active and effective the power that is latent in it.

Albert Schweitzer

We aspire by setting up ideals and striving after them.

Harry Emerson Fosdick

God gave man an upright countenance to survey the heavens, and to look upward to the stars.

Ovid

Hitch your wagon to a star.

Ralph Waldo Emerson

I saw the mountains stand
Silent, wonderful, and grand,
Looking across the land
When the golden light was falling
On distant dome and spire;
And I heard a low voice calling,
"Come up higher, come up higher,"
From the lowlands and the mire,
From the mists of earth's desire,
From the vain pursuit of pelf,
From the attitude of self:
"Come up higher, come up higher."

James S. Clark — Come Up Higher

Our ideals are our better selves.

Amos Bronson Alcott

I feel that the best thing in man or woman
is being "there." Physical bravery, which is
always inspiring, is surprisingly common; but
the sure and steady quality of being "there"
belongs to comparatively few. This is why we
hear on every hand, "If you want a thing well
done, do it yourself"; not because the man
who wants it done is best able to do it, but
because to many persons it seems a hopeless
quest to look for anyone who cares enough
for them, who can put himself vigorously
enough into their places, to give them his best,
to give them intelligent, unremitting, loyal
service until the job is done — not half-done,
or nine-tenths done, or ninety-nine hundredths
done, but done with intelligence and devotion
in every nail he drives or every comma he
writes. Being "there" is the result of three
things — intelligence, constant practice, and
something hard to define but not too fancifully
called an ideal.

Le Baron Russell Briggs

Keep thou thy dreams — the tissue of all wings
    Is woven first from them; from dreams are
        made
The precious and imperishable things,
    Whose loveliness lives on, and does not fade.

Virna Sheard

No vision and you perish;
    No ideal, and you're lost;
Your heart must ever cherish
    Some faith at any cost.

Some hope, some dream to cling to,
    Some rainbow in the sky,
Some melody to sing to,
    Some service that is high.

Harriet Du Autermont — Some Faith at Any Cost

The pure, the bright, the beautiful
    That stirred our hearts in youth,
The impulses to wordless prayer,
    The streams of love and truth,
The longing after something lost,
    The spirit's yearning cry,
The striving after better hopes —
    These things can never die.

Charles Dickens — Things That Never Die

A man who thinks that he is all that he ought
to be is obviously not what he ought to be.
Anyone who has reached his ideal has not
an ideal, and a man without an ideal is not
a man, for the world of moral action is as
inexhaustible as the world of knowledge.

C. Delisle Burns

The dreamers are the saviors of the world. As
the visible world is sustained by the invisible,
so men, through all their trials and sins and
sordid vocations, are nourished by the beautiful
visions of their solitary dreamers. Humanity
cannot forget its dreamers; it cannot let their
ideals fade and die; it lives in them; it knows
them as the realities which it shall one day see
and know.

James Allen

Some men see things as they are and say, why?
I dream things that never were and say, why
not?

George Bernard Shaw

Don't part with your illusions. When they are
gone you may still exist but you have ceased
to live.

Mark Twain

When I could not sleep for cold,
I had enough fire in my brain,
And builded, with roofs of gold,
My beautiful castles in Spain.

James Russell Lowell

Hold fast your dreams!
Within your heart
Keep one still, secret spot
Where dreams may go,
And, sheltered so,
May thrive and grow
Where doubt and fear are not.
O keep a place apart,
Within your heart,
For little dreams to go!

Think still of lovely things that are not true.
Let wish and magic work at will in you.
Be sometimes blind to sorrow. Make believe!
Forget the calm that lies
In disillusioned eyes.
Though we all know that we must die,
Yet you and I
May walk like gods and be
Even now at home in immortality.

We see so many ugly things—
Deceits and wrongs and quarrelings;
We know, alas! we know
How quickly fade
The color in the west,
The bloom upon the flower,
The bloom upon the breast
And youth's blind hour.
Yet keep within your heart
A place apart
Where little dreams may go,
May thrive and grow.
Hold fast — hold fast your dreams!

Louise Driscoll — Hold Fast Your Dreams

To have striven, to have made an effort, to
have been true to certain ideals — this alone is
worth the struggle. We are here to add what
we can *to,* not to get what we can *from,* life.

Sir William Osler

Incentives

Your world is as big as you make it.
I know, for I used to abide
In the narrowest nest in a corner,
My wings pressing close to my side.

But I sighted the distant horizon
Where the skyline encircled the sea
And I throbbed with a burning desire
To travel this immensity.

I battered the cordons around me
And cradled my wings on the breeze
Then soared to the uttermost reaches
With rapture, with power, with ease!

Georgia Douglas Johnson — Your World

Ye stars! which are the poetry of heaven,
If in your bright leaves we would read the fate
Of men and empires—'tis to be forgiven
That in our aspirations to be great
Our destinies o'erleap their mortal state,
And claim a kindred with you; for ye are
A beauty and a mystery, and create
In us such love and reverence from afar,
That fortune, fame, power, life, have named
    themselves a star.

George Gordon, Lord Byron — Stars

Our gifts and attainments are not only to be
light and warmth in our own dwellings, but
are to shine through the window, into the dark
night, to guide and cheer bewildered travellers
on the road.

Henry Ward Beecher

To accomplish anything you need an interest,
a motive, a center of your thought. You need
a star to steer by, a cause, a creed, an idea, a
passionate attachment.

M. MacNeile Nixon

O strong of heart, go where the road
Of ancient honour climbs.
Bow not your craven shoulders,
Earth conquered gives the stars.

Boethius

22

Inspiration is a fragile thing . . . just a breeze, touching the green foliage of a city park, just a whisper from the soul of a friend. Just a line of verse clipped from some forgotten magazine . . . or a paragraph standing out from the chapters of a book.

Inspiration . . . who can say where it is born, and why it leaves us? Who can tell the reasons for its being or not being? Only this . . . I think inspiration comes from the Heart of Heaven to give the lift of wings, and the breath of divine music to those of us who are earthbound.

Margaret Sangster

Human nature loses its most precious quality when it is robbed of its sense of things beyond, unexplored and yet insistent.

Alfred North Whitehead

Life is what we are alive to. It is not length but breadth. To be alive only to appetite, pleasure, pride, money-making, and not to goodness, kindness, purity, love, history, poetry, music, flowers, stars, God, and eternal hope is to be all but dead.

Maltbie D. Babcock

So long as life continues as life, it will never lose its yearning to be more than it is.

William Pepperell Montague

The margin between that which men naturally do, and that which they can do, is so great that a system which urges men on to action and develops individual enterprise and initiative is preferable, in spite of the wastes that necessarily attend that process.

Louis D. Brandeis

There is a deep tendency in human nature to become like what we imagine ourselves to be.

William Ernest Hocking

At some time in our life we feel a trembling, fearful longing to do some good thing. Life finds its noblest spring of excellence in this hidden impulse to do our best.

Robert Collyer

If you could take the human heart and listen to it, it would be like listening to a seashell. You would hear in it the hollow murmur of the infinite ocean to which it belongs, from which it draws its profoundest inspiration, and for which it yearns.

Edwin Hubbell Chapin

The vision of the better-yet-to-be is the stuff of inspiration. Given vision, our lives are lived under the light of distant stars, foreseeing upon our present workmanship the judgment of future generations.

T. V. Smith

The soul of art is beauty,
    The heart of love is youth;
The soul of courage, duty;
    The heart of science, truth;
And so man struggles upward,
    To find beyond the sod
The heart and soul of the universe,
    The Infinite, his God.

M. Grace Houseman

Far away there in the sunshine are my highest aspirations. I may not reach them, but I can look up and see their beauty, believe in them, and try to follow where they lead.

Louisa May Alcott

It is not the critic who counts; not the man who points out how the strong man stumbled, or where the doer of deeds could have done them better. The credit belongs to the man who is actually in the arena, whose face is marred by dust and sweat and blood; who strives valiantly; who errs and comes short again and again; who knows the great enthusiasms, the great devotions; who spends himself in a worthy cause; who, at best, knows in the end the triumph of high achievement, and who, at the worst, if he fails, at least fails while daring greatly, so that his place shall never be with those timid souls who knew neither victory nor defeat.

Theodore Roosevelt

Courage

Have courage for the great sorrow of life and patience for the small one; and when you have laboriously accomplished your daily task, go to sleep in peace. God is awake.

Victor Hugo

The hills ahead look hard and steep and high
And often we behold them with a sigh;
But as we near them level grows the road.
We find on every slope with every load
The climb is not so steep, the top so far,
The hills ahead look harder than they are.

And so it is with troubles though they seem
   so great
That men complain and fear and hesitate;
Less difficult the journey than we dreamed
It never proves as hard as once it seemed,
There never comes a task, a hill, a day
But as we near it — easier the way.

Douglas Malloch — Hills Ahead

I have lived eighty-six years. I have watched men climb to success, hundreds of them, and of all the elements that are important for success, the most important is faith. No great thing comes to any man unless he has courage.

James Cardinal Gibbons

Low I kneel through the night again,
  Hear my prayer, if my prayer be right!
Take for Thy token my proud heart broken.
  God, guide my arm! I go back to the fight.

Anonymous

The hero is no braver than an ordinary man, but he is brave five minutes longer.

Ralph Waldo Emerson

Courage is armor
  A blind man wears;
The calloused scar
  Of outlived repairs;
Courage is Fear
  That has said its prayers.

Karle Wilson Baker

The only life worth living is the adventurous life. Of such a life the dominant characteristic is that it is unafraid. In the first place, it is unafraid of what other people think. Like Columbus, it dares not only to assert a belief but to live it in the face of contrary opinion. It does not adapt either its pace or its objectives to the pace and objectives of its neighbors. It is not afraid of dreaming dreams that have no practical meaning. It thinks its own thoughts, it reads its own books, it develops its own hobbies, it is governed by its own conscience. The herd may graze where it pleases or stampede when it pleases, but he who lives the adventurous life will remain unafraid when he finds himself alone.

Raymond B. Fosdick

Do you fear the force of the wind,
The slash of the rain?
Go face them and fight them,
Be savage again.
Go hungry and cold like the wolf,
Go wade like the crane:
The palms of your hands will thicken,
The skin of your cheek will tan,
You'll grow ragged and weary and swarthy,
But you'll walk like a man!

Hamlin Garland — Do You Fear The Wind?

I didn't believe,
Standing on the bank of a river
Which was wide and swift,
That I would cross that bridge
Plaited from thin, fragile reeds
Fastened with bast.
I walked delicately as a butterfly
And heavily as an elephant,
I walked surely as a dancer
And wavered like a blind man.
I didn't believe that I would cross that bridge,
And now that I am standing on the other side,
I don't believe I crossed it.

Leopold Staff — The Bridge

God, grant me the serenity to accept things I cannot change, courage to change things I can, and wisdom to know the difference.

Reinhold Niebuhr

Keep your fears to yourself, but share your
courage with others.

Robert Louis Stevenson

To bow before the rigor of the storm
Is no disgrace.
To stay bowed low whene'er the calm has
    come—
Catastrophe!
Life is a gift—
Our own to breathe, to feel,
To have, to hold.
This shell of ours,
The temple of our soul,
Will wax and wane.
But we ourselves
Are God's own spark of life,
Unquenchable.
We bow before the rigor of the storm—
For we are weak.
We rise renewed whene'er the calm has come—
For we are strong!

Nell Cravens

The best lightning rod for your protection
is your own spine.

Ralph Waldo Emerson

Courage is generosity of the highest order.

Charles Caleb Colton

I do not ask to walk smooth paths
    Nor bear an easy load.
I pray for strength and fortitude
    To climb the rock-strewn road.

Give me such courage I can scale
    The hardest peaks alone,
And transform every stumbling block
    Into a stepping-stone.

Gail Brook Burkett

Back of tranquillity lies always conquered
unhappiness.

Eleanor Roosevelt

It's not life that counts but the fortitude you
bring into it.

John Galsworthy

He who loses wealth loses much; he who loses a
friend loses more; but he that loses his courage
loses all.

Miguel de Cervantes

Let me pray not to be sheltered from dangers
    but to be fearless in facing them.
Let me not beg for the stilling of my pain,
    but for the heart to conquer it.
Let me not look for allies in life's battlefield,
    but to my own strength.
Let me crave not in anxious fear to be saved,
    but hope for the patience to win my freedom.
Grant me that I may not be a coward, feeling
    your mercy in my success alone; but let me
    find the grasp of your hand in failure.

Rabindranath Tagore

Courage is the price life exacts for granting
        peace.
The soul that knows it not, knows no release
    From little things;

Knows not the livid loneliness of fear
Nor mountain heights, where bitter joy can hear
    The sound of wings.

How can life grant us boon of living, compensate
For dull gray ugliness and pregnant hate
    Unless we dare

The soul's dominion? Each time we make a
        choice, we pay
With courage to behold resistless day
    And count it fair.

Amelia Earhart — Courage

Every day is a fresh beginning;
    Listen, my soul, to the glad refrain,
And, spite of old sorrow and older sinning,
    And puzzles forecasted and possible pain,
Take heart with the day, and begin again.

Susan Coolidge — Begin Again

What you can do, or dream you can, begin it.
Courage has genius, power and magic in it;
Only engage, and then the mind grows heated.
Begin it and the work will be completed.

Anonymous

Keep your face to the sunshine and you cannot see the shadow.

Helen Keller

Courage consists not in hazarding without fear, but being resolutely minded in a just cause. The brave man is not he who feels no fear, for that were stupid and irrational, but he whose noble soul subdues its fear, and bravely dares the danger nature shrinks from.

Ferrold

Whether a man accepts from Fortune her spade and will look downward and dig, or from Aspiration her axe and cord, and will scale the ice, the one and only success which it is his to command is to bring to his work a mighty heart.

Oliver Wendell Holmes

I have hoped, I have planned, I have striven,
To the will I have added the deed;
The best that was in me I've given,
I have prayed, but the gods would not heed.

I have dared and reached only disaster,
I have battled and broken my lance;
I am bruised by a pitiless master
That the weak and the timid call Chance.

I am old, I am bent, I am cheated
Of all that Youth urged me to win;
But name me not with the defeated,
Tomorrow again, I begin.

Samuel S. E. Kiser — Unsubdued

Let us be like a bird for a moment perched
    On a frail branch while he sings;
Though he feels it bend, yet he sings his song,
    Knowing that he has wings.

Victor Hugo — Wings

The only man who never makes mistakes is the man who never does anything.

Theodore Roosevelt

The day shall not be up so soon as I
To try the fair adventure of tomorrow.

William Shakespeare

I am tired of hearing of self-made men. There is not a self-made man in the world. The so-called self-made man is the man who seized his opportunities and those given to him by circumstance and has made use of them.

Lucius Tuttle

We have tomorrow
Bright before us
Like a flame.

Yesterday
A night-gone thing,
A sun-down name.

And dawn-today
Broad arch above the road we came.

We march!

Langston Hughes — Youth

Why not go out on a limb? Isn't that where the fruit is?

Frank Scully

So I never quite despair,
    Nor let my courage fail;
And some day when skies are fair,
    Up the bay my ships will sail.

Robert Barry Coffin

Courage, the highest gift, that scorns to bend
    To mean devices for a sordid end,
Courage — an independent spark from
        Heaven's bright throne,
    By which the soul stands raised, triumphant,
        high, alone.
Courage, the mighty attribute of power above,
    By which those great in war are great in love.
The spring of all brave acts are seated here,
    As falsehoods draw their sordid birth
        from fear.

George Farquhar — Courage

The best men are not those who have waited for chances but who have taken them; beseiged the chance; conquered the chance and made chance the servitor.

Edwin H. Chapin

Physical strength is measured by what we can carry; spiritual by what we can bear.

Anonymous

Little minds are tamed and subdued by misfortune, but great minds rise above it.

Washington Irving

One can never be certain of his courage until he has faced danger.

François, Duc de La Rochefoucauld

And only when we are no longer afraid do we begin to live in every experience, painful or joyous; to live in gratitude for every moment, to live abundantly.

Dorothy Thompson

Let terror strike slaves mute;
Much danger makes great hearts most resolute.

John Marston

It is better to light one small candle than to curse the darkness.

Confucius

The world has no room for cowards. We must all be ready somehow to toil, to suffer, to die. And yours is not the less noble because no drum beats before you when you go out to your daily battlefields, and no crowds shout your coming when you return from your daily victory and defeat.

Robert Louis Stevenson

A man of courage is also full of faith.

Cicero

Every great and commanding moment in the annals of the world is the triumph of some enthusiasm.

Ralph Waldo Emerson

By the street of By-and-By, one arrives at the house of Never.

Miguel de Cervantes

It is easy to be pleasant
When life flows by like a song,
But the man worth while is one who will smile,
When everything goes dead wrong.

For the test of the heart is trouble,
And it always comes with the years,
And the smile that is worth the praises of earth
Is the smile that shines thru the tears.

Ella Wheeler Wilcox

Confidence or courage is conscious ability—the sense of power.

William Hazlitt

He who has conquered doubt and fear has conquered failure. Doubt has killed more splendid projects, shattered more ambitious schemes, strangled more effective geniuses, neutralized more superb efforts, blasted more fine intellects, thwarted more splendid ambitions than any other enemy of the race.

James Allen

Fulfill something you are able to fulfill, rather than run after what you will never achieve. Nobody is perfect. Remember the saying "None is good but God alone." And nobody can be. It is an illusion. We can modestly strive to fulfill ourselves and to be as complete human beings as possible, and that will give us trouble enough.

Carl G. Jung

Be not anxious about tomorrow. Do today's duty; fight today's temptations and do not weaken and distract yourself by looking forward to things you cannot see and could not understand if you saw them.

Charles Kingsley

The basest of all things is to be afraid.

William Faulkner

One man with courage makes a majority.

Andrew Jackson

Learning and Wisdom

Knowledge

He who knows not, and knows not that he
   knows not,
    is a fool, shun him;
He who knows not, and knows that he knows
   not,
    is a child, teach him.
He who knows, and knows not that he knows
   is asleep, wake him.
He who knows, and knows that he knows,
   is wise, follow him.

Proverb

The doorstep to the temple of wisdom is a
knowledge of our own ignorance.

Charles Haddon Spurgeon

Knowledge is happiness, because to have
knowledge — broad deep knowledge — is to
know true ends from false, and lofty things
from low. To know the thoughts and deeds
that have marked man's progress is to feel the
great heart-throbs of humanity through the
centuries; and if one does not feel in these
pulsations a heavenward striving, one must
indeed be deaf to the harmonies of life.

Helen Keller

Our minds possess by nature an insatiable
desire to know the truth.

Cicero

Thinking is the hardest work there is, which
is probably why so few engage in it.

Henry Ford

What we need, in education, is some sense of
far horizons and beautiful prospects, some
consciousness of the largeness and mystery and
wonder of life.

Arthur Christopher Benson

Education is what remains when we have
forgotten all that we have been taught.

Marquis of Halifax

A sound discretion is not so much indicated
by never making a mistake as by never
repeating it.

Christian Bovee

Man's mind stretched to a new idea never
goes back to its original dimensions.

Oliver Wendell Holmes

If I had influence with the good fairy who is
supposed to preside over the christening of all
children I should ask that her gift to each child
be a sense of wonder so indestructible that it
would last throughout life, an unfailing antidote
against the boredom and disenchantment of
later years, the sterile preoccupation with things
that are artificial, the alienation from the
sources of our strength.

Rachel Carson

The man who cannot wonder, who does not
habitually wonder and worship, is but a pair of
spectacles behind which there is no eye.

Thomas Carlyle

Only the educated are free.

Epictetus

A great many people think they are thinking when they are merely rearranging their prejudices.

William James

Logic is a machine of the mind, and if it is used honestly it ought to bring out an honest conclusion. When people say that you can prove anything by logic, they are not using words in a fair sense. What they mean is, you can prove anything by bad logic. Deep in the mystic ingratitude in the soul of man there is an extraordinary tendency to use the name for an organ, when what is meant is the abuse or decay of that organ. Thus we speak of a man suffering from "nerves" which is about as sensible as talking about a man suffering from ten fingers. We speak of "liver" and "digestion" when we mean the failure of the liver and the absence of digestion. And in the same manner, we speak of the dangers of logic, when what we really mean is the danger of fallacy.

Gilbert Keith Chesterton

Education does not mean teaching people what they do not know. It means teaching them to behave as they do not behave. It is not teaching the youth the shapes of letters and the tricks of numbers, and then leaving them to turn their arithmetic to roguery, and their literature to lust. It means, on the contrary, training them into the perfect exercise and kingly continence of their bodies and souls. It is a painful, continual and difficult work to be done by kindness, by watching, by warning, by precept, and by praise, but above all — by example.

John Ruskin

We ought not to look back unless it is to derive useful lessons from past errors and for the purpose of profiting by dear-bought experience.

George Washington

Every man who rises above the common level has received two educations: the first from his teachers; the second, more personal and important, from himself.

Edward Gibbon

I have never let my schooling interfere with my education.

Mark Twain

He is indeed a kind of semi-Solomon. He *half* knows everything.

Sydney Smith

Knowledge is the food of the soul. Must they not be utterly unfortunate whose souls are compelled to pass through life always hungering?

Plato

It's a wise man who profits by his own experience, but it's a good deal wiser one who lets the rattlesnake bite the other fellow.

Josh Billings

The years teach much which the days never know.

Ralph Waldo Emerson

God spare me sclerosis of the curiosity, for the curiosity which craves to keep us informed about the small things no less than the large is the mainspring, the dynamo, the jet propulsion of all complete living. Our curiosities are what feed our consciousness, and our consciousness is the proof that our minds are still functioning. Nothing that happens to us, nothing we do, no walk we take, nothing we see or read, no one we meet or listen to, means anything to us unless we have the mind to use our minds, and keep them refreshed.

John Mason Brown

It is not a mind, it is not a body that we erect, but it is a man, and we must not make two parts of him.

Michel de Montaigne

The atrocious crime of being a young man charged upon me, I shall neither attempt to palliate nor deny; but content myself with wishing that I may be one of those whose follies may cease with their youth, and not of that number who are ignorant in spite of experience.

Samuel Johnson

The roots of education are bitter, but the fruit is sweet.

Aristotle

Ignorance is the night of the mind, a night without moon or star.

Confucius

Do not wish for self-confidence in yourself; get it from within. Nobody can give it to you. It is one of the greatest assets of life. Self-confidence comes to you every time you are knocked down and get up. A little boy was asked how he learned to skate: "Oh, by getting up every time I fell down," he replied . . . Self-trust is the first secret of success.

Ralph Waldo Emerson

David Livingstone, the great explorer and Christian pioneer, wrote in one magnificent sentence, "I will go anywhere — provided it be forward."

Walter Russell Bowie

Education is the instruction of the intellect in the laws of Nature, under which name I include not merely things and their forces, but men and their ways; and the fashioning of the affections and of the will into an earnest and loving desire to move in harmony with those laws.

Thomas H. Huxley

Knowledge and wisdom, far from being one, have ofttimes no connection. Knowledge dwells in heads replete with thoughts of other men; wisdom in minds attentive to their own. Knowledge is proud that it knows so much; wisdom is humble that it knows no more.

William Cowper

Education makes a people easy to lead, but difficult to drive; easy to govern, but impossible to enslave.

Lord Brougham

It is better to know nothing than to know what ain't so.

Josh Billings

The wisest mind hath something yet to learn.

George Santayana

As a general rule the most successful man in life is the man who has the best information.

Benjamin Disraeli

No man really becomes a fool until he stops asking questions.

Charles P. Steinmetz

Merely having an open mind is nothing; the object of opening the mind, as of opening the mouth, is to shut it again on something solid.

Gilbert Keith Chesterton

There is four hundred times as much learning in the world as there is wisdom.

Josh Billings

The farther backward you can look, the farther forward you are likely to see.

Winston Churchill

The best cosmetic in the world is an active mind that is always finding something new.

Mary Meek Atkeson

It wasn't until quite late in life that I discovered how easy it is to say, "I don't know."

W. Somerset Maugham

What we have to learn to do, we learn by doing.

Aristotle

No man can with all the wealth in the world buy so much skill as to be a good lutenist; he must go the same way that poor people do, he must learn and take pains: much less can he buy constancy, or chastity, or courage; nay, not so much as the contempt of riches: and by possessing more than we need, we cannot obtain so much power over ourselves as not to require more.

Jeremy Taylor

Learning makes the wise wiser and the fool more foolish.

John Ray

Aristotle was asked how much educated men were superior to the uneducated: "As much," said he, "as the living are to the dead."

Diogenes Laertuis

We have learnt that nothing is simple and rational except what we ourselves have invented; that God thinks in terms neither of Euclid nor of Riemann; that science has "explained" nothing; that the more we know the more fantastic the world becomes and the profounder the surrounding darkness.

Aldous Huxley

Learning is acquired by reading books; but the much more necessary learning, the knowledge of the world, is only to be acquired by reading men, and studying all the various editions of them.

Lord Chesterfield

The end of learning is to repair the ruins of our first parents by regaining to know God aright, and out of that knowledge to love him, to imitate him, to be like him.

John Milton

An open mind is all very well in its way, but it ought not to be so open that there is no keeping anything in or out of it.

Samuel Butler

The larger the island of knowledge, the longer the shore line of wonder.

Ralph W. Sockman

Insight

The wise does at once what the fool does at last.

Baltasar Gracián

Dare to be wise; begin! He who postpones the hour of living rightly is like the rustic who waits for the river to run out before he crosses.

Horace

Not by age but by capacity is wisdom acquired.

Plautus

There is a time for some things, and a time for all things; a time for great things, and a time for small things.

Miguel de Cervantes

To be a philosopher is not merely to have subtle thoughts, nor even to found a school, but so to love wisdom as to live, according to its dictates, a life of simplicity, independence, magnanimity, and trust.

Henry David Thoreau

The ignorant man marvels at the exceptional; the wise man marvels at the common.

George Boardman

What else is Wisdom,
What of man's endeavor,
Or God's high grace, so lovely and so great—
To stand from fear set free,
To breathe and wait . . . .

Euripides

The virtue of wisdom more than anything else contains a divine element which always remains.

Plato

Wisdom is that olive that springeth from the heart, bloometh on the tongue, and beareth fruit in the actions.

Elizabeth Grymeston

Almighty God, the Giver of Wisdom, without whose help resolutions are vain, without whose blessing study is ineffectual, enable me, if it be Thy will, to attain such knowledge as may qualify me to direct the doubtful and instruct the ignorant, to prevent wrongs, and terminate contentions; and grant that I may use that knowledge which I shall attain, to Thy glory and my own salvation.

Samuel Johnson

Wisdom makes but a slow defence against trouble, though at last a sure one.

Oliver Goldsmith

Wisdom outweighs any wealth.

St. Clement of Rome

A man's wisdom is most conspicuous where he is able to distinguish among dangers and make choice of the least.

Machiavelli

A grain of gold will gild a great surface, but not so much as a grain of wisdom.

Henry David Thoreau

To flee vice is the beginning of virtue, and to have got rid of folly is the beginning of wisdom.

Horace

A man has only so much knowledge as he puts to work.

St. Francis of Assisi

Wisdom is the highest virtue, and it has in it four other virtues; of which one is prudence, another temperance, the third fortitude, the fourth justice.

Boethius

Wisdom is of the soul, is not susceptible of proof, is its own proof.

Walt Whitman

The doors of wisdom are never shut.

Benjamin Franklin

I begin to suspect that a man's bewilderment is the measure of his wisdom.

Nathaniel Hawthorne

He whose heart has been set on the love of learning and true wisdom, and has exercised this part of himself, *that* man *must* without fail have thoughts that are immortal and divine, if *he lay hold on truth.*

Plato

The invariable mark of wisdom is to see the miraculous in the common.

Ralph Waldo Emerson

The mintage of wisdom is to know that rest is rust and that the real life is love, laughter, and work.

Elbert Hubbard

The art of being wise is the art of knowing what to overlook.

William James

A man should never be ashamed to say he has been wrong, which is but saying in other words that he is wiser today than he was yesterday.

Alexander Pope

The greatest good is wisdom.

St. Augustine

[Wisdom is] the science of happiness or of the means of attaining the lasting contentment which consists in the continual achievement of a greater perfection or at least in variations of the same degree of perfection.

G. W. von Leibniz

Of all human pursuits the pursuit of wisdom is the most perfect, the most sublime, the most profitable, the most delightful.

St. Thomas Aquinas

Great wisdom is generous; petty wisdom is contentious. Great speech is impassioned, small speech cantankerous.

Chuang-tzu

A wise man who stands firm is a statesman, a foolish man who stands firm is a catastrophe.

Adlai Stevenson

Should it be said that the Greeks discovered philosophy by human wisdom, I reply that I find the Scriptures declare all wisdom to be a divine gift.

St. Clement of Rome

The only medicine for suffering, crime, and all the other woes of mankind, is wisdom.

Thomas H. Huxley

It is a characteristic of wisdom not to do desperate things.

Henry David Thoreau

It is wisdom to believe the heart.

George Santayana

To profit from good advice requires more wisdom than to give it.

John Churton Collins

My blessing with you!
And these few precepts in thy memory:
See thou character. Give thy thoughts no tongue,
Nor any unproportioned thought his act.
Be thou familiar, but by no means vulgar.
The friends thou hast, and their adoption tried,
Grapple them to thy soul with hoops of steel;
But do not dull thy palm with entertainment
Of each new-hatched, unfledged comrade.
    Beware
Of entrance to a quarrel; but being in,
Bear 't that the opposed may beware of thee.
Give every man thine ear, but few thy voice;
Take each man's censure; but reserve thy
    judgment.
Costly thy habit as thy purse can buy,
But not expressed in fancy; rich not gaudy;
For the apparel oft proclaims the man.
Neither a borrower nor a lender be;
For loan oft loses both itself and friend,
And borrowing dulls the edge of husbandry.
This above all: to thine own self be true,
And it must follow, as the night the day,
Thou canst not then be false to any man.

William Shakespeare

Common-sense in an uncommon degree is what the world calls wisdom.

Samuel Taylor Coleridge

A man who is his own doctor has a fool for his patient.

American Proverb

It is not worth while to go round the world to count the cats in Zanzibar.

Henry David Thoreau

We should be careful to get out of an experience only the wisdom that is in it — and stop there; lest we be like the cat that sits down on a hot stove lid. She will never sit down on a hot stove lid again — and that is well: but also she will never sit down on a cold one any more.

Mark Twain

It is not the rich man you should properly call happy, but him who knows how to use with wisdom the blessings of the gods, to endure hard poverty, and who fears dishonor worse than death, and is not afraid to die for cherished friends or fatherland.

Horace

Let us run if we must — even the sands do that — but let us keep our hearts young and our eyes open that nothing worth our while shall escape us. And everything is worth its while if we only grasp it and its significance.

Victor Cherbuliez

Stars and atoms have no size,
They only vary in men's eyes.

Men and instruments will blunder
— Calculating things of wonder.

A seed is just as huge a world
As any ball the sun has hurled.

Stars are quite as picayune
As any splinter of the moon.

Time is but a vague device;
Space can never be precise;

Stars and atoms have a girth,
Small as zero, ten times Earth.

There is, by God's swift reckoning
A universe in everything.

A. M. Sullivan — Measurement

There is not a heart but has its moments of longing, yearning for something better, nobler, holier than it knows now.

Henry Ward Beecher

The most beautiful thing we can experience is the mysterious. It is the source of all true art and science. He to whom this emotion is a stranger, who can no longer pause to wonder and stand rapt in awe, is as good as dead: his eyes are closed.

Albert Einstein

There is no happiness where there is no wisdom;
No wisdom but in submission to the gods.
Big words are always punished,
And proud men in old age learn to be wise.

Sophocles

Wisdom consists in perceiving when human nature and that perverse world necessitate making exceptions to abstract truths.

Wendell Phillips

Two men look out through the same bars:
One sees mud, and one the stars.

Frederick Langbridge

Character

Character is like a tree and reputation like its shadow. The shadow is what we think of; the tree is the real thing.

Abraham Lincoln

Every man has three characters — that which he exhibits, that which he has, and that which he thinks he has.

Alphonse Karr

Most people are some other people. Their thoughts are someone else's opinion, their lines a mimicry, their passions a quotation.

Oscar Wilde

It is not what he has, or even what he does which expresses the worth of a man, but what he is.

Henri Frédéric Amiel

There is no such thing as an average man. Each one of us is a unique individual. Each one of us expresses his humanity in some distinctly different way. The beauty and the bloom of each human soul is a thing apart — a separate holy miracle under God, never once repeated throughout all the millenniums of time.

Lane Weston

There is a great deal of human nature in people.

Mark Twain

If you have anything really valuable to contribute to the world, it will come through the expression of your own personality — that single spark of divinity that sets you off and makes you different from every other living creature.

Bruce Barton

I have to live with myself, and so
I want to be fit for myself to know.
I want to be able as days go by
Always to look myself in the eye.

I don't want to stand with the setting sun
And hate myself for the thing I've done.
I never can hide myself from me,
I see what others may never see.

I know what others may never know,
I never can fool myself, and so
Whatever happens I want to be
Self-respecting and conscience-free.

Edgar A. Guest — Myself

People who are faithful in that which is least wear very radiant crowns. They are the people who are great in little tasks. They are scrupulous in the rutty roads of drudgery. They win triumphs amid small irritations. They are as loyal when wearing aprons in the kitchen as if they wore purple and fine linen in the visible presence of the king.
They finish the most obscure bit of work as if it were to be displayed before an assembled heaven by Him who is the Lord of light and glory. Great souls are those who are faithful in that which is least.

John Henry Jowett

Live your life while you have it. Life is a splendid gift. There is nothing small in it. For the greatest things grow by God's Law out of the smallest. But to live your life you must discipline it. You must not fritter it away in "fair purpose, erring act, inconstant will" but make your thoughts, your acts, all work to the same end and that end, not self but God. That is what we call character.

Florence Nightingale

That I am a man, this I share with other men.
That I see and hear and that I eat and drink
is what all animals do likewise. But that I am I
is only mine and belongs to me and to nobody
else; to no other man, not to an angel, nor to
God — except inasmuch as I am one with Him.

Meister Eckhart

Put an end once and for all to this discussion
of what a good man should be, and be one.

Marcus Aurelius

Character is singularly contagious.

Samuel A. Eliot

You can within yourself find a mighty, unexplored kingdom in which you can dwell in
peace if you will.

Russell H. Conwell

If a man does not keep pace with his companions, perhaps it is because he hears the beat
of a different drummer. Let him step to the
music which he hears, however measured or
far away.

Henry David Thoreau

They say best men are molded out of faults,
And, for the most, become much more the better
For being a little bad.

William Shakespeare

Beware of too sublime a sense of your own
worth and consequence.

William Cowper

Half our mistakes in life arise from feeling
where we ought to think, and thinking where
we ought to feel.

John Churton Collins

Interesting people are people who are interested.
Bores are people who are bored.

Anonymous

Better keep yourself clean and bright: you are
the window through which you must see the
world.

George Bernard Shaw

If an animal does something they call it instinct.
If we do exactly the same thing for the same
reason they call it intelligence. I guess what they
mean is that we all make mistakes, but
intelligence enables us to do it on purpose.

Will Cuppy

So live that you would not be ashamed to sell
the family parrot to the town gossip.

Will Rogers

Make me as one that casteth not by day
A dreary shadow, but reflecting aye
One little beam, loved, warmed and golden
    caught
From the bright sun that lights our daily way.

I. P. Boynton

Don't seek to live someone else's life; it's just
not you . . . You have no right to put on a false
face, to pretend what you are not, unless you
want to rob others. Say to yourself: I am going
to bring something new into this person's life,
because he has never met anyone like me nor
will he ever meet anyone like me, for in the
mind of God, I am unique and irreplaceable.

Anonymous

What life means to us is determined not so
much by what life brings to us as by the attitude
we bring to life; not so much by what happens
to us as by our reaction to what happens.

Lewis L. Dunnington

Our world is the world within,
    Our life is the thought we take,
And never an outer sin
    Can mar it or break.

Brood not on the rich man's land,
    Sigh not for the miser's gold,
Holding in reach of your hand
    The treasure untold.

That lies in the Mines of Heart,
    That rest in the soul alone —
Bid worry and care depart,
    Come into your own!

John Kendrick Bangs — The Kingdom Of Man

The world is a looking-glass, and gives back to every man the reflection of his own face. Frown at it, and it in turn will look sourly at you; laugh at it, and with it, and it is a jolly, kind companion.

William Makepeace Thackeray

In the hills of life there are two trails. One lies along the higher sunlit fields — where those who travel see afar, and the light lingers long after the sun is down. And one lies along the lower ground — where those who journey look over their shoulders with eyes of dread, and gloomy shadows gather long before the day is done.

Harold Bell Wright

Every human being is intended to have a character of his own; to be what no other is, and to do what no other can do.

William Ellery Channing

The value of a man's advice is the way he applies it to himself.

Barry Cornwall

Every man has within himself a continent of undiscovered character. Happy is he who proves the Columbus of his soul.

Johann Wolfgang von Goethe

Of all the passions that are incident to a man, there is none so impetuous, or that produceth so terrible effect as anger; for besides that intrinsical mischief which it works in a man's own heart, in regard whereof Hugo said well, "Pride robs me of God, envy of my neighbor, anger of myself." What bloody tragedies doth this passion act every day in the world, making the whole earth nothing but either an amphitheatre for fight or a shambles for slaughter.

Joseph Hall

I never yet heard man or woman much abused, that I was not inclined to think better of them; and to transfer any suspicion or dislike to the person who appeared to take delight in pointing out the defects of a fellow creature.

Jane Porter

Criticism is dangerous, because it wounds a man's precious pride, hurts his sense of importance and arouses his resentment.

Dale Carnegie

The greatest undeveloped territory in the world lies under your hat.

Anonymous

A man's virtues should not be measured by his occasional exertions but by his ordinary days.

Will Rogers

Fellowship and Service

Friendship

The glory of friendship is not the outstretched hand, nor the kindly smile, nor the joy of companionship; it is the spiritual inspiration that comes to one when he discovers that someone believes in him and is willing to trust him with his friendship.

Ralph Waldo Emerson

In men whom men condemn as ill,
   I find so much of goodness still;
In men whom men pronounce divine,
   I find so much of sin and blot,
I hesitate to draw a line
   Between the two where God has not.

Joaquin Miller

The holy passion of Friendship is of so sweet and steady and loyal and enduring a nature that it will last through a whole lifetime, if not asked to lend money.

Mark Twain

A Common Friendship — Who talks of a Common Friendship? There is no such thing in the world. On earth no word is more sublime.

Henry Drummond

There's nothing worth the wear of winning but laughter and the love of friends.

Hilaire Belloc

Two persons will not be friends long if they cannot forgive each other's little failings.

Jean de La Bruyère

There are veins in the hills where jewels hide
   And gold lies buried deep;
There are harbor-towns where the great ships ride,
   And fame and fortune sleep;
But land and sea though we tireless rove,
And follow each trail to the end,
   Whatever the wealth of our treasure-trove,
The best we shall find is a friend.

John J. Moment — The Best Treasure

The tide of friendship does not rise high on the bank of perfection. Amiable weaknesses and shortcomings are the food of love. It is from the roughnesses and imperfect breaks in a man that you are able to lay hold of him. If a man be an entire and perfect chrysolite, you slide off him and fall back into ignorance. My friends are not perfect –– no more am I — and so we suit each other admirably. Their weaknesses keep mine in countenance, and so save me from humiliation and shame. We give and take, bear and forbear; the stupidity they utter today salves the recollection of the stupidity I uttered yesterday; in their want of it I see my own, and so feel satisfied and kindly disposed. It is one of the charitable dispensations of Providence that perfection is not essential to friendship.

Alexander Smith

It is a good thing to be rich, and a good thing to be strong, but it is a better thing to be beloved of many friends.

Euripides

Happy is the house that shelters a friend.

Thomas Fuller

When friendships are real, they are not glass threads or frost work, but the solidest things we can know.

Ralph Waldo Emerson

In prosperity our friends know us; in adversity we know our friends.

John Churton Collins

If we would build on a sure foundation in friendship, we must love our friends for *their* sake rather than for *our* own.

Charlotte Brontë

O who will walk a mile with me
    Along life's merry way?
A comrade blithe and full of glee,
Who dares to laugh out loud and free,
And let his frolic fancy play,
Like a happy child, through the flowers gay
That fill the field and fringe the way
    Where he walks a mile with me.

And who will walk a mile with me
    Along life's weary way?
A friend whose heart has eyes to see
The stars shine out o'er the darkening lea,
And the quiet rest at the end o' the day,—
A friend who knows, and dares to say,
The brave, sweet words that cheer the way
    Where he walks a mile with me.

With such a comrade, such a friend,
I fain would walk till journey's end,
Through summer sunshine, winter rain,
And then?—Farewell, we shall meet again!

Henry Van Dyke — A Mile With Me

The most agreeable of all companions is a simple, frank person, without any high pretensions to an oppressive greatness—one who loves life, and understands the use of it; obliging alike at all hours; above all, of a golden temper, and steadfast as an anchor. For such an one we gladly exchange the greatest genius, the most brilliant wit, the profoundest thinker.

Gotthold Ephraim Lessing

Every man should keep a fair-sized cemetery in which to bury the faults of his friends.

Henry Ward Beecher

Four things are specially the property of friendship: love and affection, security and joy. And four things must be tried in friendship: faith, intention, discretion and patience. Indeed, as the sage says, all men would lead a happy life if only two tiny words were taken from them, mine and thine.

St. Aelred of Rievaulx

We cannot tell the precise moment when friendship is formed. As in filling a vessel drop by drop, there is at last a drop which makes it run over; so in a series of kindnesses there is at last one which makes the heart run over.

Samuel Johnson

The language of friendship is not words but meanings.

Henry David Thoreau

Without friends no one would choose to live, though he had all other goods.

Aristotle

Friends are the end and the reward of life. They keep us worthy of ourselves.

Robert Louis Stevenson

A true friend unbosoms freely, advises justly, assists readily, adventures boldly, takes all patiently, defends courageously, and continues a friend unchangeably.

William Penn

The wise man seeks a friend in whom are those qualities which he himself may lack; for thus being united is their friendship the more completely defended against adversity.

Jeremy Taylor

Life has no blessing like an earnest friend; than treasured wealth more precious, than the power of monarchs, and the people's loud applause.

Euripides

When your pocket's empty,
  when your heart is sad,
When fellow-men distrust you,
  your name and credit bad;
The man or woman who will then
  stand by you and defend,
Must surely be without a doubt
  a true and noble friend.

Anonymous

Have friends. 'Tis a second existence. Every friend is good and wise for his friend: among them all everything turns to good. Everyone is as others wish him; that they may wish him well, he must win their hearts and so their tongues. There is no magic like a good turn, and the way to gain friendly feelings is to do friendly acts. The most and best of us depend on others; we have to live either among friends or among enemies. Seek someone every day to be a well-wisher if not a friend; by and by after trial some of these will become intimate.

Baltasar Gracian

The joy of meeting makes us love farewell;
We gather once again around the hearth,
  And thou will tell
All that thy keen experience has been
Of pleasure, danger, misadventure, mirth,
  And unforeseen.

But friend, go not again so far away;
In need of some small help I always stand,
  Come whatso may;
I know not whither leads this path of mine,
But I can tread it better when my hand
  Is clasped in thine.

Alfred de Musset — To a Comrade

All we can do is to make the best of our friends, love and cherish what is good in them, and keep out of the way of what is bad.

Thomas Jefferson

The most I can do for my friend is simply to be his friend. I have no wealth to bestow on him. If he knows that I am happy in loving him, he will want no other reward. Is not friendship divine in this?

Henry David Thoreau

A friend may well be reckoned the masterpiece of Nature.

Ralph Waldo Emerson

A brother may not be a friend, but a friend will always be a brother.

Benjamin Franklin

About the only thing in life that makes it worth while is the enjoyment of friendly relations.

George W. Norris

What sweetness is left in life, if you take away friendship? Robbing life of friendship is like robbing the world of the sun.

Cicero

Give me the avowed, the erect, the manly foe,
Bold I can meet — perhaps may turn his blows;
But of all the plagues, good Heaven,
  thy wrath can send,
Save, oh! save me from the candid friend.

George Canning

A blessed thing it is for any man or woman to have a friend; one human soul whom we can trust utterly; who knows the best and the worst of us, and who loves us in spite of all our faults; who will speak the honest truth to us, while the world flatters us to our face, and laughs at us behind our back; who will give us counsel and reproof in the day of prosperity and self-conceit; but who, again, will comfort and encourage us in the day of difficulty and sorrow, when the world leaves us alone to fight our own battle as we can.

Charles Kingsley

Endeavor to be always patient of the faults and imperfections of others, for thou hast many faults and imperfections of thy own that require a reciprocation of forbearance. If thou art not able to make thyself that which thou wishest to be, how canst thou expect to mould another in conformity to thy will?

Thomas á Kempis

A friend is a present you give yourself.

Robert Louis Stevenson

Friend: one who knows all about you and loves you just the same.

Elbert Hubbard

Courage we need for this life of ours,
Courage, calmness, power;
Glee in the present which children own,
Hope for the coming hour.

Underneath, and all the time,
A warm pulse, beating
To Nature's beauty, loved one's rhythm,
The springtime urge repeating.

What will give us courage deep,
Joy in the things that are?
The true and lasting love of friends
For us, will go most far.

Madeline Benedict — Human Need

Hearts are linked by God. The friend in whose fidelity you can count, whose success in life flushes your cheek with honest satisfaction, whose triumphant career you have traced and read with a heart-throbbing almost as if it were a thing alive, for whose honor you would answer as for your own; that friend, given to you by circumstances over which you have no control, was God's own gift.

F. W. Robertson

Once being asked how we should treat our friends, Aristotle said, "As we would wish them to treat us." Asked what a friend is, he answered, "One soul abiding in two bodies."

Diogenes Laertius

It is only the greathearted who can be true friends. The mean, the cowardly, can never know what true friendship means.

Charles Kingsley

The man that hails you Tom or Jack,
And proves, by thumping on your back,
His sense of your great merit,
Is such a friend that one had need
Be very much his friend indeed
To pardon or to bear it.

William Cowper

Friendship is better than wealth, to possess the love of a true heart, the sympathy of a noble soul, is better than to be a desolate millionaire.

George MacDonald

Because of a friend, life is a little stronger, fuller, more gracious thing for the friend's existence, whether he be near or far. If the friend is close at hand, that is best; but if he is far away he still is there to think of, to wonder about, to hear from, to write to, to share life and experience with, to serve, to honor, to admire, to love.

Arthur Christopher Benson

I didn't find my friends; the good God gave them to me.

Ralph Waldo Emerson

Some men make you feel as though the warm sun had just broken through the clouds, while others make you feel as though a sudden east wind, with its arms full of cold fog, had caught you with too thin clothing.

Edward Young

Treat your friends for what you know them to be. Regard no surfaces. Consider not what they did, but what they intended.

Henry David Thoreau

By friendship you mean the greatest love, the greatest usefulness, the most open communication, the noblest suffering, the severest truth, the heartiest counsel, and the greatest union of minds of which brave men and women are capable.

Jeremy Taylor

So long as we love, we serve. So long as we are loved by others I would almost say we are indispensable; and no man is useless while he has a friend.

Robert Louis Stevenson

The things which our friends do with and for us, form a portion of our lives; for they strengthen and advance our personality.

Johann Wolfgang von Goethe

Do not remove a fly from a friend's forehead with a hatchet.

Chinese Proverb

A friend is one who takes your hand
  And talks a speech you understand.
He's partly kindness, partly mirth —
  And faith unfaltering in your worth.
He's first to cheer you in success
  And last to leave you in distress.
A friend is constant, honest, true —
  In short, old pal, he's just like you.

Edgar A. Guest — A Real Friend

Once I found a dear friend. 'Dear me,' I said, 'he was made for me.' But now I find more and more friends who seem to have been made for me, and more and yet more made for me. Is it possible we were all made for each other all around the world?

Gilbert Keith Chesterton

I do not tremble when I meet
The stoutest of my foes,
But heaven defend me from a friend
Who comes but never goes.

John Godfrey Saxe

The only way to have a friend is to be one.

Ralph Waldo Emerson

These are the things I prize
  And hold of dearest worth:
Light of the sapphire skies,
Peace of the silent hills,
Shelter of the forests, comfort of the grass,
Music of birds, murmur of little rills,
Shadows of clouds that swiftly pass,
  And, after showers,
  The smell of flowers
And of the good brown earth —
And best of all, along the way, friendship
  and mirth.

Henry Van Dyke — The Things I Prize

The best way to keep your friends is to never owe them anything and never lend them anything.

Paul de Kock

God save me from my friends, I can protect myself from my enemies.

Marshal de Villars

Instead of loving your enemies, treat your friends a little better.

Edgar Watson Howe

Whoever looks for a friend without imperfections will never find what he seeks.

St. Syrus Ephream

In the hour of distress and misery the eye of every mortal turns to friendship; in the hour of gladness and conviviality, what is our want? It is friendship. When the heart overflows with gratitude, or with any other sweet and sacred sentiment, what is the word to which it would give utterance? A friend.

Walter Savage Landor

O grant me, Heaven, a middle state,
Neither too humble nor too great;
More than enough for nature's ends,
With something left to treat my friends.

David Mallet

A friend you have to buy won't be worth what you pay for him.

George D. Prentice

A friend that ain't in need is a friend indeed.

Kin Hubbard

The ring of coin is often the knell of friendship.

François, Duc de La Rochefoucauld

The man who will give you, as the phrase goes, a piece of his mind, who tells you of your faults to your face in what he thinks is a candid sort of fashion — such a friend as this may be the very soul of sincerity, but a very disagreeable companion.

Lady Eastlake

We are all travellers in the wilderness of this world, and the best that we find in our travels is an honest friend.

Robert Louis Stevenson

It is my joy in life to find
At every turning of the road
The strong arm of a comrade kind.
To help me onward with my load.

And since I have no gold to give,
And love alone must make amends,
My only prayer is, while I live—
God make me worthy of my friends.

Frank Dempster Sherman — A Prayer

He that blows the coals in a quarrel he has
nothing to do with has no right to complain if
the sparks fly in his face.

Benjamin Franklin

Better are the blows of a friend than the false
kisses of an enemy.

Thomas à Becket

Say not that friendship's but a name,
Sincere we none can find;
An empty bubble in the air,
A phantom of the mind.
What is life without a friend?
A dreary race to run,
A desert where no water is,
A world without a sun.

Henry Alford

We take care of our health, we lay up our
money, we make our roof tight and our
clothing sufficient, but who provides wisely
that he shall not be wanting in the best
property of all—friends?

Ralph Waldo Emerson

Surely there is no more beautiful sight to see
in all this world,—full as it is of beautiful
adjustments and mutual ministrations,—than
the growth of two friends' natures who, as
they grow old together, are always fathoming,
with newer needs, deeper depths of each other's
life, and opening richer veins of one another's
helpfulness. And this best culture of personal
friendship is taken up and made, in its infinite completion, the gospel method of the
progressive saving of the soul by Christ.

Phillips Brooks

To me, fair friend, you never can be old,
For as you were when first your eye I eyed,
Such seems your beauty still. Three winters
    cold
Have from the forests shook three summers'
    pride,
Three beauteous springs to yellow autumn
    turn'd
In process of the seasons have I seen,
Three April perfumes in three hot Junes
    burn'd,
Since first I saw you fresh, which yet are green.
Ah, yet doth beauty, like a dial-hand,
Steal from his figure, and no pace perceived;
So your sweet hue, which methinks still doth
    stand,
Hath motion, and mine eye may be deceived:
    For fear of which, hear this, thou age unbred;
    Ere you were born was beauty's summer
        dead.

William Shakespeare — Sonnet CIV

There is no friend like an old friend
    Who has shared our morning days,
No greeting like his welcome,
    No homage like his praise.
Fame is the scentless flower,
    With gaudy crown of gold;
But friendship is the breathing rose,
    With sweets in every fold.

Oliver Wendell Holmes — A Friend

Oh, the comfort, the inexpressible comfort
of feeling safe with a person; having neither
to weigh thoughts nor measure words, but to
pour them all out, just as they are, chaff and
grain together, knowing that a faithful hand
will take and sift them, keep what is worth
keeping, and then, with the breath of kindness,
blow the rest away.

Dinah Maria Mulock Craik

There is no better looking-glass than an old
friend.

Alexander Pope

Love, to endure life's sorrow and earth's woe,
Needs friendship's solid masonry below.

Ella Wheeler Wilcox

Beautiful and rich is an old friendship,
Grateful to the touch as ancient ivory,
Smooth as aged wine, or sheen or tapestry
Where light has lingered, intimate and long.
Full of tears and warm is an old friendship
That asks no longer deeds of gallantry,
Or any deed at all—save that the friend shall be
Alive and breathing somewhere, like a song.

Eunice Tietjens — Old Friendship

It seems the world was always bright
    With some divine unclouded weather,
When we, with hearts and footsteps light,
    By lawn and river walked together.

There was no talk of me and you,
    Of theories with facts to bound them,
We were content to be and do,
    And take our fortunes as we found them . . .

It seems I was not hard to please,
    Where'er you led I needs must follow;
For strength you were my Hercules,
    For wit and luster my Apollo.

The years flew onward: stroke by stroke,
    They clashed from the impartial steeple,
And we appear to other folk
    A pair of ordinary people.

One word, old friend: though fortune flies,
    If hope should fail—till death shall sever—
In one dim pair of faithful eyes
    You seem as bright, as brave as ever.

Arthur Christopher Benson — My Friend

"Stay" is a charming word in a friend's
vocabulary.

Amos Bronson Alcott

I have three chairs in my house: one for
solitude, two for friendship, and three for
company.

Henry David Thoreau

Half the pleasure of solitude comes from
having with us some friend to whom we can
say how sweet solitude is.

William Jay

He who throws away a friend is as bad as he
who throws away his life.

Sophocles

I like a friend better for having faults that
one can talk about.

William Hazlitt

As yellow gold is tried in the fire, so the faith
of friendship can only be known in the season
of adversity.

Ovid

When trouble comes your soul to try,
You love the friend who just "stands by."
Perhaps there's nothing he can do—
The thing is strictly up to you;
For there are troubles all your own,
And paths the soul must tread alone;
Times when love cannot smooth the road
Nor friendship lift the heavy load,
But just to know you have a friend
Who will "stand by" until the end,
Whose sympathy through all endures,
Whose warm handclasp is always yours—
It helps, someways, to pull you through,
Although there's nothing he can do.
And so with fervent heart you cry,
"God bless the friend who just 'stands by'."

B. Y. Williams — The Friend Who Just Stands By

Friendship is a strong and habitual inclination
in two persons to promote the good and
happiness of one another.

Eustace Budgell

A faithful friend is a sturdy shelter;
    he who finds one finds a treasure.
A faithful friend is beyond price,
    no sum can balance his worth.
A faithful friend is a life-saving remedy,
    such as he who fears God finds;
For he who fears God behaves accordingly,
    and his friend will be like himself.

Ecclesiasticus 6:14-17

A friend is the one who comes in when the
whole world has gone out.

Anonymous

Brotherhood

I would be true, for there are those who trust
  me;
I would be pure, for there are those who care;
I would be strong, for there is much to suffer;
I would be brave, for there is much to dare.
I would be friend of all — the poor — the
  friendless;
I would be giving and forget the gift;
I would be humble, for I know my weakness;
I would look up — and laugh — and love —
  and lift.

Howard Arnold Walter — My Creed

I believe that we can live on earth according
to the teachings of Jesus, and that the greatest
happiness will come to the world when man
obeys His commandment "Love ye one another."

I believe that we can live on earth according
to the fulfillment of God's will, and that when
the will of God is done on earth as it is done
in heaven, every man will love his fellow men,
and act towards them as he desires they should
act towards him. I believe that the welfare of
each is bound up in the welfare of all.

I believe that life is given us so we may grow in
love, and I believe that God is in me as the sun
is in the color and fragrance of a flower — the
Light in my darkness, the Voice in my silence.

I believe that only in broken gleams has the
Sun of Truth yet shone upon men. I believe
that love will finally establish the Kingdom of
God on earth, and that the Cornerstones of
that Kingdom will be Liberty, Truth, Brotherhood, and Service.

Helen Keller

I believe that man will not merely endure:
he will prevail. He is immortal not because he
alone among creatures has an inexhaustible
voice, but because he has a soul, a spirit
capable of compassion and sacrifice and
endurance.

William Faulkner

If you have learned to walk
A little more sure-footedly than I,
Be patient with my stumbling then
And know that only as I do my best and try
May I attain the goal
For which we both are striving.

If through experience, your soul
Has gained heights which I
As yet in dim-lit vision see,
Hold out your hand and point the way,
Lest from its straightness I should stray,
And walk a mile with me.

Anonymous

Until you become really, in actual fact, a
brother to every one, brotherhood will not
come to pass.

Fyodor Dostoyevsky

We have committed the Golden Rule to
memory; let us now commit it to life.

Edwin Markham

I dream a world where man
No other will scorn,
Where love will bless the earth
And peace its paths adorn.
I dream a world where all
Will know sweet freedom's way,
Where greed no longer saps the soul
Nor avarice blights our day.
A world I dream where black or white,
Whatever race you be,
Will share the bounties of the earth
And every man is free,
Where wretchedness will hang its head,
And joy, like a pearl,
Attend the needs of all mankind.
Of such I dream —
Our world!

Langston Hughes — I Dream A World

O brother man, fold to thy heart thy brother:
  Where pity dwells, the peace of God is there;
To worship rightly is to love each other,
  Each smile a hymn, each kindly deed a
    prayer.

John Greenleaf Whittier

Every soul that touches yours—
Be it the slightest contact—
Gets therefrom some good;
Some little grace; one kindly thought;
One aspiration yet unfelt;
One bit of courage
For the darkening sky;
One gleam of faith
To brave the thickening ills of life;
One glimpse of brighter skies—
To make this life worthwhile
And heaven a surer heritage.

George Eliot — Making Life Worth While

The one essential thing is that we strive to
have light in ourselves. Our strivings will be
recognized by others, and when people have
light in themselves, it will shine out from them.
Then we get to know each other as we walk
together in the darkness, without needing
to pass our hands over each other's faces, or
to intrude into each other's hearts.

Albert Schweitzer

Blessed is the servant who loves his brother
as much when he is sick and useless as when
he is well and can be of service to him. And
blessed is he who loves his brother as well
when he is afar off as when he is by his side,
and who would say nothing behind his back
he might not, in love, say before his face.

St. Francis of Assisi

Let me live in my house by the side of the road
   Where the race of men go by—
They are good, they are bad, they are weak,
      they are strong,
   Wise, foolish—so am I.
Then why should I sit in the scorner's seat
   Or hurl the cynic's ban?—
Let me live in my house by the side of the road
And be a friend to man.

Sam Walter Foss — The House by the Side of the Road

Are you lonely, O my brother?
   Share your little with another!
Stretch your hand to one unfriended,
   And your loneliness is ended.

John Oxenham

If you hear a kind word spoken
Of some worthy soul you know,
It may fill his heart with sunshine
If you only tell him so.

If a deed, however humble,
Helps you on your way to go,
Seek the one whose hand has helped you,
Seek him out and tell him so!

If your heart is touched and tender
Toward a sinner lost and low,
It might help him to do better
If you'd only tell him so!

Oh, my sisters, oh, my brothers,
As o'er life's rough path you go,
If God's love has saved and kept you,
Do not fail to tell men so!

Anonymous — Tell Him So

Grant us brotherhood, not only for this day
but for all our years—a brotherhood not of
words but of acts and needs.

Stephen Vincent Benét

Brotherhood is not just a Bible word. Out of
comradeship can come and will come the happy
life for all.

Heywood Broun

It is not enough that you should understand
about applied science in order that your work
may increase man's blessings. Concern for man
himself and his fate must always form the
chief interest of all technical endeavors, concern for the great unsolved problems of the
organization of labor and the distribution of
goods — in order that the creations of our
mind shall be a blessing and not a curse to
mankind. Never forget this in the midst of your
diagrams and equations.

Albert Einstein

There is a destiny that makes us brothers;
None goes his way alone:
All that we send into the lives of others
Comes back into our own.

Edwin Markham

It is the very essence of love, of nobleness, of greatness, to be willing to suffer for the good of others.

Herbert Spencer

Kindness

You cannot do a kindness too soon, because you never know how soon it will be too late.

Old Proverb

The best cure for worry, depression, melancholy, brooding, is to go deliberately forth and try to lift with one's sympathy the gloom of somebody else.

Arnold Bennett

Life is made up, not of great sacrifices or duties, but of little things in which smiles and kindness and small obligations given habitually, are what win and preserve the heart and secure comfort.

Sir Humphry Davy

Kindness is the golden chain by which society is bound together.

Johann Wolfgang von Goethe

Find him who shows most virtue in all ways
And minds his business, save that all his days,
He tries to do the gentlest deeds he can:
Take that man for your greatest gentleman.

Geoffrey Chaucer

A part of kindness consists in loving people more than they deserve.

Joseph Joubert

A kindly act is a kernel sown,
That will grow to a goodly tree,
Shedding its fruit when time has flown
Down the gulf of eternity.

John Boyle O'Reilly

Truth generally is kindness, but where the two diverge and collide, kindness should override truth.

Samuel Butler

I expect to pass this way but once; any good therefore that I can do, or any kindness that I can show to any fellow creature, let me do it now. Let me not defer or neglect it, for I shall not pass this way again.

Etienne de Grellet

No one is useless in the world who lightens the burden of it for anyone else.

Charles Dickens

Kindness is the sunshine in which virtue grows.

Robert Ingersoll

Among the pitfalls in our way,
The best of us walk blindly;
So, man, be wary, watch and pray,
And judge your brother kindly.

Alice Cary

The most delicate, the most sensible of all pleasures, consists in promoting the pleasure of others.

Jean de La Bruyère

The quality of mercy is not strained,
It droppeth as the gentle rain from heaven
Upon the place beneath: it is twice blessed;
It blesseth him that gives and him that takes:
'Tis mightiest in the mightiest: it becomes
The throned monarch better than his crown;
His scepter shows the force of temporal power,
The attribute of awe and majesty,
Wherein doth sit the dread and fear of kings;
But mercy is above that sceptered sway,
It is enthroned in the heart of kings;
It is an attribute to God himself;
And earthly power doth then show like God's
When mercy seasons justice.

William Shakespeare

The greatest pleasure I know is to do a good action by stealth, and to have it found out by accident.

Charles Lamb

Charity — the only thing we can give away without losing it.

Horace Smith

A good manner springs from a good heart,
and fine manners are the outcome of unselfish
kindness.

Anonymous

If you sit down at set of sun
And count the acts that you have done
   And counting, find
One self-denying deed, one word
That eased the heart of him who heard —
   One glance most kind,
That fell like sunshine where it went
Then you may count that day well spent.

But if, through all the livelong day
You've cheered no heart, by yea or nay —
   If, through it all
You've nothing done that you can tracc
That brought the sunshine to one face —
   No act most small
That helped some soul and nothing cost —
Then count that day as worse than lost.

George Eliot — You May Count That Day

According to the old proverb, 'Charity
covers a multitude of skins.'

O. Henry

Because I have been sheltered, fed,
By thy good care,
I cannot see another's lack
And I not share
My glowing fire, my loaf of bread,
My roof's safe shelter overhead,
That he, too, may be comforted.

Grace Noll Crowell

Do not wait for extraordinary circumstances to
do good actions: try to use ordinary situations.

Jean Paul Richter

We should give as we would receive, cheerfully,
quickly, and without hesitation, for there is
no grace in a benefit that sticks to our fingers.

Seneca

He hath a tear for pity, and a hand
Open as day for melting charity.

William Shakespeare

Politeness is like an air cushion; there may be
nothing in it, but it eases our jolts wonderfully.

Will Carleton

There is a great man who makes every man
feel small. But the real great man is the man
who makes every man feel great.

Gilbert Keith Chesterton

If an unkind word appears,
   File the thing away,
If some novelty in jeers,
   File the thing away,
If some clever little bit
   Of a sharp and pointed wit,
Carrying a sting with it,
   File the thing away.

If some bit of gossip come,
   File the thing away.
Scandalously spicy crumb,
   File the thing away.
If suspicion comes to you
   That your neighbor isn't true
Let me tell you what to do —
   File the thing away.
Do this for a little while,
   Then go out and burn the pile.

John Kendrick Bangs — On File

The greater the man, the greater the courtesy.

Alfred, Lord Tennyson

Good manners and soft words have brought
many a difficult thing to pass.

Aesop

The most skilful flattery is to let a person
talk on, and be a listener.

Joseph Addison

How sweet and gracious, even in common
   speech
Is that fine sense which men call courtesy!
Wholesome as the air and genial as the light.
Welcome in every clime as breath of flowers,
It transmutes aliens into trusting friends,
And gives the owner passport 'round the globe.

James Thomas Fields

Life is not so short but there is always time enough for courtesy.

Ralph Waldo Emerson

I can live for two months on a good compliment.

Mark Twain

Friendship cannot live with ceremony, nor without civility.

Lord Halifax

Tact is the ability to close your mouth before someone else wants to.

Anonymous

Kind words cost no more than unkind ones. Kind words produce kind actions, not only on the part of those to whom they are addressed, but on the part of those by whom they are employed: and this not incidentally only, but habitually in virtue of the principle of association.

Jeremy Bentham

Humanity

I have come to see life, not as a chase of forever impossible personal happiness, but as a field for endeavor toward the happiness of the whole human family. There is no other success. I know indeed of nothing more subtly satisfying and cheering than a knowledge of the real good will and appreciation of others. Such happiness does not come with money; nor does it flow from a fine physical state. It cannot be bought. But it is the keenest joy, after all, and the toiler's truest and best reward.

William Dean Howells

It is contact with others which teaches man all he knows.

Euripides

The faults of our neighbors with freedom we blame,
And tax not ourselves, though we practice the same.

Robert Blair

To have courage without pugnacity,
to have conviction without bigotry,
to have charity without condescension,
to have faith without credulity,
to have love of humanity without mere
    sentimentality,
to have meekness with power
and emotion with sanity—
that is brotherhood.

Charles Evans Hughes

There is no one in the whole human family to whom kindly affection is not due by reason of the bond of a common humanity, although it may not be due on the ground of reciprocal love.

St. Augustine

No man has come to true greatness who has not felt that his life belongs to his race, and that which God gives him, He gives him for mankind.

Phillips Brooks

Man is a special being, and if left to himself, in an isolated condition, would be one of the weakest creatures; but associated with his kind, he works wonders.

Daniel Webster

No man is an island entire of itself. Every man is a piece of the continent, a part of the main. If a clod be washed away by the sea, Europe is the less, as well as if a promontory were, as well as if a manor of thy friends or of thine own were. Any man's death diminishes me, because I am involved in mankind. Therefore never send to know for whom the bell tolls. It tolls for thee.

John Donne

The universe is but one great city, full of beloved ones, divine and human by nature, endeared to each other.

Epictetus

Maturing is the process by which the individual becomes conscious of the equal importance of each of his fellow men.

Alvin Goeser

We are all citizens of one world, we are all of one blood. To hate a man because he was born in another country, because he speaks a different language, or because he takes a different view on this subject or that, is a great folly. Desist, I implore you, for we are all equally human . . . Let us have but one end in view, the welfare of humanity.

Johann Amos Comenius

All is well with him who is beloved of his neighbors.

George Herbert

A man is called selfish, not for pursuing his own good, but for neglecting his neighbor's.

Richard Whately

To God be humble, to thy friend be kind,
And with thy neighbors gladly lend and borrow:
His chance tonight, it may be thine tomorrow.

Wiliam Dunbar

A virtuous deed should never be delayed, the impulse comes from heaven; and he who strives a moment to repress it, disobeys the God within his mind.

Edward Dowden

And the poorest one yet in the humblest abode
May help a poor brother a step on the road.

Charles Swain

If I can stop one Heart from breaking
I shall not live in vain
If I can ease one Life the Aching
Or cool one Pain

Or help one fainting Robin
Unto his Nest again
I shall not live in Vain.

Emily Dickinson

Every man's neighbor is his looking-glass.

James Howell

Your own safety is at stake when your neighbor's house is in flames.

Horace

Just do what you can. It's not enough merely to exist. It's not enough to say, "I'm earning enough to live and support my family. I do my work well. I'm a good father. I'm a good husband." That's all very well. *But you must do something more.* Seek always to do some good, somewhere. Every man has to seek in his own way to make his own self more noble and to realize his own true worth. You must give some time to your fellowman. Even if it's a little thing, do something for those who have need of help, something for which you get no pay but the privilege of doing it. For remember, you don't live in a world all your own. *Your brothers are here, too.*

Albert Schweitzer

Do all the good you can
By all the means you can
In all the ways you can
In all the places you can
At all the times you can
To all the people you can
As long as ever you can.

Anonymous

Men resemble the gods in nothing so much as in doing good to their fellow creatures.

Cicero

The superior man stands erect by bending above the fallen. He rises by lifting others.

Robert G. Ingersoll

No man has ever risen to the real stature of spiritual manhood until he has found that it is finer to serve somebody else than it is to serve himself.

Woodrow Wilson

To be of service is a solid foundation for contentment in this world.

Charles W. Eliot

We ought to do good to others as simply and as naturally as a horse runs, or a bee makes honey, or a vine bears grapes season after season without thinking of the grapes it has borne.

Marcus Aurelius

51

Love and Marriage

Romance

Young and in love — how magical the phrase!
How magical the fact! Who has not yearned
Over young lovers when to their amaze
They fall in love, and find their love returned,
And the lights brighten, and their eyes are clear
To see God's image in their common clay.
Is it the music of the spheres they hear?
Is it the prelude to that noble play
The drama of Joined Lives?

Alice Duer Miller — From The White Cliffs

O mistress mine, where are you roaming?
O, stay and hear; your true love's coming,
That can sing both high and low:
Trip no further, pretty sweeting;
Journeys end in lovers meeting,
Every wise man's son doth know.

What is love? 'tis not hereafter;
Present mirth hath present laughter;
What's to come is still unsure:
In delay there lies no plenty;
Then come kiss me, sweet-and-twenty,
Youth's a stuff will not endure.

William Shakespeare

He who is not impatient is not in love.

Pietro Aretino

There's nothing half so sweet in life
As love's young dream.

Thomas Moore

Love is a madness most discreet.

William Shakespeare

April's amazing meaning doubtless lies
In tall, hoarse boys and slips
Of slender girls with suddenly wider eyes
And parted lips;

For girls must wander pensive in the spring
When the green rain is over,
Doing some slow, inconsequential thing,
Plucking clover;

And any boy alone upon a bench
When his work's done will sit
And stare at the black ground and break a
  branch
And whittle it

Slowly; and boys and girls, irresolute,
Will curse the dreamy weather
Until they meet past the pale hedge and put
Their lips together.

George Dillon — April's Amazing Meaning

In dreams and love there are no impossibilities.

János Arany

To love is to place our happiness in the
happiness of another.

Gottfried von Leibnitz

No cord nor cable can so forcibly draw, or hold
so fast, as love can do with a twined thread.

Robert Burton

Courtship

Let my voice ring out and over the earth,
Through all the grief and strife,
With a golden joy in a silver mirth;
Thank God for life!

Let my voice swell out through the great abyss
To the azure dome above,
With a chord of faith in the harp of bliss:
Thank God for Love!

Let my voice thrill out beneath and above,
The whole world through:
O my love and life, O my life and love,
Thank God for you.

James Thomson — Song

There is no remedy for love but to love more.

Henry David Thoreau

There is no surprise more magical than the
surprise of being loved; it is God's finger on a
man's shoulder.

Charles Morgan

For your brother and my sister no sooner met
but they looked; no sooner looked but they
loved; no sooner loved but they sighed; no
sooner sighed but they asked one another the
reason; no sooner knew the reason but they
sought the remedy: and in these degrees have
they made a pair of stairs to marriage.

William Shakespeare

Two shall be born a whole wide world apart
And one day out of darkness they shall stand
And read life's meaning in each other's eyes.

Anonymous

Three words always grace the tongue—
Stammered, whispered, moaned, or sung:
    I love you.

Philomene Bourgeois

We don't believe in rheumatism and true love
until after the first attack.

Marie Enber-Eschnenbach

Who ever lov'd, that lov'd not at first sight!

Christopher Marlowe

That is the true season of love, when we believe
that we alone can love, that no one could ever
have loved so before us, and that no one will
love in the same way as us.

Johann Wolfgang von Goethe

He is not a lover who does not love forever.

Euripides

True love's the gift which God has given
To man alone beneath the heaven:
The silver link, the silken tie,
Which heart to heart and mind to mind
In body and in soul can bind.

Sir Walter Scott

Love is an image of God; and not a lifeless
image, nor one painted on paper, but the living
essence of the Divine Nature which beams full
of all goodness.

Martin Luther

Love is a proud and gentle thing,
    a better thing to own
Than all of the wide impossible stars
    over the heavens blown,
And the little gifts her hand gives
    are careless given or taken,
And though the whole great world break,
    the heart of her is not shaken . . .
Love is a viol in the wind,
    a viol never stilled.

And mine of all is the surest
    that ever time has willed . . .
And the things that love gives after
    shall be as they were before,
For life is only a small house . . .
    and love is an open door.

Orrick Johns — Love Is An Open Door

Oh, love, love, love!
Love is like a dizziness,
It winna let a poor body
Go about his biziness.

James Hogg

Yes, Love indeed is light from heaven;
A spark of that immortal fire.

George Gordon, Lord Byron

To live is like to love — all reason is against
it, and all healthy instinct for it.

Samuel Butler

It is a glorious privilege to live, to know, to act,
to listen, to behold, to love. To look up at the
blue summer sky; to see the sun sink slowly
beyond the line of the horizon; to watch the
worlds come twinkling into view, first one by
one, and the myriads that no man can count,
and lo! the universe is white with them; and
you and I are here.

Marco Morrow

Doubt thou the stars are fire;
Doubt thou that the sun doth move;
Doubt truth to be a liar,
But never doubt I love.

William Shakespeare

Love is a circle, that doth restless move
In the same sweet eternity of love.

Robert Herrick

Love is the enchanted dawn of every heart.

Alphonse de Lamartine

This is the miracle that happens every time
to those who really love: the more they give, the
more they possess of that precious nourishing
love from which flowers and children have their
strength and which could help all human beings
if they would take it without doubting.

Rainer Maria Rilke

I wonder what fool it was that first invented
kissing.

Jonathan Swift

There is nothing holier in this life of ours than
the first consciousness of love — the first
fluttering of its silken wings — the first rising
sound and breath of that wind which is so soon
to sweep through the soul.

Henry Wadsworth Longfellow

We are all born for love: it is the principle
of existence and its only end.

Benjamin Disraeli

Love is a second life; it grows into the soul,
warms every vein, and beats in every pulse.

Joseph Addison

Love ever gives,
Forgives, outlives,
And ever stands
With open hands.
And, while it lives,
It gives.
For this is Love's prerogative —
To give and give and give.

John Oxenham

I knew you thought of me all night,
I knew though you were far away;
I felt your love blow over me
As if a dark wind-riven sea
Drenched me with quivering spray.

There are so many ways to love
And each way has its own delights —
Then be content to come to me
Only as spray the beating sea
Drives inland through the night.

Sara Teasdale — Spray

How many other lovers, dear, have named
The slow red harvest moon as all their own?
How many others have fenced off this hill
With barbed September stars, for two alone;
Or glimpsed this woods, and laid a breathless
   claim
To all its beauty, bright with autumn's flame?

How many other hearts at dusk pretend
Theirs is the lamplight at the gray road's end?

Edna Casler Joll — Waiting Dreams

I love her with a love as still
As a broad river's peaceful might,
Which by high tower and lowly mill,
Goes wandering at its own will,
And yet does ever flow aright.

James Russell Lowell

Not from the whole wide world I chose thee—
Sweetheart, light of the land and the sea!
The wide, wide world could not enclose thee,
For thou art the whole wide world to me.

Richard Watson Gilder — Song

We love being in love, that's the truth on't.

William Makepeace Thackeray

Love is said to be blind, but I know lots of
fellows in love who can see twice as much in
their sweethearts as I can.

Josh Billings

Love is something eternal — the aspect may
change, but not the essence. There is the same
difference in a person before and after he is in
love as there is in an unlighted lamp and one
that is burning. The lamp was there and it was
a good lamp, but now it is shedding light, too,
and that is its real function.

Vincent van Gogh

The fountains mingle with the river
And the rivers with the ocean;
The winds of heaven mix forever
With a sweet emotion;
Nothing in the world is single;
All things by a law divine
In one spirit meet and mingle.
Why not I with thine?

See the mountains kiss high heaven,
And the waves clasp one another;
No sister-flower would be forgiven
If it disdained its brother;
And the sunlight clasps the earth,
And the moonbeams kiss the sea:
What are all these kissings worth
If thou kiss not me?

Percy Bysshe Shelley — Love's Philosophy

If we spend our lives in loving, we have no
leisure to complain, or to feel unhappiness.

Joseph Joubert

Those who love deeply never grow old; they
may die of old age, but they die young.

Sir Arthur Pinero

Love is the most terrible, and also the most
generous of the passions; it is the only one
which includes in its dreams the happiness of
someone else.

Alphonse Karr

Love iz like the meazles; we kant have it bad
but onst, and the later in life we have it the
tuffer it goes with us.

Josh Billings

It is strange to talk of miracles, revelations,
inspiration, and the like, as things past, while
love remains.

Henry David Thoreau

I like not only to be loved, but also to be told
that I am loved. I am not sure that you are of
the same kind. But the realm of silence is large
enough beyond the grave. This is the world
of light and speech, and I shall take leave to tell
you that you are very dear.

George Eliot

Love does not consist in gazing at each other
but in looking outward together in the same
direction.

Antoine de Saint-Exupéry

Love is a miracle,
Making hearts sing,
Love is a beautiful,
Wonderful thing.

Love is a precious gift
Worth more than gold,
And love that is true love
Never grows old.

Helen Farries — True Love Never Grows Old

The supreme happiness in life is the conviction
of being loved for yourself, or, more correctly,
being loved in spite of yourself.

Victor Hugo

Love, in the divine alchemy of life, transmutes
all duties into privileges, all responsibilities
into joys.

William George Jordan

Let me not to the marriage of true minds
Admit impediments. Love is not love
Which alters when it alteration finds,
Or bends with the remover to remove.
O, no! it is an ever-fixed mark
That looks on tempests, and is never shaken;
It is the star to every wandering bark,
Whose worth's unknown, although his height
   be taken.
Love's not Time's fool, though rosy lips and
   cheeks
Within his bending sickle's compass come;
Love alters not with his brief hours and weeks,
But bears it out even to the edge of doom.
   If this be error and upon me proved,
   I never writ, nor no man ever loved.

          William Shakespeare — Sonnet CXVI

The light of love
   shines over all,
Of love, that says
   not mine and thine,
But ours, for ours
   is thine and mine.

          Henry Wadsworth Longfellow

Many a man has fallen in love with a girl in a
light so dim he would not have chosen a suit
by it.

          Maurice Chevalier

The lesser gods are decorous
   And with a meek petition wait;
But Love comes, fixing his own hour,
   And hammers at the gate.

He comes, announcing final terms,
   And never cries his purpose twice;
For he has half of earth to give,
   And all of Paradise!

          Edwin Markham — Imperious Love

Love, love! The night of golden nights is this,
Filled with the beating of all joyous wings;
For beauty is made holy in your kiss
And love and loveliness immortal things.
And all my being quivers with the cry
Of happy, happy, happy to the sky.

          Eunice Tietjens — From The Mountain

Love's on the highroad,
Love's in the byroad —
Love's on the meadow, and Love's on the mart!
And down every byway
Where I have taken my way
I've met Love a-smiling — for Love's in my
   heart!

          Dana Burnet — Song

Since we parted yester eve,
I do love thee, love, believe,
Twelve times dearer, twelve hours longer,—
One dream deeper, one night stronger,
One sun surer, — thus much more
Than I loved thee, love, before.

          Edward Robert Bulwer-Lytton — Since We Parted

I am wild, I will sing to the trees,
   I will sing to the stars in the sky,
I love, I am loved, he is mine,
   Now at last I can die!

I am sandaled with wind and with flame,
   I have heart-fire and singing to give,
I can tread on the grass or the stars,
   Now at last I can live!

          Sara Teasdale — Joy

Love, then hath every bliss in store;
'Tis friendship and 'tis something more.
Each other every wish they give;
Not to know love is not to live.

          John Gay

All the breath and the bloom of the year
   in the bag of one bee;
   All the wonder and wealth of the mine
      in the heart of one gem;
In the core of one pearl all the shade and
   the shine of the sea;
   Breath and bloom, shade and shine, —
      wonder, wealth, and — how far
      above them —
   Truth, that's brighter than gem,
   Truth, that's purer than pearl, —
Brightest truth, purest trust in the universe —
   all were for me
   In the kiss of one girl.

          Robert Browning

Love has no other desire but to fulfill itself.
To melt and be like a running brook that sings
its melody to the night. To wake at dawn with
a winged heart and give thanks for another
day of loving.

Kahlil Gibran

True love is always young in the heart.

Honoré de Balzac

Love is a fire in whose devouring flames all
earthly ills are consumed.

Robert Bridges

In all your thoughts, and in all your acts, in
every hope and in every fear, when you soar
to the skies and when you fall to the ground,
always you are holding the other person's hand.

A. A. Milne

My bounty is as boundless as the sea,
My love as deep; the more I give to thee
The more I have, for both are infinities.

William Shakespeare

Endless torments dwell about thee: Yet who
would live, and live without thee!

Joseph Addison

Love is not blind — it sees more, not less. But
because it sees more, it is willing to see less.

Julius Gordon

Matrimony

Going my way of old
Contented more or less
I dreamt not life could hold
Such happiness.

I dreamt not that love's way
Could keep the golden height
Day after happy day,
Night after night.

Wilfrid Wilson Gibson — Marriage

An ideal wife is any woman who has an ideal
husband.

Booth Tarkington

There's a promise of love everlasting,
    Of joys even sweeter than now
In the words you're repeating together,
    The words of that beautiful vow.

There's assurance of someone to comfort,
    To count on "in sickness and health,"
And no matter if "richer or poorer,"
    True love is the greatest of wealth.

In that beautiful vow you're repeating,
    Those sweet words, "to have and to hold,"
In that promise "to love and to cherish,"
    Are treasures more precious than gold.

Through a lifetime of love, keep repeating
    The words of that beautiful vow,
And the years will hold joys that are sweeter,
    More beautiful memories than now.

Helen Farries — In the Words of That Beautiful Vow

The highest happiness on earth is in marriage.
Every man who is happily married is a successful man even if he has failed in everything
else.

William Lyon Phelps

I; —
Thou; —
We; —
They; —
Small words, but mighty.
In their span
Are bound the life and hopes of man.
For, first, his thoughts of his own self are full;
Until another comes his heart to rule.
For them, life's best is centered round their love;
Till younger lives come all their love to prove.

John Oxenham — The Little Poem of Life

A happy marriage has in it all the pleasures
of friendship, all the enjoyments of sense and
reason, and, indeed, all the sweets of life.

Joseph Addison

Marriage, rightly understood
Gives to the tender and the good
A paradise below.

John Cotton

The happiness of life is made up of minute
fractions — the little, soon forgotten charities
of a kiss or smile, a kind look, a heartfelt
compliment — countless infinitesimals of
pleasurable and genial feeling.

Samuel Taylor Coleridge

I need so much the quiet of your love
    After the day's loud strife;
I need your calm all other things above
    After the stress of life.

I crave the haven that in your dear heart lies
    After all toil is done;
I need the starshine of your lovely eyes
    After the day's great sun.

Charles Hanson Towne

There is more of good nature than of good
sense at the bottom of most marriages.

Henry David Thoreau

Of all the home remedies, a good wife is the
best.

Kin Hubbard

He is the half part of a blessed man,
Left to be finished by such a she;
And she a fair divided excellence,
Whose fullness of perfection lies in him.

William Shakespeare

No man knows what the wife of his bosom
is — what a ministering angel she is, until he
has gone with her through the fiery trials of
this world.

Washington Irving

Why man, she is mine own;
And I as rich in having such a jewel,
As twenty seas if all their sands were pearl,
The water nectar, and the rocks pure gold.

William Shakespeare

The treasures of the deep are not so precious
as are the concealed comforts of a man locked
up in a woman's love. I scent the air of
blessings when I come but near the house.

Thomas Middleton

The feller that puts off marryin' till he can
support a wife ain't very much in love.

Kin Hubbard

Ay, marriage is the life-long miracle,
The self-begetting wonder, daily fresh.

Charles Kingsley

If a man really loves a woman, of course he
wouldn't marry her for the world if he were not
quite sure that he was the best person she
could by any possibility marry.

Oliver Wendell Holmes

To love means to decide independently to live
with an equal partner, and to subordinate oneself to the formation of a new subject, a "we".

Fritz Kunkel

Such a large sweet fruit is a comfortable
marriage, that it needs a very long summer
to ripen in and then a long winter to mellow
and sweeten in.

Theodore Parker

What is there in the vale of life
Half so delightful as a wife,
When friendship, love, and peace combine
To stamp the marriage-bond divine?

William Cowper

The sum which two married people owe to
one another defies calculation. It is an infinite
debt, which can only be discharged through
all eternity.

Johann Wolfgang von Goethe

Let every husband stay a lover true,
And every wife remain a sweetheart too.

Anonymous

Before marriage man hovers above life,
observes it from without; only in marriage
does he plunge into it, entering it through the
personality of another.

Alexander Yelchaninov

A heaven on earth I have won by wooing thee.

William Shakespeare

59

There is no more lovely, friendly and charming relationship, communion or company than a good marriage.

Martin Luther

To Mamie,
For never-failing help since 1916 — in calm
    and in stress, in dark days and in bright.
Love — Ike
Christmas 1955

Dwight D. Eisenhower
Message engraved on a gold medallion
to his wife, December 25, 1955

God, the best maker of all marriages,
Combine your hearts in one.

William Shakespeare

I should like to know what is the proper function of women, if it is not to make reasons for husbands to stay home, and still stronger reasons for bachelors to go out.

George Eliot

No happiness is like unto it, no love so great as that of man and wife, no such comfort as a sweet wife.

Robert Burton

A good wife is heaven's last, best gift to man — his gem of many virtues, his casket of jewels; her voice is sweet music, her smiles his brightest day, her kiss the guardian of his innocence, her arms the pale of his safety, her industry his surest wealth, her economy his safest steward, her lips his faithful counsellors, her bosom the softest pillow of his cares.

Jeremy Taylor

Somewhere there waiteth in this world of ours
For one lone soul, another lonely soul —
Each chasing each through all the weary hours,
And meeting strangely at one sudden goal;
Then blend they — like green leaves with
    golden flowers,
Into one beautiful and perfect whole —
And life's long night is ended, and the way
Lies open onward to eternal day.

Sir Edwin Arnold

Two persons who have chosen each other out of all the species, with the design to be each other's mutual comfort and entertainment, have, in that action, bound themselves to be goodhumored, affable, discreet, forgiving, patient, and joyful, with respect to each other's frailties and perfections, to the end of their lives.

Joseph Addison

Marriage is that relation between man and woman in which the independence is equal, the dependence mutual, and the obligation reciprocal.

Louis K. Anspacher

One should believe in marriage as in the immortality of the soul.

Honoré de Balzac

If ever two were one, then surely we;
If ever man were loved by wife, then thee;
If ever wife was happy in a man,
Compare with me, ye women, if you can.
I prize thy love more than whole mines of gold,
Or all the riches that the East doth hold.
My love is such that rivers cannot quench,
Nor aught but love from thee give recompense.
Thy love is such I can no way repay;
The heavens reward thee manifold, I pray.
Then while we live in love let's so persevere
That when we live no more we may live ever.

Anne Bradstreet — To My Dear And Loving Husband

Marriage resembles a pair of shears, so joined that they can not be separated; often moving in opposite directions, yet always punishing anyone who comes between them.

Sydney Smith

One year of Joy, another of Comfort, the rest of Content, make the married Life happy.

Thomas Fuller

A good wife is a generous gift
    bestowed upon him who fears the Lord;
Be he rich or poor, his heart is content,
    and a smile is ever on his face.

Ecclesiasticus 26:3, 4

The world well tried — the sweetest thing in life
Is the unclouded welcome of a wife.

Nathaniel Parker Willis

One has no business to be married unless,
waking and sleeping, one is conscious of the
responsibility.

Abraham Flexner

Won 1880, One 1884.

William Jennings Bryan
(Inscription in wedding ring presented to his wife.)

There is no such cosy combination as man
and wife.

Menander

Marriage is the only known example of the
happy meeting of the immovable object and
the irresistible force.

Ogden Nash

The one word above all others that makes
marriage successful is 'ours.'

Robert Quillen

Every married man should believe there's but
one good wife in the world, and that's his own.

Jonathan Swift

When men enter into the state of marriage,
they stand nearest to God.

Henry Ward Beecher

Fidelity

You are my true and honorable wife,
Dear as the ruddy drops that warm my heart.

Thomas Gray

It takes a man twenty-five years to learn to be
married; it's a wonder women have the patience
to wait for it.

Clarence B. Kelland

The goal in marriage is not to think alike,
but to think together.

Robert C. Dodds

A wife is essential to great longevity; she is
the receptacle of half a man's cares, and
two-thirds of his ill-humor.

Charles Reade

Love, let us live as we have lived, nor lose
    The little names that were the first night's
        grace,
And never come the day that sees us old,
    I still your lad, and you my little lass.
Let me be older than old Nestor's years,
    And you the Sibyl, if we heed it not.
What should we know, we two, of ripe old age?
    We'll have its richness, and the years forgot.

Ausonius — To His Wife, translated from the Latin by
Helen Waddell

The best way for a husband to clinch an
argument is to take her in his arms.

Anonymous

The crowning glory of loving and being loved
is that the pair make no real progress; however
far they have advanced into the enchanted
land during the day they must start again from
the frontier the next morning.

James Barrie

This is no fallow field through which we travel,
    No barren land made waste by nature's rust;
This is no grassless plain where sand and gravel
    Are trod upon and ground to atom dust.

This is, instead, the fertile field of living
    Where you and I have scattered precious
        seed;
Where we have raised affection, and are giving,
    One to the other, what our spirits need.

Our grain is cut — the loam of life is mellow,
    A kindly sun is beaming from above.
We've reaped abundant years of ripened yellow,
    For crops are rich when two have planted
        love.

William W. Pratt — Golden Wedding

Love Is Eternal — Abraham Lincoln
Inscription of wedding ring presented to his wife,
Mary Todd Lincoln

61

We have lived and loved together
Through many changing years;
We have shared each other's gladness
And wept each other's tears;
I have known ne'er a sorrow
That was long unsoothed by thee;
For thy smiles can make a summer
Where darkness else would be.

Like the leaves that fall around us
In autumn's fading hours,
Are the traitor's smiles, that darken
When the cloud of sorrow lowers;
And though many such we've known, love,
Too prone, alas, to range,
We both can speak of one love
Which time can never change.

We have lived and loved together
Through many changing years,
We have shared each other's gladness
And wept each other's tears.
And let us hope the future
As the past has been will be:
I will share with thee my sorrows,
And thou thy joys with me.

Charles Jefferys — We Have Lived and Loved Together

A married man falling into misfortune is more
apt to retrieve his situation in the world than
a single one, chiefly because his spirits are
soothed and retrieved by domestic endearments,
and his self-respect kept alive by finding that,
although all abroad be darkness and humiliation, yet there is a little world of love at home
over which he is a monarch.

Jeremy Taylor

The happiness of married life depends upon
making small sacrifices with readiness and
cheerfulness.

John Seldon

A wife is one who shares her husband's
thought, incorporates his heart with hers in
love, and crowns him with her trust. She
is God's remedy for loneliness and God's
reward for all the toil of life.

Henry Van Dyke

She is a winsome wee thing,
She is a handsome wee thing,
She is a lo'esome wee thing,
    This sweet wee wife o' mine.

Robert Burns

My marriage was much the most fortunate
and joyous event which happened to me in the
whole of my life.

Winston Churchill

I should like to see any kind of a man,
distinguishable from a gorilla, that some good
and even pretty woman could not shape a
husband out of.

Oliver Wendell Holmes

For in what stupid age or nation
Was marriage ever out of fashion?

Samuel Butler

The satisfactions of normal married life do
not decline but mount.

Charles W. Eliot

I have this day been married fourteen years,
during which I have to bless God for the
enjoyment of a portion of felicity, resulting
from this relation in society, greater than falls
to the generality of mankind, and far beyond
anything that I have been conscious of
deserving.

John Quincy Adams — July 26, 1811

Thus let me hold thee to my heart,
    And every care resign:
And we shall never, never part,
    My life — my all that's mine!

Oliver Goldsmith

Every man who is high up loves to think he
has done it all himself; and the wife smiles,
and lets it go at that. It's only our joke. Every
woman knows that.

James Barrie

Heaven will be no heaven to me if I do not
meet my wife there.

Andrew Jackson

To Grace Coolidge . . .
For almost a quarter of a century she has
borne with my infirmities and I have rejoiced
in her graces.

Calvin Coolidge

Amid the cares of married life,
In spite of toil and business strife,
If you value your sweet wife,
    Tell her so!

Prove to her you don't forget
The bond to which your seal is set;
She's of life's sweet the sweetest yet—
    Tell her so!

Don't act as if she'd passed her prime,
As though to please her was a crime—
If e'er you loved her, now's the time:
    Tell her so!

Never let her heart grow cold—
Richer beauties will unfold;
She is worth her weight in gold

Anonymous — Tell Her So

On the banks of James River a husband
erected a tomb in memory of his wife, one of
those hundred maidens who had come to
Virginia in 1619 to marry the lonely settlers.
The stone bore the legend:
    She touched
    the soil of Virginia
    with the sole
    of her little foot
    and the wilderness
    became a home.

— Early American Epitaph

Serene will be our days and bright,
And happy will our nature be,
When love is an unerring light,
And joy its own security.

William Wordsworth

You can't appreciate home till you've left it,
money till it's spent, your wife till she's joined
a woman's club.

O. Henry

The captains and chiefs are all wedded,
    I guess—
  The leaders, the rich and the great;
Their wives, I suppose, all enjoy their success
    And dote on each triumphing mate.

And you, I know well, have strived hard
    to be there
  Front-ranked with the leaders of men,
But I am content that you are not, my dear,
    For what would our life be like then?

If maids did your bidding and cleaned up
    the house,
  And you had a chef or cook, too,
Then what would you need of your fond
    little spouse?
  Why, you'd never enjoy a good stew!

If we had the money to buy all the gowns,
  No new dress could give me much pleasure;
If all of your life were just up and no downs,
  Then how could you take my love's measure?

So men may not run at your order or word
  Passed down from some height far above,
But what could you say that's as great as
    I've heard
  In your whispers to me of our love?

Martina Foley — Dear Husband

The married man may bear his yoke with ease,
Secure at once himself and Heav'n to please;
And pass his inoffensive hours away,
In bliss all night, and innocence all day;
Tho' fortune change, his constant spouse
  remains,
Augments his joys, or mitigates his pains.

Alexander Pope

Harmony in the married state is the very first
object to be aimed at.

Thomas Jefferson

I would give up all my genius, and all my
books, if there were only some woman,
somewhere, who cared whether or not I came
home late for dinner.

Ivan Turgenev

House and Home

Blessings

Home should be a place of mutual responsbility and respect, of encouragement and cooperation and counsel, of integrity, of willingness to work, of discipline when necessary, with the tempering quality of love added to it, with a sense of belonging, and with someone to talk to.

Richard L. Evans

Happy is the family
   Whose members know what a home is for,
And keep the main aims in view;

Who give more thought to affection
   Than to the shelter that houses it;
And more attention to persons
   Than to the things amid which they live.

For a home is a shelter for love
   And a setting for joy and growth,
Rather than a place to be kept up.

It is a hallowed place,
   To which its members shall turn
With a lifting of the heart.

Leland Foster Wood — The Main Aims

The average household consists of a husband who makes the money, and a wife and kids who make it necessary.

Anonymous

Domestic Happiness, thou only bliss of
Paradise that has survived the Fall!

William Cowper

To be popular at home is a great achievement. The man who is loved by the house cat, by the dog, by the neighbor's children, and by his own wife, is a great man, even if he has never had his name in Who's Who.

Thomas Drier

The man is the brace and ceiling of his house
He is the straight walls rising from the earth.
The woman is the golden glow of lamps,
The firelight on a hearth.

A man to the home is a sheltering roof.
A wind break, refuge from storm and rain.
A woman is the warm, bright scarlet flower
Beyond the window pane.

Their children are the sun and rays that sweep
Through open doors — a blessed thing so good.
Trinity on earth that makes a "home"
Where once a mere house stood.

Emery Petho — Perfect Home

The sweetest lives are those to duty wed,
Whose deeds, both great and small,
Are close-knit strands of an unbroken thread,
Where love ennobles all.
The world may sound no trumpet, ring no bells;
The book of life the shining record tells.

Attributed to Elizabeth Barrett Browning

Our home joys are the most satisfying, the most delightful, earth affords; and the joy of parents and their children is the most holy joy of humanity. It makes their hearts pure and good, it lifts men up to their Father in heaven.

Johann Heinrich Pestalozzi

My home to me is hallowed ground
Where Paradise on earth is found.
Ardor and faith and joy divine
I pour into this task of mine . . .

To make the home a place of joys,
To bless and guide my girls and boys,
Be inspiration, helper, friend,
To him whose fate with mine must blend —
What holier mission could there be?
My home is hallowed ground to me.

Anonymous — My Home Is Hallowed Ground to Me

For mother-love and father-care,
For brothers strong and sisters fair,
For love at home and here each day,
For guidance lest we go astray,
Father in Heaven, we thank Thee.

For this new morning with its light,
For rest and shelter of the night,
For health and food, for love and friends,
For everything His goodness sends,
Father in Heaven, we thank Thee.

Christopher Morley

A happy family is but an earlier heaven.

John Bowring

The family is the miniature commonwealth
upon whose integrity the safety of the larger
commonwealth depends.

Felix Adler

The family is the only institution in the world
where the Kingdom of God can actually begin.

Elton Trueblood

Christianity begins at home. We build our
character there, and what we become in after
years is largely determined by our training
and home environment.

Tillman Hobson

God looks down well pleased to mark
In earth's dusk each rosy spark,
Lights of home and lights of love,
And the child the heart thereof.

Katharine Hinkson

Strange to see how a good dinner and feasting
reconciles everybody.

Samuel Pepys

Lord, behold our family here assembled. We
thank Thee for this place in which we dwell;
for the love that unites us; for the peace
accorded us this day; for the hope with which
we expect tomorrow; for the health, the work,
the food, and the bright skies that make our
lives delightful; for our friends in all parts of
the world.

A Family Prayer

The sober comfort, all peace which springs
From the large aggregate of little things;
On these small cares of daughter, wife, or
    friend,
The almost sacred joys of home depend.

Hannah More

Money won't buy peace in the home, but
sometimes it will negotiate an armistice.

Raymond Duncan

The common things of life are all so dear—
The waking in the warm half gloom
To find again the old familiar room,
The scents and sights and sounds that
    never tire;
The homely work, the plans, the lilt of
    baby's laugh,
The crackle of the open fire;
The waiting, then the footsteps coming near,
The opening door, your hand—clasp—and
    your kiss—
Is Heaven not after all the Now and Here?
The common things of life are all so dear.

Alice E. Allen — Life's Common Things

Home's not merely four square walls,
    Though with pictures hung and gilded;
Home is where Affection calls,
    Filled with shrines the Heart hath builded!
Home!—go watch the faithful dove,
    Sailing 'neath the heaven above us;
Home is where there's one to love!
    Home is where there's one to love us!

Charles Swain — What Is Home?

God bless our home, and help us
　To love each other true;
To make our home the kind of place
　Where everything we do
Is filled with love and kindness,
　A dwelling place for Thee,
And help us, God, each moment,
　To live most helpfully.

Anonymous

Family life is the most precious thing in the world.

Charles W. Eliot

Our families in thine arms enfold
As Thou didst keep Thy folk of old.

Oliver Wendell Holmes — Prayer

Woman knows what man has long forgotten, that the ultimate economic and spiritual unit of any civilization is still the family.

Clare Boothe Luce

Comforts

The Bible does not say very much about homes; it says a great deal about the things that make them. It speaks about life and love and joy and peace and rest! If we get a house and put these into it, we shall have secured a home.

John Henry Jowett

A house is built of logs and stone,
　Of tiles and posts and piers;
A home is built of loving deeds
　That stand a thousand years.

Victor Hugo

Whom God loves, his house is sweet to him.

Miguel de Cervantes

Home is the most popular, and will be the most enduring of all earthly establishments.

Channing Pollock

God oft hath a great share in a little house.

George Herbert

The light of all life's gladness
Shines within a happy home;
Banished every care and sadness
In the spot love calls its own.

Of all beauties, far the fairest,
Built on youth's most cherished dreams
Where Sorrow comes the rarest
And the sunshine ever gleams.

How we love its quiet splendor,
Its hearth-fires mellow glow:
How its memories, ever tender,
Linger on where'er we go.

Oh, hallowed are the places
Where happy feet have trod:
Home that happiness graces
Is indeed, a shrine of God.

Anonymous — A Happy House

Mid pleasures and palaces though we may
　roam,
Be it ever so humble, there's no place like
　home;
A charm from the sky seems to hallow us there,
Which, seek through the world, is ne'er met
　with elsewhere.
Home, home, sweet, sweet home!
There's no place like home! There's no place
　like home!

John Howard Payne — There's No Place Like Home

A child's definition of house and home: 'When you are outside, it looks like a house but when you are inside, it feels like a home.'

Anonymous

To be happy at home is the ultimate result of all ambition, the end to which every enterprise and labor tends, and of which every desire prompts the prosecution.

Samuel Johnson

The happiness of the domestic fireside is the first boon of Heaven; and it is well it is so, since it is that which is the lot of the mass of mankind.

Thomas Jefferson

Dear little house, dear shabby street,
Dear books and beds and food to eat,
How feeble words are to express
The facets of your tenderness.

How white the sun comes through the pane!
In tinkling music drips the rain!
How burning bright the furnace glows!
What paths to shovel when it snows!

Let these poor rhymes abide for proof
Joy dwells beneath a humble roof;
Heaven is not built of country seats
But little queer suburban streets!

Christopher Morley

There is magic in that little word, 'home': It is
a mystic circle that surrounds comforts and
virtues never known beyond its hallowed limits.

Robert Southey

Happiness grows at our own firesides, and
is not to be picked in strangers' gardens.

Douglas Jerrold

But what on earth is half so dear —
So longed for — as the hearth of home?

Emily Brontë

You can no more measure a home by inches,
or weigh it by ounces, than you can set up
boundaries of a summer breeze, or calculate
the fragrance of a rose. Home is the love
which is in it.

Edward Whiting

To Adam, Paradise was home. To the good
among his descendants, home is paradise.

Julius C. Hare

Cleave to thine acre; the round year
Will fetch all fruits and virtues here.
Fool and foe may harmless roam,
Loved and lovers bide at home.

Ralph Waldo Emerson

You are a King by your own Fireside, as
much as any Monarch on his Throne.

Miguel de Cervantes

A roof to keep out rain, four walls to keep out
wind, floors to keep out cold, yes — but more
than that! It is the laugh of a baby, the song
of a mother, the strength of a father; the
warmth of loving hearts, light from happy eyes;
kindness, loyalty, comradeship. Home is the
first school, and the first church for your
children. Where children are wanted, where
even the teakettle sings for happiness — that is
"Home, Sweet, Home!"

Madame Schumann-Heink

The Crown of the house is Godliness
The Beauty of the house is Order
The Glory of the house is Hospitality
The Blessing of the house is Contentment

Old Inscription

It is not vaulted roofs, palatial buildings,
Or spacious rooms to which the memory clings;
But rather small, inconsequential settings
That go to build a home — endearing things.
For it is simple things one long remembers:
A fireplace with its crackling hickory log;
A cat curled in an old red-cushioned rocker;
The dream yelp of a lazy hunting dog;
A wooden bowl of luscious, ruddy apples;
A mother's knitting needles' rhythmic click;
And father's boots, shaped by his vigorous
    stepping;
The steam before the fire; a clock's loud tick.
A house is built of wood, stone, brick, and
    mortar —
Is made secure by iron bolt and lock;
A home is built by things one long remembers:
A bowl of apples, boots, a ticking clock.

Annabelle Stewart Altwater — The Long Remembered

When home is ruled according to God's word,
angels might be asked to stay with us, and they
would not find themselves out of their element.

Charles Spurgeon

Home is where there's one to love us.

Charles Swain

A home is the total contribution of love on
the part of each one dwelling within it.

Anne Pannell

I like to see a man proud of the place in which he lives. I like to see a man live so that his place will be proud of him.

Abraham Lincoln

Every Christian family ought to be a little church, consecrated to Christ, and wholly influenced and governed by His rules.

Jonathan Edwards

With what presumption have we dared to voice,
"Thank you for home (although we hold the
    deed),
Our acre, trees, and flowers (ours by choice),
Our faithful dog and cat (though it's agreed
No one can own the latter), each good book
(A gift or purchased), all else we foresaw
That we would cherish, and have made to look
Ours by possession (nine points of the law)."

With what presumption have we called them
    ours,
And even felt unselfish when we shared them,
When, if the truth be known, they have been
    Yours
From the beginning, Lord! You have prepared
    them
For us to borrow, using as our own—
So thank You, rather, for this generous loan.

Elaine V. Emans — The Borrowers

Peace and rest at length have come,
All the day's long toil is past;
And each heart is whispering "Home,
Home at last!"

Thomas Hood

Home is where the heart is.

Pliny The Elder

But every house where Love abides
And Friendship is a guest,
Is surely home, and home sweet home,
For there the heart can rest.

Henry Van Dyke

Sweet is the smile of home; the mutual look,
When hearts are of each other sure.

John Keble

Anyone can build an altar; it requires a God to provide the flame. Anybody can build a house; we need the Lord for the creation of a home.

John Henry Jowett

Give me the simple things close to my home
    The things that are familiar, old and dear,
I do not have to wander far, or roam
    The Seven Seas—when I have splendor here.

Give me a crackling flame upon the grate
    And the warm smell of bread upon the fire.
I do not have to ride abroad in state
    To find the very core of heart's desire.

A shining tea-pot—friendly hands to pour
    And jam that smells of grapes from our
        own vine.
Could any noble king desire more?
    I am a king myself, for these are mine.

Let those who will seek promised lands afar,
    For treasures so remote I shed no tears.
Why should I strive to reach a distant star
    When heaven with all its beauty is right here!

Anonymous — The Simple Things

Stay, stay at home, my heart, and rest;
Home-keeping hearts are happiest,
For those that wander they know not where
Are full of trouble and full of care;
To stay at home is best.

Henry Wadsworth Longfellow

A woman should be as proud of her success in making her house into a perfect little world as the greatest statesman of his organizing a nation's affairs.

André Maurois

Where we love is home,
Home that our feet may leave,
    but not our hearts.

Oliver Wendell Holmes

The man who loves home best, and loves it most unselfishly, loves his country best.

Josiah Gilbert Holland

He is happiest, be he king or peasant, who finds his peace in his home.

Johann Wolfgang von Goethe

Home interprets heaven. Home is heaven for beginners.

C. H. Parkhurst

God gives all men all earth to love,
But since man's heart is small,
Ordains for each one spot should prove
Beloved over all.

Rudyard Kipling

Old Homes! old hearts! Upon my Soul forever
Their peace and gladness lie like tears and
   laughter.

Madison Cawein

Where there is room in the heart there is always room in the house.

Thomas Moore

It is one thing to feel chained to the dishpan, and another to feel that we have an important part in making a house a home. We can't hoax ourselves into feeling jolly about dishwater, but when a morning comes that we feel ourselves singing over the sink and stacking the dishes with genuine indifference—or even with a kind of tenderness—then we know that we have stumbled upon the meaning of small tasks in the heavenly economy.

Margueritte Harmon Bro

I have found such joy in simple things;
A plain clean room, a nut-brown loaf of bread,
A cup of milk, a kettle as it sings,
The shelter of a roof above my head,
And in a leaf-laced square along a floor,
Where yellow sunlight glimmers through a door.

I have found such joy in things that fill
My quiet days: a curtain's blowing grace,
A potted plant upon my window sill,
A rose fresh-cut and placed within a vase,
A table cleared, a lamp beside a chair,
And books I long have loved beside me there.

Grace Noll Crowell

Oh! through the world, where'er we roam,
Though souls be pure, and lips be kind,
The heart with fondness turns to home,
Still turns to those it left behind.

Thomas Moore

A comfortable house is a great source of happiness. It ranks immediately after health and a good conscience.

Sydney Smith

Just a little shingle roof
Held up by four square walls,
Flooded inside with smiles of sunshine
And happiness enthralls.
No costly pictures adorn the walls,
No divan's cushioned seat;
But above all this I value more
Love and home so sweet.

Effie Clouse

If it isn't heart-keeping, it isn't house-keeping.

Marcelene Cox

How can our minds and bodies be
Grateful enough that we have spent
Here in this generous room, we three,
This evening of content?
Each one of us has walked through storm
And fled the wolves along the road;
But here the hearth is wide and warm,
And for this shelter and this light
Accept, O Lord, our thanks to-night.

Sara Teasdale — Grace Before Sleep

Family

Our Father, by whose Name
   All fatherhood is known,
Who dost in love proclaim
   Each family thine own,
Bless thou all parents, guarding well,
   With constant love as sentinel,
The homes in which thy people dwell.

F. B. Tucker

Happy is he that is happy in his children.

Thomas Fuller

Let parents bequeath to their children not riches, but the spirit of reverence.

Plato

Oh God, who art our Father, take my human fatherhood and bless it with thy Spirit. Let me not fail this little son of mine. Help me to know what thou wouldst make of him, and use me to help and bless him. Make me loving and understanding, cheerful and patient and sensitive to all his needs, so that he may trust me enough to come close to me and let me come very close to him. Make me ashamed to demand of him what I do not demand of myself; but help me more and more to try to be the kind of man that he might pattern after. And this I ask in the name and by the grace of Christ.

Walter Russell Bowie — Prayer For My Son

What gift has Providence bestowed on man that is so dear to him as his children?

Cicero

How beautifully everything is arranged by nature: as soon as a child enters the world, it finds a mother ready to take care of it.

Jules Michelet

The night you were born, I ceased being my father's boy and became my son's father. That night I began a new life.

Henry Gregor Felsen

Everybody knows that a good mother gives her children a feeling of trust and stability. She is their earth. She is the one they can count on for the things that matter most of all. She is their food and their bed and the extra blanket when it grows cold in the night; she is their warmth and their health and their shelter, she is the one they want to be near when they cry. She is the only person in the whole world or in a whole lifetime who can be these things to her children. There is no substitute for her. Somehow even her clothes feel different to her children's hands from anybody else's clothes. Only to touch her skirt or her sleeve makes a troubled child feel better.

Katherine Butler Hathaway

So brief a time I have them, Lord,
To steady them with Thy bright word;
A narrow span of childish days
To set their feet in Thy green ways —
A few swift nights to know them warm,
Close-gathered now from any harm,
Looming in shadowy years ahead . . .
How can I help but be afraid?

The little wisdom I have won
Is not enough to guard my son.
The grace I grope for, deed by deed,
Cannot assuage my daughter's need;
Nor wit, nor courage hold at bay
The moment, that imperiled day,
For which no foresight may prepare —
Not even love, not even prayer.

Be to them, God, all I would be
In that far time I shall not see;
And guide me now, their friend, their mother,
To hear their prayers, to smooth the cover,
And leave their window wide upthrust
Beneath that Heaven of my trust,
Whose pity marked a sparrow's fall
And bends in mercy over all.

Frances Stoakley Lankford — A Mother's Prayer

I love these little people, and it is not a slight thing, when they, who are so fresh from God, love us.

Charles Dickens

Our children. Yet not ours,
They are their own
Whom no one can possess.
For all the future holds of good or ill
They are their own.
Unless, dear Lord, unless
By miracles of grace
And mercy infinite
They are possessed by Thee
And so become more their own
By being Thine.

Minton Johnston

I like 'em all, babies and all. Boys are a great care, but darn it, they're worth it.

William Sumner

There's only one pretty child in the world, and every mother has it.

Cheshire Proverb

A mother's love for the child of her body differs essentially from all other affections, and burns with so steady and clear a flame that it appears like the one unchangeable thing in this earthly mutable life, so that when she is no longer present it is still a light to our steps and a consolation.

W. H. Hudson

Many fathers will agree with the wit who said: "When I was young my parents told me what to do; now my children tell me what to do. I wonder when I'll be able to do what I want to do?"

Anonymous

Never did I meet with a father that would not cheerfully part with his last shilling to save or bless his son.

N. K. Daggett

What a father says to his children is not heard by the world, but it will be heard by posterity.

Jean Paul Richter

Most of all the other beautiful things in life come by twos and threes, by dozens and hundreds. Plenty of roses, stars, sunsets, rainbows, brothers and sisters, aunts and cousins, but only one *mother* in the whole world.

Kate Douglas Wiggin

It makes a man sort of humble to have been a kid when everything was the kid's fault and a parent at a time when everything is the parent's fault.

Anonymous

The sweetest sounds to mortals given
Are heard in Mother, Home, and Heaven.

William Goldsmith Brown

Take a vine of a good soil,
And the daughter of a good mother.

Italian Proverb

Blessed be the hand that prepares a pleasure for a child, for there is no saying when and where it may bloom forth.

Douglas Jerrold

The mother's heart is the child's schoolroom.

Henry Ward Beecher

It is not flesh and blood, but the heart which makes us fathers and sons.

Friedrich von Schiller

One night a father overheard his son pray: "Dear God, make me the kind of man my Daddy is."
Later that evening the father prayed: "Dear God, help me to be the kind of man my son wants me to be."

Anonymous

A mother is not a person to lean on, but a person to make leaning unnecessary.

Dorothy Canfield Fisher

"Isn't there one child you really love the best?" a mother was asked. And she replied, "Yes. The one who is sick until he gets well; the one who's away, until he gets home."

Anonymous

Children are a great comfort in your old age— and they help you reach it faster too.

Lionel M. Kauffman

My hair stands on end at the costs and charges of these boys. Why was I ever a father! Why was my father ever a father!

Charles Dickens

He who gives a child a treat
Makes joy-bells ring in Heaven's street,
And he who gives a child a home
Builds palaces in Kingdom come.

John Masefield

Before I got married I had six theories about bringing up children; now I have six children and no theories.

Lord Rochester

There's a blessing on the hearth,
A special providence for fatherhood.

Robert Browning

A wise woman once said to me: "There are
only two lasting bequests we can hope to give
our children. One of these is roots; the other,
wings."

Hodding Carter

Every child born into the world is a new
thought of God, an ever-fresh and radiant
possibility.

Kate Douglas Wiggin

One laugh of a child will make the holiest day
more sacred still.

Robert G. Ingersoll

O fingers small of shell-tipped rose,
How should you know you hold so much?
Two full hearts beating you enclose,
Hopes, fears, prayers, longings, joys and woes—
All yours to hold, O little hands!

Laurence Binyon

Lead a child to beauty,
But let him make
His own discovery of a star
In each snowflake.

Lead a child to courage,
Yet let him seek
His own good time to demonstrate
He is not weak.

Lead a child to good:
Then on some glad
Day he must find it is another
Name for God.

Elaine V. Emans — Discovery

Never fear spoiling children by making them
too happy. Happiness is the atmosphere in
which all good affections grow — the wholesome warmth necessary to make the heart-
blood circulate healthily and freely.

Ann Eliza Bray

And when with envy time transported,
    Shall think to rob us of our joys,
You'll in your girls again be courted,
    And I'll go wooing in my boys.

Gilbert Cooper

Thou art thy mother's glass, and she in thee
Calls back the lovely April of her prime.

William Shakespeare

A picture memory brings to me:
I look across the years and see
Myself beside my mother's knee.

I feel her gentle hand restrain
My selfish moods, and know again
A child's blind sense of wrong and pain.

But wiser now, a man gray grown,
My childhood's needs are better known.
My mother's chastening love I own.

John Greenleaf Whittier

There never was a woman like her. She was
gentle as a dove and brave as a lioness . . .
The memory of my mother and her teachings
were after all the only capital I had to start life
with, and on that capital I have made my way.

Andrew Jackson

My father had never lost his temper with us,
never beaten us, but we had for him that
feeling often described as fear, which is something quite different and far deeper than alarm.
It was that sense which, without irreverence,
I have thought to find expressed by the great
evangelists when they speak of the fear of God.
One does not fear God because he is terrible,
but because he is literally the soul of goodness
and truth, because to do him wrong is to do
wrong to some mysterious part of oneself, and
one does not know exactly what the consequences may be.

Joyce Cary

Certain it is that there is no kind of affection
so purely angelic as the love of a father to a
daughter.

Joseph Addison

Every little child in all the world has been a little safer since the coming of the Child of Bethlehem.

Roy L. Smith

When the voices of children are heard on the
    green
And laughing is heard on the hill,
My heart is at rest within my breast
    And everything else is still.

'Then come home, my children, the sun is
    gone down
And the dews of night arise;
Come, come, leave off play, and let us away
Till the morning appears in the skies.'

'No, no, let us play, for it is yet day
And we cannot go to sleep;
Besides in the sky the little birds fly
And the hills are all cover'd with sheep.'

'Well, well, go and play till the light fades away
And then go home to bed.'
The little ones leaped and shouted and laughed
    And all the hills echoed.

William Blake

You may have tangible wealth untold;
Caskets of jewels and coffers of gold.
Richer than I you can never be —
I had a Mother who read to me.

Strickland Gillilan

Now, my son, I wish for you,
And I wish you joy of it —
Joy of power in all you do,
Deeper passion, better wit
Than I had who had enough,
Quicker life and length thereof,
More of every gift but love.

Love I have beyond all men,
Love that now you share with me —
What have I to wish you then
But that you be good and free,
And that God to you may give
Grace in stronger days to live?

Thomas MacDonagh — Wishes For My Son

When one becomes a father, then first one becomes a son. Standing by the crib of one's own baby, with that world-old pang of compassion and protectiveness toward this so little creature that has all its course to run, the heart flies back in yearning and gratitude to those who felt just so toward one's self. Then for the first time one understands the homely succession of sacrifices and pains by which life is transmitted and fostered down the stumbling generations of men.

Christopher Morley

A child that is loved has many names.

Hungarian Proverb

Across the years he could recall
His father one way best of all.

In the stillest hour of night
The boy awakened to a light.

Half in dreams, he saw his sire
With his great hands full of fire.

The man had struck a match to see
If his son slept peacefully.

He held his palms each side the spark
His love had kindled in the dark.

His two hands were curved apart
In the semblance of a heart.

He wore, it seemed to his small son,
A bare heart on his hidden one,

A heart that gave out such a glow
No son awake could bear to know.

It showed a look upon a face
Too tender for the day to trace.

One instant, it lit all about,
And then secret heart went out.

But it shone long enough for one
To know that hands held up the sun.

Robert P. Tristram Coffin — The Secret Heart

74

A baby is God's opinion that the world
should go on.

Carl Sandburg

I walk upon the rocky shore;
Her strength is in the ocean's roar.
I glance into the shaded pool;
Her mind is there so calm and cool.
I hear sweet rippling of the sea;
Naught but her laughter 'tis to me.
I gaze into the starry skies;
And there I see her wondrous eyes.
I look into my inmost mind;
And here her inspiration find.
In all I am and hear and see;
My precious mother is to me.

Josephine Rice Creelman

What the mother sings to the cradle goes all
the way down to the grave.

Henry Ward Beecher

Laughter of children brings
    The kitchen down with laughter.
While the old kettle sings
Laughter of children brings
To a boil all savory things.
    Higher than beam or rafter,
Laughter of children brings
    The kitchen down with laughter.

So ends an autumn day,
    Light ripples on the ceiling,
Dishes are stacked away;
So ends an autumn day,
The children jog and sway
    In comic dances wheeling.
So ends an autumn day,
    Light ripples on the ceiling.

They trail upstairs to bed,
    And night is a dark tower.
The kettle calls: instead
They trail upstairs to bed,
Leaving warmth, the coppery-red
    Mood of their carnival hour.
They trail upstairs to bed,
    And night is a dark tower.

Barbara Howes — Early Supper

O Lord, who knowest every need of mine,
Help me to bear each cross and not repine;
Grant me fresh courage every day,
Help me to do my work alway
    Without complaint!

O Lord, Thou knowest well how dark the way,
Guide Thou my footsteps, lest they stray;
Give me fresh faith for every hour,
Lest I should ever doubt Thy power
    And make complaint!

Give me a heart, O Lord, strong to endure,
Help me to keep it simple, pure,
Make me unselfish, helpful, true
In every act, whate'er I do,
    And keep content.

Help me to do my woman's share,
Make me courageous, strong to bear
Sunshine or shadow in my life!
Sustain me in the daily strife
    To keep content!

Anonymous — A Woman's Prayer

We never know the love of the parent till we
become parents ourselves. When we first bend
over the cradle of our own child, God throws
back the temple door, and reveals to us the
sacredness and mystery of a father's and
a mother's love to ourselves.

Henry Ward Beecher

One father is more than a hundred
schoolmasters.

George Herbert

Life is a flame that is always burning itself
out, but it catches fire again every time a child
is born.

George Bernard Shaw

Give a little love to a child and you get a
great deal back.

John Ruskin

Parents scarcely bring up children now;
they finance them.

John Brooks

My mother was the making of me. She was so true and so sure of me I felt I had something to live for — someone I must not disappoint. The memory of my mother will always be a blessing to me.

Thomas A. Edison

Thanksgiving

Lord, behold our family here assembled. We thank Thee for this place in which we dwell; for the love that unites us; for the peace accorded us this day; for the hope with which we expect tomorrow; for the health, the work, the food, and the bright skies that make our lives delightful; for our friends in all parts of the world.

A Family Prayer

God give you blessings at Christmas time;
Stars for your darkness, sun for your day,
Light on the path as you search for the Way,
    And a mountain to climb.

God grant you courage this coming year,
Fruit for your striving, friends if you roam,
Joy in your labor, love in your home,
    And a summit to clear.

Myra Scovel — Christmas Wish

A scarlet tulip nodding in the breeze.
The dewy freshness of an April morn.
    A calf just born.
The endless vastness of the pounding sea.
The quiet peace of snow that falls at night.
    The geese in flight.
The smell of earth fresh-turned beneath the
      plow.
A misty rainbow arching through the sky.
    A butterfly.
The gentle whisper of cascading leaves.
A gang of puppies romping in the sun.
    The day's work done.
We take Thy blessings, Lord, all through the
      year
Without a word of thanks until, today,
    We pause to pray.

Barbara Parsons Hildreth — Thought for Thanksgiving

Our Father, you have given us this day our daily bread. The grain is ripe. Some fields are cut, and the strong, good smell of earth hovers over them. Harvest is not far away.
It may not be a bumper crop this year. Even so, we have our daily bread. For this, I give thanks. For daily bread. For the cotton cloth on my kitchen table, and the sun coming in the window. And for the burnished sheen on that apple I polished.
It may not be a magazine-cover kitchen, Lord. The stove is old, but it still bakes good bread. *Daily* bread. There is a peace here in my kitchen, a sunniness that is more than that which comes through the window.
The table may not be glamorously spread for supper tonight, Lord. But there will be savory stew. There will be homemade jelly. And there will be bread. Daily bread. This, with thee, is enough.
I give thanks.
My cup runneth over.
Amen.

Jo Carr & Imogene Sorley — November

We thank thee for our daily bread,
For faith by which the soul is fed;
For burdens given us to bear,
For hope that lifts the heart's despair.

We thank thee, Lord, for eyes to see
The truth that makes, and keeps, men free;
For faults — and the strength to mend them,
For dreams — and courage to defend them.

We have so much to thank thee for,
Dear Lord, we beg but one boon more;
Peace in the hearts of all men living,
Peace in the whole world this Thanksgiving.

Joseph Auslander — A Prayer For Thanksgiving

Help us rightly to remember the birth of Jesus, that we may share in the song of the angels, the gladness of the shepherds, and the worship of the Wise Men.

Robert Louis Stevenson

Joy and Happiness

Cheerfulness

The difference between polished iron and iron
that is unpolished is the difference between
cheerfulness and no cheerfulness. Cheerfulness
in a man is that which when people meet him
makes them happy.

Henry Ward Beecher

The men whom I have seen succeed have
always been cheerful and hopeful, who went
about their business with a smile on their
faces, and took the changes and chances of
this mortal life like men.

Charles Kingsley

Gentleness and cheerfulness, these come
before all morality; they are the perfect duties
. . . If your morals make you dreary, depend
upon it they are wrong. I do not say "Give
them up," for they may be all you have; but
conceal them like vice, lest they should
spoil the lives of better and simpler people.

Robert Louis Stevenson

All people smile in the same language.

Anonymous

Contentment, and indeed usefulness, comes as
the infallible result of great acceptances, great
humilities — of not trying to make ourselves
this or that, but of surrendering ourselves to the
fullness of life — of letting life flow through
us. To be used — that is the sublimest thing
we know.

David Grayson

Talk happiness. The world is sad enough
Without your woes. No path is wholly rough;
Look for the places that are smooth and clear,
And speak of those, to rest the weary ear
Of Earth, so hurt by one continuous strain
Of human discontent and grief and pain.

Talk faith. The world is better off without
Your uttered ignorance and morbid doubt.
If you have faith in God, or man, or self,
Say so. If not, push back upon the shelf
Of silence all your thoughts, till faith shall
   come;
No one will ever grieve because your lips are
   dumb.

Talk health. The dreary, never-changing tale
Of mortal maladies is worn and stale.
You cannot charm, or interest, or please
By harping on that minor chord, disease.
Say you are well, or all is well with you,
And God shall hear your words and make
   them true.

Ella Wheeler Wilcox — Optimism

Optimism is a kind of heart stimulant — the
digitalis of failure.

Elbert Hubbard

Cheerfulness and content are great beautifiers
and are famous preservers of youthful looks.

Charles Dickens

Let us be of good cheer, remembering that
the misfortunes hardest to bear are those which
never come.

Amy Lowell

O Holy Spirit, descend plentifully into my heart. Enlighten the dark corners of this neglected dwelling and scatter there Thy cheerful beams.

St. Augustine

I have tried too in my time to be a philosopher; but I don't know how, cheerfulness was always breaking in.

Oliver Edwards

The voluntary path to cheerfulness, if our spontaneous cheerfulness be lost, is to sit up cheerfully, and act and speak as if cheerfulness were already there. To feel brave, *act* as if we were brave, use all our will to that end, and courage will very likely replace fear. If we act as if from some better feeling, the bad feeling soon folds its tent like an Arab and silently steals away.

William James

Ignore dull days; forget the showers;
Keep count of only shining hours.

Louis Untermeyer — Lesson from a Sun-Dial

Nothing is all wrong. Even a clock that has stopped running is right twice a day.

Anonymous

A happy life is not built up of tours abroad and pleasant holidays, but of little clumps of violets noticed by the roadside, hidden away almost so that only those can see them who have God's peace and love in their hearts; in one long continuous chain of little joys, little whispers from the spiritual world, and little gleams of sunshine on our daily work.

Edward Wilson

In green gardens, hidden away
From sight of revel and sound of strife,—
Here I have leisure to breathe and move,
And to do my work in a nobler way;
To sing my songs, and to say my say;
To dream my dreams, and to love my love;
To hold my faith, and to live my life,
Making the most of its shadowy day.

Violet Fane

When spring arrives and lilacs blow
I'm not compelled to shovel snow.
In summer no one bothers me
To feed the fire, nor skate, nor ski.
In autumn no one longer needs
To waste the morning pulling weeds.
And winter brings no dewy dawn
When I must rise to mow the lawn.

So I am glad the seasons through
For what I do not have to do.

Arthur Guiterman — Contentment

When we cannot find contentment in ourselves, it is useless to seek it elsewhere.

François, Duc de La Rochefoucauld

No one is happy unless he is reasonably well satisfied with himself, so that the quest for tranquillity must of necessity begin with self-examination.

William S. Ogdon

An attitude so precious that it becomes a virtue is a gentle and constant equality of temper. What an unutterable charm does it give to the society of a man who possesses it! How is it possible to avoid loving him whom we always find with serenity on his brow, and a smile on his countenance!

Edward Stanley

True contentment is the power of getting out of any situation all that there is in it.

Gilbert Keith Chesterton

Happy the man, of mortals happiest he,
    Whose quiet mind from vain desires is free;
Whom neither hopes deceive, nor fears torment,
    But lives at peace, within himself content.

George Granville

But all the pleasure that I find
Is to maintain a quiet mind.

Edward Dyer

Be cheerful. Of all the things you wear, your expression is the most important.

Anonymous

Real joy comes not from ease or riches or from the praise of men, but from doing something worthwhile.

Wilfred T. Grenfell

How restful are unhurried things!—
The spreading light of dawn's gray hour,
Slow, rhythmic motion of birds' wings,
The opening petals of a flower . . .

Dim shadows moving on a wall,
The moon's calm light above the bay,
Soft murmurings that rise and fall
Within the dusk that hushes day.

My journey, too, may bring content
To the still place of heart's desire;
There, tranquilly, to pitch my tent—
Watch flames scale heavenward from my fire.

Ida Norton Munson — Journeys

A man's moments of serenity are few, but a few will sustain him a lifetime.

Richard E. Byrd

If peace be in the heart
The wildest winter storm is full of solemn
    beauty,
The midnight lightning flash but shows the
    path of duty,
Each living creature tells some new and
    joyous story,
The very trees and stones all catch a ray of
    glory,
If peace be in the heart.

Charles Francis Richardson

Leisure is an affair of mood and atmosphere rather than simply of the clock. It is not a chronological occurrence but a spiritual state. It is unhurried pleasurable living among one's native enthusiasms. Leisure consists of those pauses in our lives when experience is a fusion of stimulation and repose. Genuine leisure yields at once a feeling of vividness and a sense of peace. It consists of moments so clear and pleasant in themselves that one might wish they were eternal.

Irwin Edman

The happiest people seem to be those who have no particular cause for being happy except the fact that they are so — a good reason, no doubt.

William Ralph Inge

God cannot endure that unfestive, mirthless attitude of ours in which we eat our bread in sorrow, with pretentious, busy haste, or even with shame. Through our daily meals He is calling us to rejoice, to keep holiday in the midst of our working day.

Dietrich Bonhoeffer

A little thought will show you how vastly your own happiness depends on the way other people bear themselves toward you. The looks and tones at your breakfast table, the conduct of your fellow-workers or employers, the faithful or unreliable men you deal with, what people say to you on the street, the letters you get, the friends or foes you meet — these things make up very much of the pleasure or misery of your day. Turn the idea around, and remember that just so much are you adding to the pleasure or the misery of other people's days. And this is the half of the matter which you can control. Whether any particular day shall bring to you more of happiness or of suffering is largely beyond your power to determine. Whether each day of your life shall *give* happiness or suffering rests with yourself.

George S. Merriam

The year's at the spring
And day's at the morn;
Morning's at seven:
The hillside's dew-pearled;
The lark's on the wing;
The snail's on the thorn;
God's in his heaven—
All's right with the world!

Robert Browning

A man looking at the present in the light of the future, and taking his whole being into account, may be contented with his lot: that is Christian contentment.

Henry Ward Beecher

Content is the philosopher's stone, that turns
all it touches into gold.

Benjamin Franklin

My creed is this:
Happiness is the only good.
The place to be happy is here.
The time to be happy is now.
The way to be happy is to help make others so.

Robert G. Ingersoll

Mirth

Laughter—while it lasts, slackens and unbraces
the mind, weakens the faculties, and causes a
kind of remissness and dissolution in all the
powers of the soul: and thus far it may be
looked upon as a weakness in the composition
of human nature. But if we consider the
frequent reliefs we receive from it, and how
often it breaks the gloom which is apt to
depress the mind and dampen our spirit, with
transient, unexpected gleams of joy, one would
take care not to grow too wise for so great a
pleasure of life.

Joseph Addison

The children were shouting together,
    And racing along the sands,
A glimmer of dancing shadows,
    A dovelike flutter of hands.

The stars were shouting in heaven,
    The sun was chasing the moon:
The game was the same as the children's,
    They danced to the self-same tune.

The whole of the world was merry,
    One joy from the vale to the height,
Where the blue woods of twilight encircled
    The lovely lawns of the light.

A. E. (George William Russell) — Frolic

There is the laughter which is born out of the
pure joy of living, the spontaneous expression
of health and energy — the sweet laughter of the
child. This is a gift of God.

J. E. Boodin

Give me a sense of humor, Lord;
Give me the grace to see a joke,
To get some happiness from life,
And pass it on to other folk.

Chester Cathedral

Mirth is the sweet wine of human life. It should
be offered sparkling with zestful life unto God.

Henry Ward Beecher

The laughter of man is the contentment of God.

John Weiss

Laugh and be merry, remember, better the
    world with a song,
Better the world with a blow in the teeth
    of a wrong.
Laugh, for the time is brief, a thread the
    length of a span.
Laugh, and be proud to belong to the old
    proud pageant of man.

Laugh and be merry: remember, in olden
    time,
God made Heaven and Earth for the joy
    He took in a rhyme,
Made them and filled them full with the
    strong red wine of His mirth,
The splendid joy of the stars: the joy
    of the earth.

So we must laugh and drink from the deep
    blue cup of the sky,
Join the jubilant song of the great stars
    sweeping by,
Laugh, and battle, and work, and drink
    of the wine outpoured
In the dear green earth, the sign of the
    joy of the Lord.

Laugh and be merry together, like brothers
    akin,
Guesting awhile in the rooms of a beautiful
    inn,
Glad till the dancing stops, and the lilt of
    the music ends.
Laugh till the game is played; and be you
    merry, my friends.

John Mascfield — Laugh and Be Merry

Mirth is God's medicine. Everybody ought to bathe in it. Grim care, moroseness, anxiety—all this rust of life ought to be scoured off by the oil of mirth. It is better than emery. Every man ought to rub himself with it. A man without mirth is like a wagon without springs, in which everyone is caused disagreeably to jolt by every pebble over which it runs.

Henry Ward Beecher

Morally considered, laughter is next to the Ten Commandments.

H. W. Shaw

No man who has once heartily and wholly laughed can be altogether irreclaimably bad.

Thomas Carlyle

Laughing is the sensation of feeling good all over, and showing it principally in one spot.

Josh Billings

The gift of gayety may itself be the greatest good fortune, and the most serious step toward maturity.

Irwin Edman

Mirthfulness is in the mind and you cannot get it out.—It is just as good in its place as conscience or veneration.

Henry Ward Beecher

Gladness

Joy is the gigantic secret of the Christian.

Gilbert Keith Chesterton

When we speak of joy, we do not speak of something we are after, but of something that will come to us when we are after God and duty.

Horace Bushnell

Joys divided are increased.

Josiah Gilbert Holland

Uncertainty and expectation are the joys of life.

Richard Congreve

Oh, the wild joys of living! the leaping from
    rock up to rock.
The strong rending of boughs from the
    fir-tree, the cool silver shock
Of the plunge in a pool's living water, the
    hunt of the bear,
And the sultriness showing the lion is couched
    in his lair.
How good is man's life, the mere living!
    How fit to employ
All the heart and the soul and the senses for
    ever in joy!

Robert Browning

One of the sanest, surest, and most generous joys of life comes from being happy over the good fortune of others.

Archibald Rutledge

Take what God gives, O heart of mine,
    And build your house of happiness.
Perchance some have been given more;
    But many have been given less.
The treasure lying at thy feet,
    Whose value you but faintly guess,
Another builder looking on,
    Would barter heaven to possess.

B. Y. Williams — House Of Happiness

If you want to be happy,
    Begin where you are,
Don't wait for some rapture
    That's future and far.
Begin to be joyous, begin to be glad
    And soon you'll forget
That you ever were sad.

Anonymous

The sun does not shine for a few trees and flowers, but for the wide world's joy.

Henry Ward Beecher

All the animals excepting man know that the principal business of life is to enjoy it.

Samuel Butler

All who joy would win must share it.
Happiness was born a twin.

George Gordon, Lord Byron

There's night and day, brother, both sweet things; sun, moon, and stars, brother. Life is very sweet.

George Borrow

There is, above all, the laughter that comes from the eternal joy of creation, the joy of making the world new, the joy of expressing the inner riches of the soul — laughter from triumphs over pain and hardship in the passion for an enduring ideal, the joy of bringing the light of happiness, of truth and beauty into a dark world. This is divine laughter par excellence.

J. E. Boodin

Contentment

If one only wished to be happy, this could be easily accomplished; but we wish to be happier than other people, and this is always difficult, for we believe others to be happier than they are.

Baron de Montesquieu

Man is the artificer of his own happiness.

Henry David Thoreau

Who drives the horses of the sun
  Shall lord it but a day.
Better the lowly deed were done
  And kept the humble way.

The rust will find the sword of fame;
  The dust will hide the crowd,
Aye, none shall nail so high his name
  Time will not tear it down.

The happiest heart that ever beat
  Was in some quiet breast
That found the common daylight sweet
  And left to heaven the rest.

John Vance Cheney — The Happiest Heart

It is neither wealth nor splendor, but tranquillity and occupation, which give happiness.

Thomas Jefferson

There is but one way to tranquillity of mind and happiness. Let this therefore be always ready at hand with thee, both when thou wakest early in the morning, and when thou goest late to sleep, to account no external thing thine own, but commit all these to God.

Epictetus

It is the law of our nature to desire happiness. This law is not local, but universal; not temporary, but eternal.

Horace Mann

How soon a smile of God can change the world!
How we are made for happiness — how work
Grows play, adversity a winning fight!

Robert Browning

False happiness is like false money; it passes for a time as well as the true, and serves some ordinary occasions; but when it is brought to the touch, we find the lightness and alloy, and feel the loss.

Alexander Pope

Happiness depends, as Nature shows,
Less on exterior things than most suppose.

William Cowper

Happiness is like manna; it is to be gathered in grains, and enjoyed every day. It will not keep; it cannot be accumulated; nor have we got to go out of ourselves or into remote places to gather it, since it is rained down from Heaven, at our very doors.

Tryon Edwards

To watch the corn grow, or the blossoms set; to draw hard breath over the ploughshare or spade; to read, to think, to love, to pray, are the things that make men happy.

John Ruskin

Happiness includes chiefly the idea of satisfaction after full honest effort. No one can possibly be satisfied and no one can be happy who feels that in some paramount affair he has failed to take up the challenge of life.

Arnold Bennett

If thou of all thy mortal goods bereft
And from thy store alone two loaves are left,
Sell, sell thou one. Then with thy toll
Buy hyacinth — and speed thy soul.

Muslik-ud-Din

It is not easy to find happiness in ourselves,
and impossible to find it elsewhere.

Agnes Repplier

The inner half of every cloud
  Is bright and shining;
I therefore turn my clouds about,
And always wear them inside out
  To show the lining.

Ellen Thorneycroft Fowler

If you would make a man happy, do not add
to his possessions but subtract from the sum of
his desires.

Seneca

If you observe a really happy man you will
find him building a boat, writing a symphony,
educating his son, growing double dahlias in
his garden, or looking for dinosaur eggs in the
Gobi desert. He will not be striving for it as
a goal itself. He will have become aware that
he is happy in the course of living life twenty-
four crowded hours of the day.

W. Beran Wolfe

There is a wonderful mythical law of nature
that the three things we crave most in life —
happiness, freedom, and peace of mind — are
always attained by giving them to someone else.

Peyton Conway March

Happiness! It is useless to seek it elsewhere
than in the warmth of human relations. Our
sordid interests imprison us within their walls.
Only a comrade can grasp us by the hand
and haul us free.

Antoine de Saint-Exupéry

The happiest life, seen in perspective, can
hardly be better than a stringing together of
odd little moments.

Norman Douglas

Happiness? It is an illusion to think that more
comfort means more happiness. Happiness
comes of the capacity to feel deeply, to enjoy
simply, to think freely, to risk life, to be needed.

Storm Jameson

Happiness is like a crystal,
Fair and exquisite and clear,
Broken in a million pieces,
Shattered, scattered far and near.
Now and then along life's pathway,
Lo! some shining fragments fall;
But there are so many pieces
No one ever finds them all.

You may find a bit of beauty,
Or an honest share of wealth,
While another just beside you
Gathers honor, love or health.
Vain to choose or grasp unduly,
Broken is the perfect ball;
And there are so many pieces
No one ever finds them all.

Yet the wise as on they journey
Treasure every fragment clear,
Fit them as they may together
Imaging the shattered sphere,
Learning ever to be thankful,
Though their share of it is small;
For it has so many pieces
No one ever finds them all.

Priscilla Leonard — Happiness

Happiness is not a reward; it is a consequence.

Robert G. Ingersoll

The belief that youth's the happiest time of
life is founded on a fallacy. The happiest
person is the person who thinks the most
interesting thoughts, and we grow happier as
we grow older.

William Lyon Phelps

Go not abroad for happiness. For see
  It is a flower that blooms at thy door.
Bring love and justice home, and then no more
  Thou'lt wonder in what dwelling joy may be.

Minot J. Savage

83

Perfect happiness, I believe, was never intended by the Deity to be the lot of one of His creatures in this world; but that He has very much put in our power the nearness of our approaches to it, is what I have steadfastly believed.

Thomas Jefferson

The days that make us happy make us wise.

John Masefield

Happiness is in the taste, and not in the things themselves; we are happy from possessing what we like, not from possessing what others like.

François, Duc de La Rochefoucauld

Remember this — that very little is needed to make a happy life.

Marcus Aurelius

There is that in me — I do not know what
  it is . . . but I know it is in me . . .
I do not know it — it is without a name —
  it is a word unsaid;
It is not in any dictionary, utterance, symbol.
Something it swings in more than the earth
  I swing on.
To it the creation is the friend whose
  embracing awakes me . . .
It is not chaos or death — it is form, union,
  plan, it is eternal life — it is happiness.

Walt Whitman

Happiness doesn't come from doing what we like to do but from liking what we have to do.

Wilfred Peterson

To be of use in this world is the only way to be happy.

Hans Christian Andersen

Happiness is not in strength, or wealth, or power, or all three. It lies in ourself, in true freedom, in the conquest of ignoble fear, in perfect self-government, in power of contentment and peace, and the even flow of life, even in poverty, exile, disease, and the very Valley of the Shadow of Death.

Epictetus

We have no more right to consume happiness without producing it than to consume wealth without producing it.

George Bernard Shaw

If you ever find happiness by hunting for it, you will find it, as the old woman did her lost spectacles, safe on her own nose all the time.

Josh Billings

It's pretty hard to tell what does bring happiness; poverty and wealth have both failed.

Kin Hubbard

The Constitution guarantees me the right to life, but I die; to liberty, but if I try being too free, I'm locked up; and to the pursuit of happiness — but happiness has the right to run whenever being pursued and I've never been able to tree her yet. Here I am at ever-so-many years of age, blown and exhausted with the chase, and happiness is still able to do her hundred yards in ten seconds flat whenever I approach.

Finley Peter Dunne

The foolish man seeks happiness in the distance; the wise grows it under his feet.

James Oppenheim

Happiness is like coke — something you get as a by-product in the process of making something else.

Aldous Huxley

Many persons have a wrong idea about what constitutes true happiness. It is not attained through self-gratification, but through fidelity to a worthy purpose.

Helen Keller

Happiness is a by-product of an effort to make someone else happy.

Gretta Palmer

Man's happiness does not lie in freedom, but in acceptance of duty.

André Gide

Happy the man, and happy he alone,
He who can call today his own;
He who, secure within, can say,
"Tomorrow, do thy worst, for I have lived
    today.
Be fair, or foul, or rain or shine,
The joys I have possessed, in spite of fate,
    are mine.
Not heaven itself upon the past has power;
But what has been, has been, and I have had
    my hour."

John Dryden — Happy The Man

We live in the future. Even the happiness of
the present is made up mostly of that delightful
discontent of which the hope of better things
inspires.

Josiah Gilbert Holland

The search for happiness is one of the chief
sources of unhappiness.

Eric Hoffer

The grand essentials to happiness in this life
are something to do, something to love, and
something to hope for.

Joseph Addison

Grant to us, O Lord, the royalty of inward
happiness, and the serenity which comes from
living close to Thee. Daily renew in us the
sense of joy, and let the eternal spirit of the
Father dwell in our souls and bodies, filling us
with light and grace, so that, bearing about
with us the infection of a good courage, we
may be diffusers of life, and may meet all ills
and accidents with gallant and highhearted
happiness, giving Thee thanks always for all
things.

L. H. Soule — Prayer

To be without some of the things you want
is an indispensable part of happiness.

Bertrand Russell

Happiness to be true must be oriented on
landmarks much greater than one's own little
personal joys and gratifications.

Dagobert D. Runes

All happiness depends on courage and work.
I have had many periods of wretchedness, but
with energy and above all, with illusions, I
pulled through them all.

Honoré de Balzac

Is it so small a thing to have enjoyed the
sun, to have lived light in the spring, to have
loved, to have thought, to have done?

Matthew Arnold

There can be no happiness if the things we
believe in are different from the things we do.

Freya Stark

I have come to see life, not as a chase of
forever impossible personal happiness, but as
a field for endeavor toward the happiness of
the whole human family. There is no other
success. I know indeed of nothing more subtly
satisfying and cheering than a knowledge of
the real good will and appreciation of others.
Such happiness does not come with money;
nor does it flow from a fine physical state. It
cannot be bought. But it is the keenest joy,
after all, and the toiler's truest and best reward.

William Dean Howells

What right have I to make every one in the
house miserable because I am miserable?
Troubles must come to all, but troubles need
not be wicked, and it is wicked to be a
destroyer of happiness.

Amelia E. Barr

We are all of us fellow passengers on the same
planet, and we are all of us equally responsible
for the happiness and well-being of the world
in which we happen to live.

Hendrik Willem van Loon

Those who bring sunshine into the lives of
others cannot keep it from themselves.

James M. Barrie

Happiness is like a kiss — in order to get any
good out of it you have to give it to somebody
else.

Anonymous

85

There can be no real and abiding happiness without sacrifice. Our greatest joys do not result from our efforts toward self-gratification, but from a loving and spontaneous service to other lives. Joy comes not to him who seeks it for himself, but to him who seeks it for other people.

H. W. Sylvester

You have to believe in happiness,
 Or happiness never comes.
I know that a bird chirps none the less
 When all that he finds is crumbs.
You have to believe the buds will blow
Believe in the grass in the days of snow;
 Ah, that's the reason a bird can sing—
 On his darkest day he believes in Spring.

You have to believe in happiness—
 It isn't an outward thing.
The Spring never makes the song, I guess,
 As much as the song the Spring.
Aye, many a heart could find content
If it saw the joy on the road it went
 The joy ahead when it had to grieve—
 For the joy is there—but you have to believe.

Douglas Malloch — You Have to Believe

Those only are happy who have their minds fixed on some object other than their own happiness; on the happiness of others, on the improvement of mankind, even on some art or pursuit followed not as a means but as itself an ideal end. Aiming thus at something else, they find happiness by the way . . . Ask yourself whether you are happy, and you cease to be so. The only chance is to treat, not happiness, but some end external to it, as the purpose of life.

John Stuart Mill

He is a wise man who does not grieve for the things which he has not, but rejoices for those he has.

Epictetus

Happiness adds and multiplies as we divide it with others.

A. Nielen

The way to happiness is to make others so.

Ralph G. Ingersoll

I went to purchase happiness —
 Exorbitant the price!
"None of your worldly treasure,"
 Said the merchant, "will suffice."

"But give yourself to others,
 And on the scales you'll weigh
A thousand fold in fervent joy
 You will receive today."

Anonymous

To be happy you must forget yourself.

Edward Robert Bulwer-Lytton

Grief can take care of itself, but to get the full value of a joy you must have somebody to divide it with.

Mark Twain

There is no duty we so much underrate as the duty of being happy.

Robert Louis Stevenson

He who enjoys doing and enjoys what he has done is happy.

Johann Wolfgang von Goethe

Think of the hopes that lie before you
 Not of the waste that lies behind;
Think of the treasures you have gathered,
 Not the ones you failed to find;
Think of the service you may render,
 Not of serving self alone;
Think of the happiness of others,
 And in this you'll find your own.

Robert E. Farley

I accept life unconditionally. Life holds so much — so much to be so happy about always. Most people ask for happiness on condition. Happiness can be felt only if you don't set conditions.

Artur Rubinstein

Happiness is a habit — cultivate it.

Elbert Hubbard

Lord God, how full our cup of happiness!
We drink and drink—and yet it grows not less;
But every morn the newly risen sun
Finds it replenished, sparkling, over-run!
Hast Thou not given us raiment, warmth, and
   meat,
And in due season all earth's fruits to eat?
Work for our hands and rainbows for our eyes,
And for our souls the wings of butterflies?
A father's smile, a mother's fond embrace,
The tender light upon a lover's face?
The talk of friends, the twinkling eye of mirth,
The whispering silence of the good green earth?
Hope for our youth, and memories for age,
And psalms upon the heavens' moving page?
And dost Thou not of pain a mingling pour
To make the cup but overflow the more?

Gilbert Thomas

Most folk are about as happy as they make up
their minds to be.

Abraham Lincoln

Happiness in this world, when it comes, comes
incidentally. Make it the object of pursuit, and
it leads us a wild-goose chase, and is never
attained. Follow some other object, and very
possibly we may find that we have caught
happiness without dreaming of it; but likely
enough it is gone the moment we say to
ourselves, "Here it is!" like the chest of gold
that treasure-seekers find.

Nathaniel Hawthorne

To fill the hour, and leave no crevice for a
repentance or an approval,—that is happiness.

Ralph Waldo Emerson

Every person in the world may not become
a personage. But every person may become a
personality. The happiest people are those who
think the most interesting thoughts. Interesting
thoughts can only live in cultivated minds.
Those who decide to use leisure as a means of
mental development, who love good music,
good books, good pictures, good plays at the
theater, good company, good conversation—
what are they? They are the happiest people
in the world; and they are not only happy in
themselves, they are the cause of happiness
in others.

William Lyon Phelps

If I have faltered more or less
In my great task of happiness;
If I have moved among my race
And shown no glorious morning face;
If beams from happy human eyes
Have moved me not; if morning skies,
Books, and my food, and summer rain
Knocked on my sullen heart in vain:—
Lord, thy most pointed pleasure take
And stab my spirit broad awake;
Or, Lord, if too obdurate I,
Choose thou, before that spirit die,
A piercing pain, a killing sin,
And to my dead heart run them in!

Robert Louis Stevenson — The Celestial Surgeon

Be happy with what you have and are, be
generous with both, and you won't have to
hunt for happiness.

William E. Gladstone

Life and Living

Meaning

There is such a thing as taking ourselves and the world too seriously, or at any rate too anxiously. Half of the secular unrest and dismal, profane sadness of modern society comes from the vain idea that every man is bound to be a critic of life, and to let no day pass without finding some fault with the general order of things, or projecting some plan for its general improvement. And the other half comes from the greedy notion that a man's life does consist, after all, in the abundance of things that he possesses, and that it is somehow or other more respectable and pious to be always at work trying to make a larger living, than it is to lie on your back in the green pastures and beside the still waters, and thank God that you are alive.

Henry Van Dyke

May you live all the days of your life.

Jonathan Swift

Be a life long or short, its completeness depends on what it was lived for.

David Starr Jordan

Do not pray for easy lives; pray to be stronger men! Do not pray for tasks equal to your powers, pray for powers equal to your tasks. Then the doing of your work shall be no miracle, but you shall be a miracle. Every day you shall wonder at yourself, at the richness of life which has come to you by the grace of God.

Phillips Brooks

Life is something like this trumpet. If you don't put anything in it you don't get anything out. And that's the truth.

W. C. Handy

However mean your life is, meet it and live it; do not shun it and call it hard names. It is not so bad as you are. It looks poorest when you are richest. The fault-finder will find faults even in paradise. Love your life.

Henry David Thoreau

Life is not a having and a getting, but a being and a becoming.

Matthew Arnold

The pleasantest things in the world are pleasant thoughts; and the art of life is to have as many of them as possible.

Michel de Montaigne

The truth is that life is delicious, horrible, charming, frightful, sweet, bitter, and that it is everything.

Anatole France

I looked more widely around me. I studied the lives of the masses of humanity, and I saw that, not two or three, or ten, but hundreds, thousands, millions, had so understood the meaning of life that they were able both to live and to die. All these men were well acquainted with the meaning of life and death, quietly labored, endured privation and suffering, lived and died, and saw in all this, not a vain, but a good thing.

Count Leo Tolstoy

89

Live all you can; it's a mistake not to. It doesn't so much matter what you do in particular so long as you have your life. If you haven't had that what *have* you had?

Henry James

There are obviously two educations. One should teach us how to make a living. The other should teach us how to live.

James Truslow Adams

Be not afraid of life. Believe that life *is* worth living, and your belief will help create the fact.

William James

Let your boat of life be light, packed with only what you need — a homely home and simple pleasures, one or two friends, worth the name, someone to love and someone to love you, a cat, a dog, and a pipe or two, enough to eat and enough to wear, and a little more than enough to drink; for thirst is a dangerous thing.

Jerome K. Jerome

My code of life and conduct is simply this: work hard; play to the allowable limit; disregard equally the good and bad opinion of others; never do a friend a dirty trick . . . never grow indignant over anything . . . live the moment to the utmost of its possibilities . . . and be satisfied with life always, but never with oneself.

George Jean Nathan

A man should always consider how much he has more than he wants, and how much more unhappy he might be than he really is.

Joseph Addison

Drink the brimming cup of life to the full and to the end — and thank God and nature for its trials and challenges, its punishments and rewards, its gifts of beauty, wisdom, labor and love.

Will Durant

To him that lives well every form of life is good.

Samuel Johnson

Nor love thy life, nor hate; but whilst thou liv'st
Live well; how long, how short, permit to
   Heaven.

John Milton

The person who limits his interests to the means of living without consideration of the content or meaning of his life is defeating God's great purpose when he brought into existence a creature with the intelligence and godlike powers that are found in man.

Arthur H. Compton

How good is man's life, the mere living!

Robert Browning

Perhaps it would be a good idea, fantastic as it sounds, to muffle every telephone, stop every motor and halt all activity for an hour some day, to give people a chance to ponder for a few minutes on what it is all about, why they are living and what they really want.

James Truslow Adams

Life, happy or unhappy, successful or unsuccessful, is extraordinarily interesting.

George Bernard Shaw

It takes a lot of patience and God
   To build a life,
It takes a lot of courage
   To meet the stress and strife;
It takes a lot of loving
   To make the wrong come right;
It takes a lot of patience and God
   To build a life

Anonymous

Part of me remained forever at Latitude 80° 08′ South: what survived of my youth, my vanity, perhaps, and certainly my skepticism. On the other hand I did take away something that I had not fully possessed before: appreciation of the sheer beauty and miracle of being alive, and a humble set of values. All this happened four years ago. Civilization has not altered my ideas. I live more simply now, and with more peace.

Admiral Richard E. Byrd

90

Let me but live my life from year to year,
  With forward face and unreluctant soul;
  No hurrying to, nor turning from, the goal;
Not mourning for the things that disappear
In the dim past, nor holding back in fear
  From what the future veils; but with a whole
  And happy heart, that pays its toll
To Youth and Age, and travels on with cheer.

So let the way wind up the hill or down,
  O'er rough or smooth, the journey will be
    joy:
  Still seeking what I sought when but a boy,
New friendship, high adventure, and a crown,
My heart will keep the courage of the quest,
And hope the road's last turn will be the best.

                    Henry Van Dyke — Life

Life was meant to be lived, and curiosity
must be kept alive. One must never, for whatever reason, turn his back on life.

                    Eleanor Roosevelt

Anyone can carry his burden, however hard,
until nightfall. Anyone can do his work, however hard, for one day. Anyone can live
sweetly, lovingly, purely, till the sun goes down.
And this is all that life really means.

                    Robert Louis Stevenson

Try to care about something in this vast
world besides the gratification of small selfish
desires. Try to care for what is best in thought
and action — something that is good apart
from the accidents of your own lot. Look on
other lives besides your own. See what their
troubles are, and how they are borne.

                    George Eliot

I am convinced that my life belongs to the
whole community; and as long as I live, it is
my privilege to do for it whatever I can,
for the harder I work the more I live.
I rejoice in life for its own sake. Life is no
brief candle to me. It is a sort of splendid
torch which I got hold of for a moment, and
I want to make it burn as brightly as possible
before turning it over to future generations.

                    George Bernard Shaw

To give life a meaning one must have a
purpose larger than one's self.

                    Will Durant

If we would only give, just once, the same
amount of reflection to what we want to get
out of life that we give to the question of what
to do with a two weeks' vacation, we would
be startled at our false standards and the
aimless procession of our busy days.

                    Dorothy Canfield Fisher

The great use of life is to spend for something
that will outlast it.

                    William James

Glad that I live am I;
That the sky is blue;
Glad for the country lanes,
And the fall of dew.

After the sun the rain,
After the rain the sun;
This is the way of life,
Till the work be done.

All that we need to do,
Be we low or high,
Is to see that we grow
Nearer the sky.

        Lizette Woodworth Reese — A Little Song of Life

I went [to Walden Pond] because I wished to
live deliberately, to front only the essential
facts of life, and see if I could not learn what
it had to teach, and not, when I came to die,
discover that I had not lived. I did not wish to
live what was not life, living is so dear; nor
did I wish to practise resignation, unless it was
quite necessary. I wanted to live deep and
suck out all the marrow of life.

                    Henry David Thoreau

Life is neither a banquet nor a dreary pil-
grimage; it is neither a trading concern where
all dividends that are fairly earned are
punctually paid, nor a lotus-eater's paradise;
it is a school of manhood.

                    Burnett H. Streeter

To be glad of life, because it gives you the chance to love and to work and to play and to look up at the stars; to be satisfied with your possessions, but not contented with yourself until you have made the best of them; to despise nothing in the world except falsehood and meanness, and to fear nothing except cowardice; to be governed by your admirations rather than by your disgusts; to covet nothing that is your neighbor's except his kindness of heart and gentleness of manner; to think seldom of your enemies, often of your friends and every day of Christ; and to spend as much time as you can with body and with spirit, in God's out-of-doors — these are the little guideposts on the footpath of peace.

Henry van Dyke

Everyone shares the responsibility in the future. But this responsibility can materialize into a constructive effort only if people realize the full meaning of their lives, the significance of their endeavors and their struggles, and if they keep their faith in the high destiny of Man.

Lecomte du Noüy

Life is occupied both in perpetuating itself and in surpassing itself.

Simone de Beauvoir

There is more to life than increasing its speed.

Mahatma Gandhi

Health enough to make work a pleasure.
Wealth enough to support your needs.
Strength to battle with difficulties and
  overcome them.
Grace enough to confess your sins and
  forsake them.
Patience enough to toil until some good
  is accomplished.
Charity enough to see some good in your
  neighbor.
Love enough to move you to be useful and
  helpful to others.
Faith enough to make real the things of God.
Hope enough to remove all anxious fears
  concerning the future.

Johann Wolfgang von Goethe — For a Contented Life

To live content with small means;
To seek elegance rather than luxury, and
  refinement rather than fashion;
To be worthy, not respectable, and wealthy,
  not rich;
To study hard, think quietly, talk gently, act
  frankly;
To listen to stars and birds, to babes and
  sages, with open heart;
To bear all cheerfully, do all bravely, await
  occasions, hurry never.
In a word, to let the spiritual, unbidden and
  unconscious, grow up through the common.
This is to be my symphony.

William Ellery Channing — My Symphony

To be honest, to be kind, to earn a little and to spend a little less, to make upon the whole a family happier for his presence; to renounce when that shall be necessary and not be embittered; to keep a few friends but these without capitulation; above all on the same grim condition, to keep friends with himself; here is a task for all that a man has of fortitude and delicacy.

Robert Louis Stevenson

The art of living successfully consists of being able to hold two opposite ideas in tension at the same time: first, to make long-term plans as if we were going to live forever; and, second, to conduct ourselves daily as if we were going to die tomorrow.

Sydney Harris

Life's supreme adventure is the adventure of living. Life's greatest achievement is the continual remaking of yourself so that at last you do know how to live.
The man who is set for the building up of a self he can live with in some kind of comfort and with the hope of continued improvement chooses deliberately what he will let himself think and feel, thoughts of admiration and high desire, emotions that are courageous and inspiring. It is by these that we grow into more abundant and truer life, a more harmonious inner state and a more stalwart personality.

Winfred Rhoades

What we need is to take the gas and hot air out of the real business of living, and send it sizzling off in sky-rockets for the entertainment of our idle hours.

Marjorie Barstow Greenbie

I will be a man among men; and no longer a dreamer among shadows. Henceforth be mine a life of action and reality! I will work in my own sphere, nor wish it other than it is. This alone is health and happiness.

Henry Wadsworth Longfellow

Action

Life's a pretty precious and wonderful thing. You can't sit down and let it lap around you . . . you have to plunge into it; you have to dive through it! And you can't save it, you can't store it up; you can't board it in a vault. You've got to taste it; you've got to use it. The more you use, the more you have . . . that's the miracle of it!

Kyle Crichton

The life of man is made up of action and endurance; the life is fruitful in the ratio in which it is laid out in noble action or in patient perseverance.

Henry Parry Liddon

Doing is the great thing. For if, resolutely, people do what is right, in time they come to like doing it.

John Ruskin

Do not stop thinking of life as an adventure.

Eleanor Roosevelt

Reflect that life, like every other blessing,
Derives its value from its use alone;
Not for itself, but for a nobler end,
The Eternal gave it, and that end is virtue.

Samuel Johnson

Adventure is not outside a man; it is within.

David Grayson

We should act with as much energy as those who expect everything from themselves; and we should pray with as much earnestness as those who expect everything from God.

Charles Caleb Colton

The proper function of man is to live, not to exist. I shall not waste my days in trying to prolong them. I shall use my time.

Jack London

The world is blessed most by men who do things, and not by those who merely talk about them.

James Oliver

We live in deeds, not years; in thoughts, not
  breaths;
In feelings, not in figures on a dial.
We should count time by heart-throbs.
  He most lives
Who thinks most — feels the noblest
  — acts the best.

Philip James Bailey

There are many ways of going forward, but there is only one way of standing still.

Franklin Delano Roosevelt

Happiness is activity.

Aristotle

If one advances confidently in the direction of his dreams, and endeavors to live the life which he has imagined, he will meet with a success unexpected in common hours . . . If you have built castles in the air, your work need not be lost; that is where they should be. Now put foundations under them.

Henry David Thoreau

What a large volume of adventures may be grasped within this little span of life by him who interests his heart in everything, and who, having eyes to see what time and chance are perpetually holding out to him as he journeyeth on his way, misses nothing he can fairly lay his hands on.

Laurence Sterne

I do not believe in a fate that falls on men however they act; but I do believe in a fate that falls on them unless they act.

Gilbert Keith Chesterton

Outlook

For all your days prepare,
    And meet them ever alike:
When you are the anvil, bear—
    When you are the hammer, strike.

Edwin Markham

The tests of life are to make, not break us. Trouble may demolish a man's business but build up his character. The blow at the outward man may be the greatest blessing to the inner man. If God, then, puts or permits anything hard in our lives, be sure that the real peril, the real trouble, is that we shall lose if we flinch or rebel.

Maltbie D. Babcock

God did not make us to be eaten up by anxiety, but to walk erect, free, unafraid in a world where there is work to do, truth to seek, love to give and win.

Joseph Fort Newton

Most of the shadows of this life are caused by standing in our own sunshine.

Ralph Waldo Emerson

One cannot always be a hero, but one can always be a man.

Johann Wolfgang von Goethe

We do not succeed in changing things according to our desire, but gradually our desire changes. The situation that we hoped to change because it was intolerable becomes unimportant. We have not managed to surmount the obstacle, as we were absolutely determined to do, but life has taken us round it, led us past it, and then if we turn round to gaze at the remote past, we can barely catch sight of it, so imperceptible has it become.

Marcel Proust

Thank God for life; life is not sweet always.
Hands may be heavy laden, heart care-full;
Unwelcome nights follow unwelcome days,
And dreams divine end in awakenings dull;
Still it is life; and life is cause for praise.
This ache, this restlessness, this quickening sting
Prove me no torpid and inanimate thing —
Prove me of Him who is the life, the spring.
I am alive — and that is beautiful.

Anonymous

Afflictions, like God's angels, will move away when they have done their errand.

Agnes Carter Mason

God will not look you over for medals, degrees or diplomas, but for scars.

Elbert Hubbard

Prosperity asks fidelity; adversity exacts it.

Seneca

Never a tear bedims the eye
That time and patience will not dry.

Bret Harte

Many might go to heaven with half the labor they go to hell.

Ralph Waldo Emerson

Trials are medicines which our gracious and wise physician prescribes, because we need them; and he proportions the frequency and weight of them to what the case requires. Let us trust his skill and thank him for his prescription.

Joseph Fort Newton

Little minds are tamed and subdued by misfortune, but great minds rise above it.

Washington Irving

To be thrown upon one's resources is to be cast into the very lap of fortune.

Anonymous

I am an old man and have known a great many troubles, but most of them never happened.

Mark Twain

94

It is not what the world gives me
In honor, praise or gold;
It is what I do give the world,
So others do unfold.

If by my work through life I can
Another soul unfold,
Then I have done what cannot be
Made good, by praise or gold.

One tiny thought in tiny word
May give a great one birth,
And, if that thought was caused by me,
I lived a life of worth.

Richard F. Wolfe — Worth

There is so much good in the worst of us,
And so much bad in the best of us,
That it ill behooves any of us
To find fault with the rest of us.

Anonymous

Give me a man capable of a devotion to
anything, rather than a cold, calculating man
of all the virtues.

Bret Harte

Talk not of wasted affection! affection
    never was wasted;
If it enrich not the heart of another, its
    waters, returning
Back to their springs, like the rain, shall
    fill them full of refreshment:
That which the fountain sends forth
    returns again to the fountain.

Henry Wadsworth Longfellow

Praise is well, compliment is well, but affection
— that is the last and final and most precious
reward that any man wins, whether by character
or achievement.

Mark Twain

If a man is worth knowing at all, he is worth
knowing well.

Alexander Smith

Loyalty is the holiest good in the human heart.

Seneca

Unless you find some sort of loyalty, you
cannot find unity and peace in your active
living.

Josiah Royce

Success is speaking words of praise,
In cheering other people's ways,
In doing just the best you can,
With every task and every plan,
It's silence when your speech would hurt,
Politeness when your neighbor's curt,
It's deafness when the scandal flows,
And sympathy with others' woes,
It's loyalty when duty calls,
It's courage when disaster falls,
It's patience when the hours are long,
It's found in laughter and in song,
It's in the silent time of prayer,
In happiness and in despair,
In all of life and nothing less,
We find the thing we call success.

Anonymous — Success

A narrow window may let in the light,
A tiny star dispel the gloom of night,
A little deed a mighty wrong set right.

A rose, abloom, may make a desert fair,
A single cloud may darken all the air,
A spark may kindle ruin and despair.

A smile, and there may be an end to strife;
A look of love, and Hate may sheathe the
    knife;
A word — ah, it may be a word of life!

Florence Earle Coates — A Narrow Window

True worth is in *being,* not seeming,
In doing, each day that goes by,
Some little good, not in dreaming
Of great things to do by and by,
For whatever men say in their blindness,
And spite of the fancies of youth,
There's nothing so kingly as kindness,
And nothing so royal as truth.

Alice Cary

It is better to be faithful than famous.

Theodore Roosevelt

95

Money and time are the heaviest burdens of
life, and the unhappiest of all mortals are those
who have more of either than they know
how to use.

Samuel Johnson

Defeat may serve as well as victory
To shake the soul and let the glory out.
When the great oak is straining in the wind,
The boughs drink in new beauty and the trunk
Sends down a deeper root on the windward side.
Only the soul that knows the mighty grief
Can know the mighty rapture. Sorrows come
To stretch out spaces in the heart for joy.

Edwin Markham — Victory in Defeat

All the misfortunes of men spring from their
not knowing how to live quietly at home in
their own rooms.

Blaise Pascal

Worry is a thin stream of fear trickling through
the mind. If encouraged, it cuts a channel into
which all other thoughts are drained.

Arthur Somers Roche

Toiling, — rejoicing, — sorrowing,
    Onward through life he goes;
Each morning sees some task begin,
    Each evening sees it close;
Something attempted, something done,
    Has earned a night's repose.

Thanks, thanks to thee, my worthy friend,
    For the lesson thou hast taught!
Thus at the flaming forge of life
    Our fortunes must be wrought;
Thus on its sounding anvil shaped,
    Each burning deed and thought!

Henry Wadsworth Longfellow

When I hear somebody sigh that "Life is
hard," I am always tempted to ask, "Compared
to what?"

Sydney Harris

It is foolish to tear one's hair in grief as though
sorrow would be made less by baldness.

Cicero

Sweet are the uses of adversity;
Which, like the toad, ugly and venomous,
Wears yet a precious jewel in his head;
And this our life, exempt from public haunt,
Finds tongues in trees, books in the running
    brooks,
Sermons in stones, and good in everything.

William Shakespeare

I do not ask, O Lord,
A life all free from pain;
I do not seek to be
In this vast world of need
Without my load of care.
For this I know, the cross
Is my eternal gain,
And he who struggles on
At last shall enter in,
And be victorious there.

So, Lord, just keep me fit within,
And give me strength to fight,
And I will follow through the din,
From darkness up to light.

Daniel A. Poling — Prayer

Time

Enjoy the blessings of the day . . . and the
evils bear patiently; for this day only is ours:
we are dead to yesterday, and not born to
tomorrow.

Jeremy Taylor

The psychologist William Moulton Marston
asked 3000 persons: "What have you to live
for?"
He was shocked to find that 94 per cent were
simply enduring the present while they waited
for the future; waited for "something" to
happen; waited for children to grow up and
leave home; waited for next year; waited for
another time to take a long-dreamed-about
trip; waited for someone to die; waited for
tomorrow without realizing that all anyone
ever has is today because yesterday is gone
and tomorrow never comes.

Douglas Lurton

Dost thou love life? Then do not squander Time, for that's the stuff life is made of.

Benjamin Franklin

Waste of wealth is sometimes retrieved; waste of health, seldom; but waste of time, never.

Thomas Campion

Live every day of your life as though you expected to live forever.

Douglas MacArthur

We're never done preparing. Every act we perform, even if it seems at the time practically our whole purpose in life, is really nothing but preparation for something we'll do at some future time. So long as we live we're never done. Today prepares for tomorrow, and next year prepares for the year after it. Our life is a sort of savings bank in which we deposit our acts and our experiences to use when we need them — and we always need them. Someone once said that we don't live long enough to learn enough to make ourselves really useful. Just the same, the more we learn and the more we prepare, the nearer we are to usefulness. So don't be discouraged because life is nothing but a series of preparations. It would be terribly dull if we came to a time when there was nothing else for which to prepare.

Anonymous — Preparation

Tomorrow — oh, it will never be
  If we should live a thousand years!
Our time is all today, today,
  The same, though changed, and
    while it flies
With still small voice the moments say:
  "Today, today, be wise, be wise."

James Montgomery

The supply of time is a daily miracle. You wake up in the morning and lo! Your purse is magnificently filled with 24 hours of the unmanufactured tissue of the universe of life. It is yours! The most precious of your possessions.

Arnold Bennett

How small a portion of our life it is that we really enjoy! In youth we are looking forward to things that are to come. In old age we are looking backward to things that have past. In manhood, although we appear to be more occupied in things that are present, yet even that is too often absorbed in vague determination to be vastly happy on some future day when we have time.

Charles Caleb Colton

Write it on your heart that every day is the best day in the year. He is rich who owns the day, and no one owns the day who allows it to be invaded with fret and anxiety. Finish every day and be done with it. You have done what you could. Some blunders and absurdities, no doubt, crept in. Forget them as soon as you can, tomorrow is a new day; begin it well and serenely, with too high a spirit to be cumbered with your old nonsense. This new day is too dear, with its hopes and invitations, to waste a moment on the yesterdays.

Ralph Waldo Emerson

Our main business is not to see what lies dimly at a distance but to do what lies clearly at hand.

Thomas Carlyle

I have a rendezvous with Life,
In days I hope will come,
Ere youth has sped, and strength of mind,
Ere voices sweet grow dumb.
I have a rendezvous with Life,
When Spring's first heralds hum.

Countee Cullen

One of the most tragic things I know about human nature is that all of us tend to put off living. We are all dreaming of some magical rose garden over the horizon — instead of enjoying the roses that are blooming outside our windows today.

Dale Carnegie

The less one has to do, the less time one finds to do it in.

Lord Chesterfield

Are you in earnest? Seize this very minute:
What you can do, or dream you can, begin it;
Boldness has genius, power, and magic in it.
Only engage and the mind grows heated;
Begin and then the work will be completed.

Johann Wolfgang von Goethe

No good e'er comes of leisure idly spent:
And Heaven ne'er helps the man who will not
   work.

Sophocles

We know nothing of tomorrow; our business
is to be good and happy today.

Sydney Smith

Look to this day! For it is life,
   The very life of life.
In its brief course lie all the varieties
And realities of your existence.
   The bliss of growth,
   The glory of action,
   The splendor of beauty,
For yesterday is but a dream,
And tomorrow is only a vision;
   But today well lived
Makes every yesterday a dream of happiness,
And every tomorrow a vision of hope.
Look well, therefore, to this day!

Anonymous

As soon as you feel too old to do a thing, do it.

Margaret Deland

The riders in a race do not stop short when
they reach the goal. There is a little finishing
canter before they come to a standstill. There
is time to hear the kind voice of friends and
to say to one's self: "The work is done." But
just as one says that, the answer comes: "The
race is over, but the work never is done
while the power to work remains." The canter
that brings you to a standstill need not be only
coming to rest. It cannot be while you still
live. For to live is to function. That is all there
is in living.

Justice Oliver Wendell Holmes, Jr.
Radio address on his ninetieth birthday
(March 8, 1931)

Though much is taken, much abides; and
   though
We are not now that strength which in old days
Moved earth and heaven, that which we are,
   we are,—
One equal temper of heroic hearts,
Made weak by time and fate, but strong in will
To strive, to seek, to find, and not to yield.

Alfred, Lord Tennyson

Growing old is no more than a bad habit
which a busy man has no time to form.

André Maurois

On his eightieth birthday, John Quincy Adams
responded to a query concerning his well-being
by saying: "John Quincy Adams is well. But
the house in which he lives at present is
becoming dilapidated. It is tottering upon its
foundation. Time and the seasons have nearly
destroyed it. Its roof is pretty well worn out.
Its walls are much shattered and it trembles
with every wind. I think John Quincy Adams
will have to move out of it soon. But he
himself is quite well, quite well."

Anonymous

To me old age is always fifteen years older
than I am.

Bernard Baruch

At fifty a man's real life begins. He has
acquired upon which to achieve; received
from which to give; learned from which to
teach; cleared upon which to build.

Edward William Bok

When one finds company in himself and his
pursuits, he cannot feel old, no matter what
his years may be.

Amos Bronson Alcott

Age is no cause for veneration. An old
crocodile is still a menace and an old crow
sings not like a nightingale.

Dagobert D. Runes

Youth is the time for the adventures of the
body, but age for the triumphs of the mind.

Logan Pearsall Smith

When I was young I was amazed at Plutarch's statement that the elder Cato began at the age of eighty to learn Greek. I am amazed no longer. Old age is ready to undertake tasks youth shirked because they would take too long.

W. Somerset Maugham

To be seventy years young is sometimes far more cheerful and hopeful than to be forty years old.

Oliver Wendell Holmes

"Nothing, so it seems to me," said the stranger, "is more beautiful than the love that has weathered the storms of life . . . The love of the young for the young, that is the beginning of life. But the love of the old for the old, that is the beginning of — of things longer."

Jerome K. Jerome

Your lordship, though not clean past your youth, hath yet some smack of age in you, some relish of the saltness of time.

William Shakespeare

Let me grow lovely, growing old —
    So many fine things do:
Laces, and ivory, and gold,
    And silks need not be new.

Karle Wilson Baker

To him whose elastic and vigorous thought keeps pace with the sun, the day is a perpetual morning.

Henry David Thoreau

All would live long, but none would be old.

Benjamin Franklin

I like spring, but it is too young. I like summer, but it is too proud. So I like best of all autumn, because its leaves are a little yellow, its tone mellower, its colors richer, and it is tinged a little with sorrow. Its golden richness speaks not of the innocence of spring, nor of the power of summer, but of the mellowness and kindly wisdom of approaching age. It knows the limitations of life and is content.

Lin Yutang

If wrinkles must be written upon our brows, let them not be written upon the heart. The spirit should not grow old.

James A. Garfield

It is too late! Ah, nothing is too late
Till the tired heart shall cease to palpitate.
Cato learned Greek at eighty; Sophocles
Wrote his grand Oedipus, and Simonides
Bore off the prize of verse from his compeers,
When each had numbered more than four score
    years . . .
Chaucer, at Woodstock with the nightingales,
At sixty wrote the Canterbury Tales;
Goethe at Weimar, toiling to the last,
Completed Faust when eighty years past.

Robert Longfellow

(NOTE: To which group may be added Michelangelo working on the design for St. Peter's Dome in his eighties; Titian painting until killed by the plague at ninety-nine; and, more recently, Grandma Moses, who was still painting at one hundred.)

Wrinkles should merely indicate where smiles have been.

Mark Twain

Though I look old, yet I am strong and lusty;
For in my youth I never did apply
Hot and rebellious liquors in my blood,
Nor did not with unbashful forehead woo
The means of weakness and debility;
Therefore my age is as a lusty winter,
Frosty, but kindly.

William Shakespeare

A long life may not be good enough, but a good life is long enough.

Benjamin Franklin

So long as enthusiasm lasts, so long is youth still with us.

David Starr Jordan

Let a man understand that you think he is faithful, and he will be.

Seneca

An old man, going a lone highway,
Came at the evening, cold and gray,
To a chasm, vast and deep and wide,
Through which was flowing a sullen tide.
The old man crossed in the twilight dim;
The sullen stream had no fears for him;
But he turned when safe on the other side
And built a bridge to span the tide.

"Old man," said a fellow pilgrim near,
"You are wasting strength with building here;
Your journey will end with the ending day;
You never again must pass this way;
You have crossed the chasm, deep and wide —
Why build you at the eventide?"

The builder lifted his old gray head:
"Good friend, in the path I have come," he said,
"There followeth after me today
A youth whose feet must pass this way.
This chasm that has been naught to me
To that fair-haired youth may a pitfall be.
He, too, must cross in the twilight dim;
Good friend, I am building the bridge for him."

Will Allen Drumgoole — The Bridge Builder

So long as you are learning, you are not
growing old. It's when a man stops learning
that he begins to grow old.

Joseph Hergesheimer

It is not what the best men do, but what they
are, that constitutes their truest benefaction to
their fellow-men. Certainly, in our little sphere,
it is not the most active people to whom we
owe the most. It is the lives like the stars,
which simply pour down on us the calm light
of their bright and faithful being, up to which
we must look, and out of which we gather
the deepest calm and courage.

Phillips Brooks

Folks want a lot of loving every minute —
The sympathy of others and their smile!
Till life's end, from the moment they begin it,
Folks need a lot of loving all the while.

Strickland Gillilan

I live for those who love me,
For those who know me true,
For the Heaven that smiles above me,
    And awaits my coming too;
For the cause that lacks assistance,
For the wrong that needs resistance,
For the future in the distance,
    And the good that I can do.

G. Linnaeus Banks — For Those Who Love Me

The young man who has not wept is a savage,
and the old man who will not laugh is a fool.

George Santayana

Not to be able to grow old is just as ridiculous
as to be unable to outgrow childhood.

Carl G. Jung

There are three classes into which all women
past seventy years of age I have ever known,
were divided: that dear old soul; that old
woman; that old witch.

Samuel Taylor Coleridge

On his bold visage middle age
Had slightly pressed its signet sage,
Yet had not quench'd the open truth
And fiery vehemence of youth;
Forward and frolic glee was there,
The will to do, the soul to dare.

Sir Walter Scott

Nature is full of freaks, and now puts an old
head on young shoulders, and then a young
heart beating under fourscore winters.

Ralph Waldo Emerson

Pride and Patriotism

Origins

The land was ours before we were the land's.
She was our land more than a hundred years
Before we were her people. She was ours
In Massachusetts, in Virginia,
But we were England's, still colonials,
Possessing what we still were unpossessed by,
Possessed by what we now no more possessed.
Something we were withholding made us weak
Until we found out that it was ourselves
We were withholding from our land of living,
And forthwith found salvation in surrender.
Such as we were we gave ourselves outright
(The deed of gift was many deeds of war)
To the land vaguely realizing westward,
But still unstoried, artless, unenhanced,
Such as she was, such as she would become.

Robert Frost — The Gift Outright

In the Name of God, Amen. We, whose names
are underwritten, the Loyal Subjects of our
dread Sovereign Lord King James, by the
Grace of God, of Great Britain, France, and
Ireland, King, Defender of the Faith, etc.
Having undertaken for the Glory of God, and
Advancement of the Christian Faith, and the
Honour of our King and Country, a Voyage to
plant the first Colony in the northern Parts
of Virginia; Do by these Presents, solemnly and
mutually, in the Presence of God and one
another, covenant and combine ourselves together into a civil Body Politick, for our better
Ordering and Preservation, and Furtherance
of the Ends aforesaid: And by Virtue hereof do
enact, constitute, and frame, such just and

equal Laws, Ordinances, Acts, Constitutions,
and Officers, from time to time, as shall be
thought most meet and convenient for the
general Good of the Colony; unto which we
promise all due Submission and Obedience. In
Witness whereof we have hereunto subscribed
our names at Cape-Cod the eleventh of November, in the Reign of our Sovereign Lord
King James, of England, France, and Ireland,
the eighteenth, and of Scotland, the fifty-fourth,
Anno Domini, 1620.

Mr. John Carver	Digery Priest
Mr. William Bradford	Thomas Williams
Mr. Edward Winslow	Gilbert Winslow
Mr. William Brewster	Edmund Margesson
Isaac Allerton	Peter Brown
Myles Standish	Richard Britteridge
John Alden	George Soule
John Turner	Edward Tilly
Francis Eaton	John Tilly
James Chilton	Francis Cooke
John Craxton	Thomas Rogers
John Billington	Thomas Tinker
Joses Fletcher	John Ridgdale
John Goodman	Edward Fuller
Mr. Samuel Fuller	Richard Clark
Mr. Christopher Martin	Richard Gardiner
Mr. William Mullins	Mr. John Allerton
Mr. William White	Thomas English
Mr. Richard Warren	Edward Doten
John Howland	Edward Liester
Mr. Steven Hopkins	

The Mayflower Compact, 11 November 1620

This spot marks the final resting place of the
Pilgrims of the Mayflower. In weariness and
hunger and in cold, fighting the wilderness
and burying their dead in common graves that
the Indians should not know how many had

perished, they here laid the foundations of a state in which all men for countless ages should have liberty to worship God in their own way. All ye who pass by and see this stone remember, and dedicate yourselves anew to the resolution that you will not rest until this lofty ideal shall have been realized throughout the earth.

Plymouth Rock Inscription

. . . Whence came all these people? They are a mixture of English, Scotch, Irish, French, Dutch, Germans, and Swedes. From this promiscuous breed, that race now called Americans have arisen.

In this great American asylum, the poor of Europe have by some means met together, and in consequence of various causes; to what purpose should they ask one another what countrymen they are? Urged by a variety of motives, here they came. Everything has tended to regenerate them: new laws, a new mode of living, a new social system. Here they are become men.

He is an American who, leaving behind him all his ancient prejudices and manners, receives new ones from the new mode of life he has embraced, the new government he obeys, and the new rank he holds. He becomes an American by being received in the broad lap of our great *alma mater*. Here individuals of all nations are melted into a new race of men whose labors and posterity will one day cause great changes in the world. Americans are the western pilgrims, who are carrying along with them the great mass of arts, sciences, vigor, and industry which began long since in the East. They will finish the great circle . . . The American is a new man, who acts upon new principles; he must therefore entertain new ideas, and form new opinions. From involuntary idleness, servile dependence, penury, and useless labor, he has passed to toils of a very different nature, rewarded by ample subsistence.

This is an American.

J. Hector St. John Crèvecoeur, 1774 —
This is an American

Let us not forget the religious character of our origin. Our fathers were brought here by their high veneration for the Christian religion. They journeyed by its light, and labored in its hope. They sought to incorporate its principles with the elements of their society, and to diffuse its influence through all their institutions — civil, political and literary. Let us cherish these sentiments, and extend this influence still more widely, in the full conviction that this is the happiest society, which partakes in the highest degree of the mild and peaceable spirit of Christianity.

Daniel Webster

I hope future ages will quote our proceedings with applause. It is one of the great duties of the democratical part of the constitution to keep itself pure. It is known in my Province that some other Colonies are not so numerous or rich as they are. I am for giving all the satisfaction in my power.
The distinctions between Virginians, Pennsylvanians, New Yorkers, and New Englanders, are no more. I am not a Virginian, but an American.

Patrick Henry, The First Continental Congress 1774

Creeds

Where the northern ocean darkens,
Where the rolling rivers run,
Past the cold and empty headlands,
Toward the slow and westering sun,
There our fathers, long before us,
Armed with freedom, faced the deep;
What they won with love and labor,
Let their children watch and keep.
By our dark and dreaming forests,
By our free and shining skies,
By our green and ripening prairies,
Where the western mountains rise;
God who gave our fathers freedom,
God who made our fathers brave,
What they built with love and anguish,
Let their children watch and save.

Robert Nathan — Watch, America

I believe in America because in it we are free
  —free to choose our government, to speak
  our minds, to observe our different religions;
Because we are generous with our freedom—
  we share our rights with those who disagree
  with us;
Because we hate no people and covet no
  people's land;
Because we are blessed with a natural and
  varied abundance;
Because we set no limit to a man's achievement:
  in mine, factory, field, or service in business
  or the arts, an able man, regardless of class
  or creed, can realize his ambition;
Because we have great dreams—and because
  we have the opportunity to make those
  dreams come true.

Wendell L. Willkie — Credo

You cannot dedicate yourself to America unless you become in every respect and with every purpose of your will thorough Americans.

Woodrow Wilson

I was born an American; I live an American; I shall die an American; and I intend to perform the duties incumbent upon me in that character to the end of my career. I mean to do this with absolute disregard of personal consequences. What are the personal consequences? What is the individual man, with all the good or evil that may betide him, in comparison with the good or evil which may befall a great country, and in the midst of great transactions which concern that country's fate? Let the consequences be what they will, I am careless. No man can suffer too much, and no man can fall too soon, if he suffer, or if he fall, in the defense of the liberties and constitution of his country.

Daniel Webster

I consider it as an indispensable duty to close this last act of my official life by commending the interests of our dearest country to the protection of Almighty God, and those who have the superintendence of them to his holy keeping.

George Washington's Farewell, 1783

America First —
Not merely in matters material, but in things
  of the spirit.
Not merely in science, inventions, motors and
  skyscrapers, but in ideals, principles,
  character.
Not merely in the calm assertion of rights,
  but in the glad assumption of duties.
Not flaunting her strength as a giant, but
  bending in helpfulness over a sick and
  wounded world like a Good Samaritan.
Not in splendid isolation, but in courageous
  cooperation.
Not in pride, arrogance, and disdain of other
  races and peoples, but in sympathy, love,
  and understanding.
Not in treading again the old worn, bloody
  pathway which ends inevitably in chaos and
  disaster, but in blazing a new trail, along
  which, please God, other nations will follow,
  into the new Jerusalem where wars shall be
  no more.
Some day some nation must take that path —
  unless we lapse once again into utter
  barbarism — and that honor I covet for
  my beloved America.
And so, in the spirit and with these hopes,
  I say with all my heart and soul,
  "America First."

G. Ashton Oldham — America First

When an American says he loves his country, he means not only that he loves the New England hills, the prairies glistening in the sun, the wide and rising plains, the great mountains, and the sea. He means that he loves the inner air, an inner light in which freedom lives and in which a man can draw a breath of self-respect.

Adlai Stevenson

Only those Americans who are willing to die for their country are fit to live.

Douglas MacArthur

So it's home again, and home again,
  America for me,
My heart is turning home again, and
  there I long to be.

Henry Van Dyke

American liberty is a religion. It is a thing of the spirit. It is an aspiration on the part of the people for not alone a free life but a better one.

Wendell L. Willkie

Whether God blesses America or not does not depend so much upon God as it does upon us Americans.

C. H. Kopf

Behind all these men you have to do with, behind officers, and government, and people even, there is the country herself, your country, and . . . you belong to her as you belong to your own mother.

Edward Everett Hale

I am an American and therefore what I do, however small, is of importance.

Struthers Burt

When, in the course of human events, it becomes necessary for one people to dissolve the political bands which have connected them with another, and to assume among the powers of the earth the separate and equal station to which the laws of nature and of nature's God entitle them, a decent respect to the opinions of mankind requires that they should declare the causes which impel them to the separation. We hold these truths to be self-evident; that all men are created equal, that they are endowed by their creator with certain unalienable rights; that among these are life, liberty, and the pursuit of happiness; that to secure these rights, governments are instituted among men, deriving their just powers from the consent of the governed; that whenever any form of government becomes destructive to these ends, it is the right of the people to alter or to abolish it, and to institute new government, laying its foundation on such principles, and organizing its powers in such form, as to them shall seem most likely to effect their safety and happiness. And for the support of this declaration, with a firm reliance on the protection of divine providence, we mutually pledge to each other our lives, our fortunes, and our sacred honor.

Declaration of Independence (July 4, 1776)

Our nation, the immortal spirit of our domain, lives in us—in our hearts and minds and consciences. There it must find its nutriment or die.

Grover Cleveland

Let our object be our country, our whole country, and nothing but our country. And, by the blessing of God, may that country itself become a vast and splendid monument, not of oppression and terror, but of wisdom, of peace, and of liberty upon which the world may gaze with admiration forever.

Daniel Webster

I believe in the United States of America as a Government of the people, by the people, for the people; whose just powers are derived from the consent of the governed; a democracy in a republic, a sovereign Nation of many sovereign States; a perfect Union one and inseparable; established upon those principles of freedom, equality, justice and humanity for which American patriots sacrificed their lives and fortunes. I therefore believe it is my duty to my country to love it; to support its Constitution; to obey its laws; to respect its flag, and to defend it against all enemies.

William Tyler Page — The American's Creed[1]
[1]Adopted by the House Representatives April 3, 1918

Let us ever remember that our interests are in concord and not in conflict, and that our true greatness rests on our victories of peace rather than those of war.

Anonymous

The true test of civilization is not the census nor the size of cities or crops, — no, but the kind of man the country turns out.

Ralph Waldo Emerson

He who loves not his country can love nothing.

George Gordon, Lord Byron

Territory is but the body of a nation. The people who inhabit its hills and valleys are its soul, its spirit, its life.

James A. Garfield

The General ever desirous to cherish a virtuous
ambition in his soldiers, as well as to foster
and encourage every species of Military merit,
directs that whenever any singularly meritorious
action is performed, the author of it shall be
permitted to wear on his facings over the left
breast, the figure of a heart in purple cloth
or silk, edged with narrow lace or binding. Not
only instances of unusual gallantry, but also of
extraordinary fidelity and essential Service in
any way shall meet with a due reward. . . .
Men who have merited this last distinction to
be suffered to pass all guards and sentinels
which officers are permitted to do.
The road to glory in a patriot army and a free
country is thus open to all — this order is
also to have retrospect to the earliest stages of
the war, and to be considered as a permanent
one.

The Purple Heart Badge of Military Merit,
which Washington established by a general order of
Aug. 7, 1782

A man's country is not a certain area of land,
of mountains, rivers and woods,—but it is a
principle; and patriotism is loyalty to that
principle.

George William Curtis

Freedom is a breath of air,
Pine-scented, or salty like the sea;
Freedom is a field new-plowed . . .
Furrows of democracy!

Freedom is a forest,
Trees tall and straight as men!
Freedom is a printing press . . .
The power of the pen!

Freedom is a country church,
A cathedral's stately spire;
Freedom is a spirit
That can set the soul on fire!

Freedom is man's birthright,
A sacred, living rampart;
A pulsebeat of humanity . . .
The throb of a nation's heart!

Clara Smith Reber — Freedom

I have seen the glories of art and architecture
and of river and mountain. I have seen the
sun set on the Jungfrau and the moon rise over
Mont Blanc. But the fairest vision on which
these eyes ever rested was the flag of my
country in a foreign port. Beautiful as a flower
to those who love it, terrible as a meteor to
those who hate it, it is the symbol of the power
and the glory and the honor of millions of
Americans.

George F. Hoar

The Flag is many things. It is a mark of
identification of ships at sea and of armies in
the field. It is a means of communication.
When you see our Flag in front of a home, it
says for all the world to read, "Here lives a
family that is American in spirit as well as in
name." The Flag is a mirror, reflecting to each
person his own ideals and dreams. It is a
history. Its thirteen stripes and fifty stars embrace a record written greatly during these
years since 1776. It is a mark of pride in a
great word — the word "American." It is an
aspiration of what small children want their
lives to be. It is a memory at the end of life of
all that life has been. It is a ribbon of honor
for those who have served it well — in peace
and war. It is a warning not to detour from
the long road that has brought our country and
its people to a degree of prosperity and happiness never even approached under any other
banner.

Edward F. Hutton

America lives in the heart of every man
everywhere who wishes to find a region where
he will be free to work out his destiny as he
chooses.

Woodrow Wilson

So, then, to every man his chance — to every
man, regardless of his birth, his shining, golden
opportunity — to every man the right to live,
to work, to be himself, and to become whatever
thing his manhood and his vision can combine
to make him — this, seeker, is the promise of
America.

Thomas Wolfe

Before all else we seek, upon our common
labor as a nation, the blessings of Almighty
God. And the hopes in our hearts fashion
the deepest prayers of our whole people.
May we pursue the right — without self-
righteousness.
May we know unity — without conformity.
May we grow in strength — without pride in
self.
May we, in our dealings with all peoples of
the earth, ever speak truth and serve justice.
May the light of freedom, coming to all
darkened lands, flame brightly — until at
last the darkness is no more.
May the turbulence of our age yield to a true
time of peace, when men and nations share
a life that honors the dignity of each, the
brotherhood of all.

> Dwight D. Eisenhower — Our Common Labor

It is a fabulous country, the only fabulous
country; it is the only place where miracles
not only happen, but where they happen all
the time.

> Thomas Wolfe

Americanism is a question of principle, of
purpose, of idealism, of character; it is not a
matter of birthplace or creed, or line of descent.

> Anonymous

Justice

What are the American ideals? They are the
development of the individual through liberty
and the attainment of the common good
through democracy and social justice.

> Louis D. Brandeis

Anglo-Saxon civilization has taught the individual to protect his own rights; American
cvilization will teach him to respect the
rights of others.

> William Jennings Bryan

An American is one who loves justice and
believes in the dignity of man.

> Harold L. Ickes

The citizens of the United States of America
have a right to applaud themselves for having
given to Mankind examples of an enlarged
and liberal policy, a policy worthy of imitation.
All possess alike liberty of conscience and
immunities of citizenship. For happily the
Government of the United States, which gives
bigotry no sanction, to persecution no assistance requires only that they who live under its
protection should demean themselves as good
citizens, in giving it on all occasions their
effectual support.
It would be inconsistent with the frankness of
my character not to avow that I am pleased
with your favorable opinion of my administra-
tion, and fervent wishes for my felicity. May
the Children of the Stock of Abraham, who
dwell in this land, continue to merit and enjoy
the good will of the other Inhabitants, while
every one shall sit in safety under his own vine
and fig-tree, and there shall be none to make
him afraid. May the father of all mercies scatter
light and not darkness in our paths, and make
us all in our several vocations useful here,
and in his own due time and way everlastingly
happy.

> George Washington to Moses Seixas, Sexton of the
> Hebrew Congregation of Newport, Rhode Island,
> August 17, 1790

Of the various executive abilities, no one
excited more anxious concern than that of
placing the interests of our fellow-citizens in
the hands of honest men, with understanding
sufficient for their stations. No duty is at the
same time more difficult to fulfill. The
knowledge of character possessed by a single
individual is of necessity limited. To seek out
the best through the whole Union, we must
resort to the information which from the best
men, acting disinterestedly and with the purest
motives, is sometimes incorrect.

> Thomas Jefferson

Government is a trust, and the officers of the
government are trustees; and both the trust
and the trustees are created for the benefit of
the people.

> Henry Clay

Just what is it that America stands for? If she stands for one thing more than another it is for the sovereignty of self-governing people.

Woodrow Wilson

America calls for government with a soul.

Franklin Delano Roosevelt

To be an American is of itself almost a moral condition, an education, and a career.

George Santayana

An American is one who will fight for his freedom and that of his neighbor.

Harold L. Ickes

As mankind become more liberal, they will be more apt to allow, that all those who conduct themselves as worthy members of the community are equally entitled to the protection of civil government. I hope ever to see America among the foremost nations in examples of justice and liberality. And I presume, that your fellow-citizens will not forget the patriotic part which you took in the accomplishment of their revolution, and the establishment of their government; or the important assistance, which they received, from a Nation in which the Roman Catholic religion is professed . . . May the members of your Society in America, animated alone by the pure spirit of Christianity, and still conducting themselves as the faithful subjects of our free government, enjoy every temporal and spiritual felicity.

George Washington to a Committee of Roman Catholics, March 15, 1790

America! America!
  God shed his grace on thee
And crown thy good with brotherhood
  From sea to shining sea!

Katherine Lee Bates

America is not a mere body of traders; it is a body of free men. Our greatness is built upon our freedom — is moral, not material. We have a great ardor for gain; but we have a deep passion for the rights of man.

Woodrow Wilson

Our country hath a gospel of her own
To preach and practice before all the world—
The freedom and divinity of man,
The glorious claims of human brotherhood,
And the soul's fealty to none but God.

James Russell Lowell — America's Gospel

An American is one who will sacrifice property, ease and security in order that he and his children may retain the rights of free men.

Harold L. Ickes

God send us men with hearts ablaze
  All truth to love, all wrong to hate;
These are the patriots nations need,
  These are the bulwark of the state.

Frederick A. Gillman

Our country, right or wrong. When right, to be kept right; when wrong, to be put right.

Carl Schurz

There is nothing wrong with America that the faith, love of freedom, intelligence and energy of her citizens cannot cure.

Dwight David Eisenhower

Civil liberties means liberties for those we like and those we don't like, or even detest.

Felix Frankfurter

Greatness

It is by no means necessary that a great nation should always stand at the heroic level. But no nation has the root of greatness in it unless in time of need it can rise to the heroic level.

Theodore Roosevelt

It is to the United States that all free men must look for the light and the hope of the world. Unless we dedicate ourselves completely to this struggle, unless we combat hunger with food, fear with trust, suspicion with faith, fraud with justice — and threats with power — nations will surrender to the futility, the panic, on which wars are fed.

General Omar Bradley

It is now your turn to figure on the face of the earth, and in the annals of the world. You possess a country which in less than a century will probably contain fifty millions of inhabitants. You have, with a great expense of blood and treasure, rescued yourselves and your posterity from the domination of Europe. Perfect the good work you have begun, by forming such arrangements and institutions as bid fair for ensuring to the present and future generations the blessings for which you have successfully contended.

May the Almighty Ruler of the Universe, who has raised you to Independence, and given you a place among the nations of the earth, make the American Revolution an Era in the history of the world, remarkable for the progressive increase of human happiness!—

Doctor David Ramsay 1789

I am certain that, however great the hardships and the trials which loom ahead, our America will endure and the cause of human freedom will triumph.

Cordell Hull

I sought for the greatness and genius of
   America in her commodious harbors and
   her ample rivers, and it was not there.
I sought for the greatness and genius of
   America in her fertile fields and boundless
   forests, and it was not there.
I sought for the greatness and genius of
   America in her rich mines and her vast
   world commerce, and it was not there.
I sought for the greatness and genius of
   America in her public school system and her
   institutions of learning, and it was not there.
I sought for the greatness and genius of
   America in her democratic congress and her
   matchless constitution, and it was not there.
Not until I went into the churches of America
   and heard her pulpits flame with righteousness did I understand the secret of her genius
   and power.
America is great because America is good, and
   if America ever ceases to be good, America
   will cease to be great.

Alexis de Tocqueville

The Americans of all nations at any time upon the earth have probably the fullest poetical nature. The United States themselves are essentially the greatest poem. In the history of the earth hitherto the largest and most stirring appear tame and orderly to their ampler largeness and stir. Here at last is something in the doings of man that corresponds with the broad doings of the day and night. Here is not merely a nation but a teeming nation of nations. Here is action untied from strings necessarily blind to particulars and details magnificently moving in vast masses. Here is the hospitality which forever indicates heroes. Other states indicate themselves in their deputies — but the genius of the United States is not best or most in its executives or legislatures, nor in its ambassadors or authors or colleges or churches or parlors, nor even in its newspapers or inventors — but always most in the common people.

Walt Whitman

America is but another name for opportunity. Our whole history appears like a last effort of divine Prudence on behalf of the human race.

Ralph Waldo Emerson

The American Dream . . . has been a dream of being able to grow to the fullest development as man and woman.

James Truslow Adams

I would not hesitate to say that the United States is the finest society on a grand scale that the world has thus far produced.

Alfred North Whitehead

There has been a calculated risk in every stage of American development. The nation was built by men who took risks: pioneers who were not afraid of the wilderness, brave men who were not afraid of failure, scientists who were not afraid of truth, thinkers who were not afraid of progress, dreamers who were not afraid of action.

Brooks Atkinson

Vision and Reality

Honesty

I am not bound to win but I am bound to be true. I am not bound to succeed but I am bound to live up to what light I have. I must stand with anybody that stands right: stand with him while he is right and part with him when he goes wrong.

Abraham Lincoln

I hope I shall always possess firmness and virtue enough to maintain what I consider the most enviable of all titles, the character of an "Honest Man."

George Washington

Honesty of thought and speech and written word is a jewel, and they who curb prejudice and seek honorably to know and speak the truth are the only builders of a better life.

John Galsworthy

If a man does really think there is no distinction between virtue and vice, why, sir, when he leaves our houses let us count our spoons.

Samuel Johnson

I grew convinced that "truth," "sincerity" and "integrity" in dealings between man and man were of the utmost importance to the felicity of life; and I formed written resolutions, which still remain in my journal book, to practice them ever while I lived.

Benjamin Franklin

The larger view always and through all shams, all wickednesses, discovers the Truth that will, in the end, prevail, and all things surely, inevitably, resistlessly work together for good.

Frank Norris

It was a maxim he had often tried, That right was right, and there he would abide.

George Crabbe

Goodness

The Good is that which satisfies want, craving, which fulfills or makes complete the need which stirs to action.

John Dewey

Goodness is richer than greatness. It lifts us nearer to God. It is manifested according to our abilities, within our sphere. Every day I bless God that the great necessary work of the world is so faithfully carried on by humble men in narrow spaces and by faithful women in narrow circles, performing works of simple goodness.

Edwin Hubbell Chapin

The good life is not only good for one's conscience; it is good for art, good for knowledge, good for health, good for fellowship.

Lewis Mumford

There is never an instant's truce between virtue and vice. Goodness is the only investment that never fails.

Henry David Thoreau

109

It is vain to ask God to make us good. He never makes any one good. We may ask Him to help us to become good; that He always does.

Washington Gladden

The good is always beautiful, the beautiful is good.

John Greenleaf Whittier

Goodness conditions usefulness. A grimy hand may do a gracious deed, but a bad heart cannot. What a man says and what a man is must stand together,—must consist. His life can ruin his lips or fill them with power. It is what men see that gives value to what we say. Being comes before saying or doing. Well may we pray, "Search me, O God! Reveal me to myself. Cleanse me from secret faults, that those who are acquainted with me, who know my downsittings and my uprisings, may not see in me the evil way that gives the lie to my words."

Maltbie D. Babcock

I believe . . . that every human mind feels pleasure in doing good to another.

Thomas Jefferson

Everything good in a man thrives best when properly recognized.

Josiah Gilbert Holland

Did it ever strike you that goodness is not merely a beautiful thing, but by far the most beautiful thing in the whole world? So that nothing is to be compared for value with goodness; that riches, honor, power, pleasure, learning, the whole world and all in it, are not worth having in comparison with being good; and the utterly best thing for a man is to be good, even though he were never to be rewarded for it.

Charles Kingsley

What a sublime doctrine it is that goodness cherished now is Eternal Life already entered upon!

William Ellery Channing

Good will is the mightiest practical force in the universe.

Charles Fletcher Dole

Tell him to live by yes and no — yes to everything good, no to everything bad.

William James

We have a call to do good, as often as we have the power and occasion.

William Penn

The good must triumph.

Fannie Hurst

Scream as we may at the bad, the good prevails.

C. A. Bartol

Goodness is the only investment that never fails.

Henry David Thoreau

Virtue is bold, and goodness never fearful.

William Shakespeare

Beauty

We do not please God any more by eating bitter aloes than by eating honey. A cloudy, foggy, rainy day is not more heavenly than a day of sunshine. A funeral march is not so much like the music of the angels as the songs of birds on a May morning. There is no more religion in the gaunt, naked forest in winter than in the laughing blossoms of spring, and the rich ripe fruits of autumn. It was not the pleasant things in the world that came from the Devil, and the dreary things that came from God.

R. W. Dale

The works of the Magician of the Beautiful are not like ours and in the least fragment His artistry is no less present than in the stars. We may enter the infinite through the minute no less than through contemplation of the vast.

A.E. (George William Russell)

110

Never lose an opportunity of seeing anything that is beautiful; for beauty is God's handwriting — a wayside sacrament. Welcome it in every fair face, in every fair sky, in every fair flower, and thank God for it as a cup of blessing.

Ralph Waldo Emerson

The soul, by an instinct stronger than virtue, ever associates beauty with truth.

H. T. Tuckerman

Whatever is in any way beautiful has its source of beauty in itself, and is complete in itself; praise forms no part of it. So it is none the worse nor the better for being praised.

Marcus Aurelius

Who hath not proved how feebly words essay
To fix one spark of beauty's heavenly ray?
Who doth not feel until his failing sight
Faints into dimness with its own delight
His changing cheek, his sinking heart confess
The might, the majesty of loveliness?

George Gordon, Lord Byron

Beauty is a pledge of the possible conformity between the soul and nature, and consequently a ground of faith in the supremacy of the good.

George Santayana

Friendships, family ties, the companionship of little children, an autumn forest flung in prodigality against a deep blue sky, the intricate design and haunting fragrance of a flower, the counterpoint of a Bach fugue or the melodic line of a Beethoven sonata, the fluted note of bird song, the glowing glory of a sunset: the world is aflame with things of eternal moment.

E. Margaret Clarkson

The human heart yearns for the beautiful in all ranks of life.

Harriet Beecher Stowe

The fruition of beauty is no hit or miss — it is as inevitable as life — it is exact and plumb as gravitation.

Walt Whitman

Life has loveliness to sell —
    All beautiful and splendid things,
Blue waves whitened on a cliff,
    Soaring fire that sways and sings,
And children's faces looking up
    Holding wonder like a cup.

Life has loveliness to sell —
    Scent of pine trees in the rain,
Music like a curve of gold,
    Eyes that love you, arms that hold,
And for the spirit's safe delight,
    Holy thoughts that star the night.

Spend all that you have for loveliness,
    Buy it and never count the cost;
For one white singing hour of peace
    Count many a year of strife well lost,
And for a breath of ecstasy
    Give all that you have been, or could be.

Sara Teasdale — Barter

Beauty is so precious, the enjoyments it gives are so refined and pure, so congenial with our tenderest and noblest feelings, and so akin to worship, that it is painful to think of the multitude of men as living in the midst of it, and living almost as blind to it as if, instead of the fair earth and glorious sky, they were living in a dungeon.

William Ellery Channing

Beauty is the index of a larger fact than wisdom.

Oliver Wendell Holmes

Beauty hath so many charms one knows not how to speak against it; and when a graceful figure is the habitation of a virtuous soul — when the beauty of the face speaks out the modesty and humility of the mind, it raises our thoughts up to the great Creator; but after all, beauty, like truth, is never so glorious as when it goes the plainest.

Laurence Sterne

Truth and beauty are but different faces of the same All.

Ralph Waldo Emerson

Beauty, like truth and justice, lives within us; like virtue and like moral law, it is a companion of the soul.

George Bancroft

Though we travel the world over to find the beautiful, we must carry it with us, or we find it not.

Ralph Waldo Emerson

In every man's heart there is a secret nerve that answers to the vibrations of beauty.

Christopher Morley

A thing of beauty is a joy forever:
Its loveliness increases; it will never
Pass into nothingness; but still will keep
A bower quiet for us, and a sleep
Full of sweet dreams, and health, and
   quiet breathing.

John Keats

Beauty as we feel it is something indescribable; what it is or what it means can never be said.

George Santayana

To gild refined gold, to paint the lily,
To throw a perfume on the violet,
To smooth the ice, or add another hue
Unto the rainbow, or with taper-light
To seek the beauteous eye of heaven to garnish,
Is wasteful and ridiculous excess.

William Shakespeare

It seems to me that we can never give up longing and wishing while we are thoroughly alive. There are certain things we feel to be beautiful and good, and we must hunger after them.

George Eliot

There is in every creature a fountain of life, which, if not choked back by stones and other dead rubbish, will create a fresh atmosphere, and bring to life beauty.

Margaret Fuller

The perception of beauty is a moral test.

Henry David Thoreau

We are living in a world of beauty but how few of us open our eyes to see it!

Lorado Taft

To see a world in a grain of sand
And a heaven in a wildflower:
Hold infinity in the palm of your hand,
And eternity in an hour.

William Blake

The ancients called beauty the flowering of virtue.

Ralph Waldo Emerson

Beauty breaks through not only at a few highly organized points, it breaks through almost everywhere. Even the minutest things reveal it as well as do the sublimest things, like the stars. Whatever one sees through the microscope, a bit of mould, for example, is charged with beauty. Everything from a dewdrop to Mount Shasta is the bearer of beauty. And yet beauty has no function, no utility. Its value is intrinsic, not extrinsic. It is its own excuse for being. It greases no wheels, it bakes no puddings. It is a gift of sheer grace, a gratuitous largesse. It must imply behind things a Spirit that enjoys beauty for its own sake and that floods the world everywhere with it. Wherever it can break through, it does break through, and our joy in it shows that we are in some sense kindred to the giver and revealer of it.

Rufus M. Jones

Every trait of beauty may be referred to some virtue, as to innocence, candor, generosity, modesty, or heroism.

Abbé de St. Pierre

Into my heart's treasury
I slipped a coin
That time cannot take
Nor thief purloin, —
Oh, better than minting
Of a gold-crowned king
Is the safe-kept memory
Of a lovely thing.

Sara Teasdale — The Coin

112

The most natural beauty in the world is honesty and moral truth. — For all beauty is truth. — True features make the beauty of the face; true proportions, the beauty of architecture; true measures, the beauty of harmony and music.

Lord Shaftesbury

The beauty seen, is partly to him who sees it.

Christian N. Bovee

Socrates called beauty a short-lived tyranny; Plato, a privilege of nature; Theophrastus, a silent cheat; Theocritus, a delightful prejudice; Carneades, a solitary kingdom; Aristotle, that it was better than all the letters of recommendation in the world; Homer, that it was a glorious gift of nature, and Ovid, that it was a favor bestowed by the gods.
The fountain of beauty is the heart, and every generous thought illustrates the walls of your chamber.
If virtue accompanies beauty it is the heart's paradise; if vice be associated with it, it is the soul's purgatory. — It is the wise man's bonfire, and the fool's furnace.

Francis Quarles

Every day stop before something beautiful long enough to say, "Isn't that b-e-a-u-t-i-f-u-l!"

Alice Freeman Palmer

The best part of beauty is that which no picture can express.

Francis Bacon

Beauty is the mark God sets on virtue.

Ralph Waldo Emerson

Truth

Truth is within ourselves; it takes no rise
From outward things, whate'er you may
    believe.
There is an inmost center in us all,
Where truth abides in fullness: . . . perfect
Clear perception which is truth.

Robert Browning

Truth is justice's handmaid, freedom is its child, peace is its companion, safety walks in its steps, victory follows in its train; it is the brightest emanation from the Gospel; it is the attribute of God.

Sydney Smith

Truth and love are two of the most powerful things in the world; and when they both go together they cannot easily be withstood.

Ralph Cudworth

A man who seeks truth and loves it must be reckoned precious to any human society.

Frederick the Great

Such is the irresistible nature of truth that all it asks, and all it wants, is the liberty of appearing. The sun needs no inscription to distinguish him from darkness.

Thomas Paine

The greatest homage we can pay to truth is to use it.

Ralph Waldo Emerson

There is nothing so powerful as truth; and often nothing as strange.

Daniel Webster

The greatest friend of Truth is Time, her greatest enemy is Prejudice, and her constant companion is Humility.

Charles Caleb Colton

Truth and sincerity have a certain distinguishing native lustre about them which cannot be perfectly counterfeited; they are like fire and flame, that cannot be painted.

Benjamin Franklin

No pleasure is comparable to the standing upon the vantage-ground of truth.

Francis Bacon

Truth is one forever absolute, but opinion is truth filtered through the moods, the blood, the disposition of the spectator.

Wendell Phillips

Truth is wherever you decide to face it.

John Berry

There is nothing so strong or safe in an emergency of life as the simple truth.

Charles Dickens

Truth has no special time of its own. Its hour is now — always.

Albert Schweitzer

I say unto you: Cherish your doubts,
    For doubt is the handmaiden of truth.
Doubt is the servant of discovery;
    She is the key unto the door of knowledge.
Let no man fear for the truth, that doubt
        may consume her;
Only he that would shut out his doubts
        denieth the truth.

Robert Weston — Honest Doubt

Give me liberty to know, to utter, and to argue freely according to conscience above all liberties . . . Though all the winds of doctrine were let loose to play upon the earth, so Truth be in the field, we do injuriously, by licensing and prohibiting, to misdoubt her strength. Let her and Falsehood grapple; who ever knew Truth put to the worse, in a free and open encounter?

John Milton

Truth — is as old as God —
His Twin identity
And will endure as long as He
A Co-Eternity.

Emily Dickinson

The heart should have fed upon the truth, as insects on a leaf, till it be tinged with the color, and show its food in every minutest fibre.

Samuel Taylor Coleridge

Men in earnest have no time to waste in patching fig leaves for the naked truth.

James Russell Lowell

Truth is stranger than fiction—to some people.

Mark Twain

Truth never yet fell dead in the streets; it has such affinity with the soul of man, the seed however broadcast will catch somewhere and produce its hundredfold.

Theodore Parker

For us, with the rule of right and wrong given us by Christ, there is nothing for which we have no standard. And there is no greatness where there is not simplicity, goodness and truth.

Count Leo Tolstoy

The ideals which have always shone before me and filled me with the joy of living are goodness, beauty, and truth.

Albert Einstein

Newton:
Fools have said
That knowledge drives out wonder from the
    world;
They'll say it still, though all the dust's ablaze
With miracles at their feet; while Newton's
    laws
Foretell that knowledge one day shall be song,
And those whom Truth has taken to her heart
Find that it beats in music.

"I know not how my work may seem to
    others—"
So wrote our mightiest mind—"but to myself
I seem a child that wandering all day long
Upon the sea-shore gathers here a shell,
And there a pebble, colored by the wave,
While the great ocean of truth, from sky to
    sky
Stretches before him, boundless, unexplored."

Alfred Noyes — Watchers of the Sky

Those who know the truth are not equal to those who love it.

Confucius

Thought, intelligence, is the dignity of a man, and no man is rising but in proportion as he is learning to think clearly and forcibly, or directing the energy of his mind to the acquisition of truth.

William Ellery Channing

114

The exact contrary of what is generally believed is often the truth.

Jean de La Bruyère

Every great discovery I ever made, I gambled that the truth was there, and then I acted on it in faith that I could prove its existence.

Arthur Compton

Truth should be the last lesson of the child, and the last aspiration of manhood.

John Greenleaf Whittier

Nothing that was worthy of the past departs; no truth or goodness realized by man ever dies, or can die; but is all still here, and recognized or not, lives and works through endless changes.

Thomas Carlyle

All the great things are simple, and many can be expressed in a single word: freedom; justice; honor; duty; mercy; hope.

Winston S. Churchill

The passion for truth has underlying it a profound conviction that what is real is best; that when we get to the heart of things we shall find there what we most need.

George S. Merriam

Truth and sincerity have a certain distinguishing native lustre about them which cannot be perfectly counterfeited; they are like fire and flame, that cannot be painted.

Benjamin Franklin

Scientific truth is marvellous, but moral truth is divine; and whoever breathes its air and walks by its light has found the lost paradise.

Horace Mann

As scarce as truth is, the supply has always been in excess of the demand.

Josh Billings

The truth always matches, piece by piece, with other parts of the truth.

Woodrow Wilson

All truth is safe and nothing else is safe, but he who keeps back truth, or withholds it from men, from motives of expediency, is either a coward or a criminal.

Max Fuller

The people have a right to the truth as they have a right to life, liberty and the pursuit of happiness.

Frank Norris

Every scientific truth goes through three stages. First, people say it conflicts with the Bible. Next, they say it has been discovered before. Lastly, they say they have always believed it.

Louis Agassiz

Truth is tough. It will not break like a bubble at a touch; nay, you will kick it about all day, like a football, and it will be round and full at evening.

Oliver Wendell Holmes

Truth may be stretched, but cannot be broken, and always gets above falsehood, as oil does above water.

Miguel de Cervantes

I would rather plant a single acorn that will make an oak of a century and a forest of a thousand years than sow a thousand morning glories that give joy for a day and are gone tomorrow. For the same reason, I would rather plant one living truth in the heart of a child that will multiply through the ages than scatter a thousand brilliant conceits before a great audience that will flash like sparks for an instant and like sparks disappear forever.

Edward Leigh Pell

Assuming that the true opinion abides in the mind, but abides as a prejudice — a belief independent of, and proof against, argument — this is not the way in which truth ought to be held by a rational being. This is not knowing the truth. Truth thus held, is but one superstition the more.

John Stuart Mill

115

World and Nature

Earth

Nothing is more beautiful than the loveliness
of the woods before sunrise.

George Washington Carver

I never loved your plains,
   Your gentle valleys,
Your drowsy country lanes
   And pleached alleys.

I want my hills — the trail
   That scorns the hollow —
Up, up the ragged shale
   Where few will follow.

Up, over wooded crest,
   And mossy boulder,
With strong thigh, heaving chest,
   And swinging shoulder.

So let me hold my way,
   By nothing halted,
Until, at close of day,
   I stand exalted.

High on my hills of dream —
   Dear hills that know me!
And then how fair will seem
   The land below me!

How pure, at vesper-time
   The far bells chiming!
God, give me hills to climb
   And strength for climbing!

Arthur Guiterman — Hills

I must go down to the seas again, to the lonely
   sea and the sky,
And all I ask is a tall ship and a star to steer
   her by,
And the wheel's kick and the wind's song and
   the white sail's shaking,
And a gray mist on the sea's face, and a gray
   dawn breaking.

I must go down to the seas again, for the call
   of the running tide
Is a wild call and a clear call that may not be
   denied;
And all I ask is a windy day with the white
   clouds flying,
And the flung spray and the blown spume,
   and the sea gulls crying.

I must go down to the seas again, to the
   vagrant gypsy life,
To the gull's way and the whale's way where
   the wind's like a whetted knife;
And all I ask is a merry yarn from a laughing
   fellow-rover,
And quiet sleep and a sweet dream when the
   long trick's over.

John Masefield — Sea Fever

The man who lives with Nature, understands
her moods and adapts himself to her ways, is
by this very conformity molded to a certain
largeness and nobility of soul, saved from
certain petty sins, and finds courage, sincerity,
and perseverance rising up within him to
match the elemental forces of the mountains
or the sea, with which his life is interwoven.

Albert W. Palmer

I love my prairies, they are mine
From zenith to horizon line,
Clipping a world of sky and sod
Like the bended arm and wrist of God.

I love their grasses. The skies
Are larger, and my restless eyes
Fasten on more of earth and air
Than seashore furnishes anywhere.

I love the hazel thickets; and the breeze,
The never resting prairie winds. The trees
That stand like spear points high
Against the dark blue sky
Are wonderful to me. I love the gold
Of newly shaven stubble, rolled
A royal carpet toward the sun, fit to be
The pathway of a deity.

I love the life of pasture lands; the song of birds
Are not more thrilling to me than the herd's
Mad bellowing or the shadow stride
Of mounted herdsmen at my side.

I love my prairies, they are mine
From high sun to horizon line.
The mountains and the cold gray sea
Are not for me, are not for me.

Hamlin Garland — My Prairies

The man who has seen the rising moon break
out of the clouds at midnight has been present
like an archangel at the creation of light and
of the world.

Ralph Waldo Emerson

O God, we thank thee for the world in which
thou hast placed us, for the universe whose
vastness is revealed in the blue depths of the
sky, whose immensities are lit by shining stars
beyond the strength of mind to follow. We
thank thee for every sacrament of beauty; for
the sweetness of flowers, the solemnity of the
stars; the sound of streams and swelling seas;
for far-reaching lands and mighty mountains
which rest and satisfy the soul, the purity of
dawn which calls to holy dedication, the peace
of evening which speaks of everlasting rest.

William E. Orchard — Prayer

"Let trees be made, for earth is bare,"
    Spake the voice of the Lord in thunder:
The roots ran deep and trees were there,
    And earth was full of wonder.

For the white birch leaned, the oak held
        straight,
    The pines marched down the mountain,
The orchards bowed with their blossomed
        weight
    And the elm rose up like a fountain.

The palm stood as proud as Aaron's rod,
    The willow billowed slowly;
So came the trees at the call of God,
    And all the trees are holy.

Arthur Guiterman — The Coming of the Trees

Today I have grown taller from walking with
    the trees,
The seven-sister poplars, who go softly in a
    line;
And I think my heart is whiter from its parley
    with a star
That trembled out at nightfall and hung above
    the pine.
The call note of a redbird from the cedars in
    the dusk
Woke his happy note within me to an answer
    free and fine,
And a sudden angel beckoned from a column
    of blue smoke—
Lord, who am I that they should stoop: these
    holy folk of Thine?

Karle Wilson Baker — Good Company

Climb the mountains and get their good
tidings. Nature's peace will flow into you as
sunshine flows into trees. The winds will flow
their own freshness into you and the storms
their energy, while cares will drop off like
autumn leaves.

John Muir

A lake is the landscape's most beautiful and
expressive feature. It is earth's eye, looking
into which the beholder measures the depth of
his own nature.

Henry David Thoreau

Oh! I have slipped the surly bonds of earth
    And danced the skies on laughter-silvered
        wings;
Sunward I've climbed, and joined the tumbling
    mirth
    Of sun-split clouds — and done a hundred
        things
You have not dreamed of — wheeled and
    soared and swung
    High in the sunlit silence. Hov'ring there,
I've chased the shouting wind along, and flung
    My eager craft through footless halls of air.

Up, up the long, delirious, burning blue
    I've topped the wind-swept heights with
        easy grace
Where never lark, or even eagle flew —
And, while with silent lifting mind I've trod
    The high untrespassed sanctity of space,
Put out my hand and touched the face of God.

John Gillespie Magee, Jr. — High Flight

There they stand, the innumerable stars,
shining in order like a living hymn, written
in light.

Nathaniel Parker Willis

God wrote His loveliest poem on the day
He made the first tall silver poplar tree,
And set it high upon a pale-gold hill
For all the new enchanted earth to see.

And then God took the music of the winds,
And set each leaf aflutter and athrill —
Today I read His poem word by word
Among the silver poplars on the hill.

Grace Noll Crowell — Silver Poplars

Love all God's creation, the whole and every
grain of sand in it. Love every leaf, every
ray of God's light. Love the animals, love the
plants, love everything. If you love everything,
you will perceive the divine mystery in things.
Once you perceive it, you will begin to comprehend it better every day. And you will
come at last to love the whole world with an
all-embracing love.

Fyodor Dostoyevsky

Seasons

First, April, she with mellow showers
Opens the way for early flowers;
Then after her comes smiling May,
In a more sweet and rich array;
Next enters June, and brings us more
Gems than those two that went before;
Then, lastly, July comes and she
More wealth brings in than all those three.

Robert Herrick

As spring comes we become more aware of
the magnanimity of Nature, a sort of elemental
big-heartedness and inclusive impartiality that
is a reflection of the character of God. Spring
sunshine will not fall on beautiful, graceful
birch trees alone, but upon the less lovable
scrub pine, alders, and willows, too. April
showers will not pick and choose, playing
favorites with the daffodils and crocuses, and
shunning objectionable dandelions and lowly
violets, blessing the arbutus and avoiding the
bloodroot and wild strawberry. The great sun
will warm the acres of saint and sinner alike.
Warm rains will beat with equal benefit upon
the gardens of the grateful and the grumbling.

Harold E. Kohn

Oh, give us pleasure in the flowers today;
And give us not to think so far away
As the uncertain harvest; keep us here
All simply in the springing of the year.

Oh, give us pleasure in the orchard white,
Like nothing else by day, like ghosts by night;
And make us happy in the happy bees,
That swarm dilating round the perfect trees.

And make us happy in the darting bird
That suddenly above the bees is heard,
The meteor that thrusts in with needle bill,
And off a blossom in mid air stands still.

For this is love and nothing else is love,
The which it is reserved for God above
To sanctify to what far ends He will,
But which it only needs that we fulfill.

Robert Frost — A Prayer In Spring

The wind is sewing with needles of rain;
With shining needles of rain
It stitches into the thin
Cloth of earth — in,
In, in, in,

Oh, the wind has often sewed with me! —
One, two, three.

Spring must have fine things
To wear, like other springs.
Of silken green the grass must be
Embroidered. One and two and three.

Then every crocus must be made
So subtly as to seem afraid
Of lifting color from the ground;
And after crocuses, the round
Heads of tulips and all the fair
Intricate garb that Spring will wear.
The wind must sew with needles of rain,
With shining needles of rain
Stitching into the thin
Cloth of earth — in,
In, in, in —

For all the springs of futurity.
One, two, three.

Hazel Hall — Two Sewing

Apple blossoms look like snow,
They're different though,
Snow falls softly, but it brings
Noisy things:
Sleighs and bells, forts and fights,
Cosy nights.

But apple blossoms when they go,
White and slow,
Quiet all the orchard space,
Till the place
Hushed with falling sweetness seems
Filled with dreams.

John Farrar — A Comparison

Our Lord has written the promise of the
Resurrection, not in books alone, but in every
leaf in springtime.

Martin Luther

It is a most exciting thing
To take a garden in the Spring:

To wonder what its borders hold;
What secrets lurk beneath the mold?

What kinds of roses you have got;
Whether the lilac blooms, or not.

Whether the peach tree, on the wall,
Has ever had a peach at all. . . .

It is a most exciting thing
To take a garden in the Spring;

And live in such delicious doubt,
Until the final flower is out.

Reginald Arkell

Four ducks on a pond,
A grass-bank beyond,
A blue sky of spring,
White clouds on the wing —
What a little thing
To remember for years!
To remember with tears!

William Allingham

Loveliest of trees, the cherry now
Is hung with bloom along the bough,
And stands about the woodland ride
Wearing white for Eastertide.

Now, of my threescore years and ten,
Twenty will not come again,
And take from seventy springs a score,
It only leaves me fifty more.

And since to look at things in bloom
Fifty springs are little room,
About the woodlands I will go
To see the cherry hung with snow.

Alfred Edward Housman — Loveliest of Trees

The kiss of the sun for pardon,
    The song of the birds for mirth—
One is nearer God's heart in a garden
    Than anywhere else on earth.

Dorothy Frances Gurney — The Garden

120

The sun was warm but the wind was chill.
You know how it is with an April day
When the sun is out and the wind is still,
You're one month on in the middle of May.
But if you so much as dare to speak,
A cloud comes over the sunlit arch,
A wind comes off a frozen peak,
And you're two months back in the middle
    of March.

                          Robert Frost

My mind lets go a thousand things
Like dates of wars and deaths of kings
And yet recalls the very hour —
'Twas noon by yonder village tower,
And on the last blue noon in May —
The wind came briskly up this way,
Crisping the brook beside the road;
Then, pausing here, set down its load
Of pine-scents, and shook listlessly
Two petals from that wild rose-tree.

           Thomas Bailey Aldrich — Memory

There's nothing like our country lanes with
    all their shady trees,
The leaves and branches stirring high above
    us in the breeze,
The sweet, rich smell of growing things
    enhance the beauty there,
As flowers bright and beautiful leave fragrance
    in the air.
The branches of the stalwart trees sway gently
    overhead,
The green grass makes a carpet soft along
    the roads we tread;
A soothing breeze stirs daily here refreshing
    passersby
Who linger longingly beneath the leaf-flecked,
    country sky.
The birds sing merrily on high within their
    cosy nests,
The bees and insects softly hum while on their
    daily quests,
Where many a city family go to ease their
    aches and pains
By picnicking on Sundays in our shady
    country lanes.

             Laura Munro — Country Lanes

In all the world there is no lovelier thing
    Than this wild crab upon a sunny hill!
Its pale-pink glory is so startling,
    The windless day is suddenly so still—
I dare not breathe lest I should shatter quite
    This radiant mass of color and of light.

I dare not touch one little clustered spray
    Lest some wild bee from out a blossom's
        heart
Should take his heavy-bodied, bungling way
    And the delicate shaken petals fall apart.
O wind be kind! O bees in hurrying past,
    Go softly that this loveliness may last.

        Grace Noll Crowell — Crab Apple Blossoms

I meant to do my work today—
But a brown bird sang in the apple tree,
And a butterfly flitted across the field,
And all the leaves were calling me.

And the wind went sighing over the land
Tossing the grasses to and fro,
And a rainbow held out its shining hand—
So what could I do but laugh and go?

             Richard LeGallienne —
          I Meant To Do My Work Today

I walked among the tender grasses
    Sparkling in the dew,
I heard the whispering of the trees,
The morning call of birds, the murmur
    of the bees,
I watched the buds so quietly unfold
    to kiss the sun;
I felt the calm and gentle breeze when
    day is done,
And then I know
That God would walk and talk within
    my garden too.

            Gertrude Thompson Miller

If spring came but once in a century instead
of once a year, or burst forth with the sound of
an earthquake and not in silence, what wonder
and expectation there would be in all hearts
to behold the miraculous change.

           Henry Wadsworth Longfellow

Winter is cold-hearted;
   Spring is yea and nay;
Autumn is a weathercock,
   Blown every way:
Summer days for me,
When every leaf is on its tree,

When Robin's not a beggar,
   And Jenny Wren's a bride,
And larks hang, singing, singing, singing,
   Over the wheat-fields wide,
   And anchored lilies ride,
And the pendulum spider
   Swings from side to side,

And blue-black beetles transact business,
   And gnats fly in a host,
And furry caterpillars hasten
   That no time be lost,
And moths grow fat and thrive,
And ladybirds arrive.

Before green apples blush,
   Before green nuts embrown,
Why, one day in the country
   Is worth a month in town —
   Is worth a day and a year
Of the dusty, musty, lag-last fashion
   That days drone elsewhere.

          Christina Rossetti — Summer Days

The summer is over,
The trees are bare,
There is mist on the garden
And frost in the air.
The meadows are empty
And gathered the sheaves —
But isn't it lovely
Kicking up leaves!

John from the garden
Has taken the chairs;
It's dark in the evening
And cold on the stairs.
Winter is coming
And everyone grieves —
But isn't it lovely
Kicking up leaves!

          Rose Fyleman — October

There is something in the autumn that
   is native to my blood,
Touch of manner, hint of mood;
And my heart is like a rhyme,
With the yellow and the purple and the
   crimson keeping time.

The scarlet of the maples can shake me
   like a cry
Of bugles going by.
And my lonely spirit thrills
To see the frosty asters like smoke upon
   the hills.

There is something in October sets the
   gypsy blood astir;
We must rise and follow her,
When from every hill aflame,
She calls and calls each vagabond by name.

          Bliss Carman — A Vagabond Song

Oh, the splendor of the universe! For many
of us autumntime is the most glorious of all
the year.
God has dipped His paint brush in His palette
of colors and splashed the hills and woods and
fields with robes of saffron and crimson and
gold and yellow and brown and scarlet.
The maples and chestnuts and oaks vie with
one another in autumnal beauty. The sumac
dazzles the eye with brilliant scarlet. The
sunsets are too gorgeous for human description.
In this amazing garden of beauty our lips
involuntarily sing forth the praises of the
psalmist: "Bless Jehovah, O my soul; and all
this is within me, bless his holy name."

          Charles Kingsley

The morns are meeker than they were,
The nuts are getting brown;
The berry's cheek is plumper,
The rose is out of town.

The maple wears a gayer scarf,
The field a scarlet gown.
Lest I should be old-fashioned,
I'll put a trinket on.

          Emily Dickinson

I heard the wild geese flying
In the dead of the night,
With beats of wings and cry
I heard the wild geese flying.

And dreams in my heart sighing
Followed their northward flight.
I heard the wild geese flying
In the dead of the night.

Elinor Chipp — Wild Geese

O World, I cannot hold thee close enough!
  Thy winds, thy wide grey skies!
  Thy mists that roll and rise!
Thy woods, this autumn day, that ache and sag
And all but cry with colour! That gaunt crag
To crush! To lift the lean of that black bluff!
World, World, I cannot get thee close enough!
Long have I known a glory in it all,
  But never knew I this;
  Here such a passion is
As stretcheth me apart. Lord, I do fear
Thou'st made the world too beautiful this year,
My soul is all but out of me—let fall
No burning leaf; prithee, let no bird call.

Edna St. Vincent Millay — God's World

I like the fall,
The mist and all.
I like the night owl's
Lonely call —
And wailing sound
Of wind around.

I like the gray
November day,
And bare, dead boughs
That coldly sway
Against my pane.
I like the rain.

I like to sit
And laugh at it —
And tend
My cozy fire a bit.
I like the fall —
The mist and all. —

Dixie Willson

Generations of mankind have discovered that gardening is work for philosophers, and that the daily planting and weeding will make a philosopher out of him who never was before. I mean philosopher in the true sense, not simply a placid soul who can accept life without protest, but a mind awakened, fertile, discriminating.

John Erskine

Stars over snow,
  And in the west a planet
Swinging below a star —
  Look for a lovely thing and you will find it,
It is not far —
  It never will be far.

Sara Teasdale — Night

Piped a tiny voice hard by,
Gay and polite, a cheerful cry,
"Chic-chicadee-dee!" Saucy note
Out of a sound heart and a merry throat,
As if it said, "Good day, good sir.
Fine afternoon, old passenger!
Happy to meet you in these places
When January brings new faces!"

Ralph Waldo Emerson — The Chickadee

In the winter time we go
Walking in the fields of snow;

Where there is no grass at all;
Where the top of every wall,

Every fence and every tree,
Is as white as white can be.

Pointing out the way we came,
Everyone of them the same —

All across the fields there be
Prints in silver filigree;

And our mothers always know,
By our footprints in the snow,

Where the children go.

James Stephens — White Fields

123

I heard a bird sing
In the dark of December
A magical thing
And sweet to remember.

"We are nearer to Spring
Than we were in September,"
I heard a bird sing
In the dark of December.

Oliver Herford — I Heard a Bird Sing

Whose woods these are I think I know.
His house is in the village, though;
He will not see me stopping here
To watch his woods fill up with snow.

My little horse must think it queer
To stop without a farmhouse near
Between the woods and frozen lake
The darkest evening of the year.

He gives his harness bells a shake
To ask if there is some mistake.
The only other sound's the sweep
Of easy wind and downy flake.

The woods are lovely, dark and deep,
But I have promises to keep,
And miles to go before I sleep,
And miles to go before I sleep.

Robert Frost —
Stopping By a Woods On a Snowy Evening

Creatures

Heaven is in my hand, and I
Touch a heart-beat of the sky,
Hearing a blackbird's cry.

Strange, beautiful, unquiet thing,
Lone flute of God, how can you sing
Winter to spring?

You have outdistanced every voice and word,
And given my spirit wings until it stirred
Like you — a bird!

Joseph Auslander — A Blackbird Suddenly

All things bright and beautiful,
All creatures great and small,
All things wise and wonderful,
The Lord God made them all.

Cecil Frances Alexander

I believe a leaf of grass is no less than the
journey-work of the stars,
And the pismire is equally perfect, and a grain
of sand, and the egg of the wren,
And the tree-toad is a chef-d'oeuvre for the
highest,
And the running blackberry would adorn the
parlors of heaven,
And the narrowest hinge in my hand puts to
scorn all machinery,
And the cow crunching with depress'd head
surpasses any statue,
And a mouse is miracle enough to stagger
sextillions of infidels.

Walt Whitman

Dear Father, hear and bless
Thy beasts and singing birds,
And guard with tenderness
Small things that have no words.

Anonymous

Across the narrow beach we flit,
One little sandpiper and I,
And fast I gather, bit by bit,
The scattered driftwood bleached and dry.
The wild waves reach their hands for it,
The wild wind raves, the tide runs high,
As up and down the beach we flit, —
One little sandpiper and I.

Above our heads the sullen clouds
Scud black and swift across the sky;
Like silent ghosts in misty shrouds.
Comrade, where wilt thou be tonight,
When the loosed storm breaks furiously?
My driftwood fire will burn so bright!
To what warm shelter canst thou fly?
I do not fear for thee, though wroth
The tempest rushes through the sky:
For are we not God's children both,
Thou, little sandpiper, and I?

Celia Thaxter — The Sandpiper

He shakes his mane upon the breeze
And gallops through the grasses;
He does not like the encircling trees —
He likes to see what passes.

He trots along much at his ease
And snatches as he passes,
Then shakes his mane upon the breeze
And gallops through the grasses.

He does not like the buzz of bees
That fades and then repasses;
He loves the open swish of trees
And the wide hum of grasses;
He shakes his mane upon the breeze.

Marion Canby — Connecticut Rondel

Recollect that the Almighty, who gave the
dog to be companion of our pleasures and our
toils, hath invested him with a nature noble
and incapable of deceit.

Sir Walter Scott

Dear God, give me time.
Men are always so driven!
Make them understand that I can never hurry.
Give me time to eat,
Give me time to plod,
Give me time to sleep,
Give me time to think.

*Carmen Bernos de Gasztold — Prayer of The Ox
translated by Rumer Godden*

Why do some people talk with such assurance
about what they are going to do with the
world, as though they owned it when really
our share is such a small one? Birds and
butterflies, bees and flying insects fill the air;
tiny animals climb and burrow and scuttle.
And underneath the ground a whole world of
life goes on that we never see — moles with
grey velvet coats push along, their strong front
feet swinging through the earth with a swim-
mer's breast stroke. Behind them come the
groundmice on sly, flying feet, and tucked
under a stone is a grey worm, rolled up for
the winter. There is myriad life under, on, and
above the earth.

Beatrix Potter

All along the backwater,
   Through the rushes tall,
Ducks are a-dabbling,
   Up tails all!

Ducks' tails, drakes' tails,
   Yellow feet a-quiver,
Yellow bills all out of sight
   Busy in the river!

Slushy green undergrowth
   Where the roaches swim —
Here we keep our larder,
   Cool and full and dim.

Everyone for what he likes!
   We like to be
Heads down, tails up,
   Dabbling free!

High in the blue above
   Swifts whirl and call —
We are down a-dabbling,
   Up tails all!

Kenneth Grahame — Duck's Ditty

Once as I travelled through a quiet evening,
I saw a pool, jet-black and mirror still.
Beyond, the slender paperbacks stood crowding;
Each on its own white image looked its fill,
And nothing moved but thirty egrets wading —
Thirty egrets in a quiet evening.

Once in a lifetime, lovely past believing,
Your lucky eyes may light on such a pool.
As though for many years I had been waiting,
I watched in silence, till my heart was full
Of clear dark water, and white trees unmoving,
And, whiter yet, those egrets wading.

Judith Wright

A robin redbreast in a cage
Puts all Heaven in a rage.

William Blake

Animals are such agreeable friends; they ask
no questions, they pass no criticisms.

George Eliot

125

He's nothing much but fur
And two round eyes of blue,
He has a giant purr
And a midget mew.

He darts and pats the air,
He starts and cocks his ear,
When there is nothing there
For him to see and hear.

He runs around in rings,
But why we cannot tell;
With sideways leaps he springs
At things invisible —

Then half-way through a leap
His startled eyeballs close,
And he drops off to sleep
With one paw on his nose.

Eleanor Farjeon — A Kitten

When I would be content and increase confidence in the power and wisdom of Almighty God, I will walk the meadows by some stream, and there contemplate the lilies that take no care, and those very many other little living creatures that are not only created, but fed, (man knows not how) by the God of Nature, and therefore trust in Him.

Izaak Walton

I heard a bird at break of day
    Sing from the autumn trees
A song so mystical and calm,
    So full of certainties,
No man, I think, could listen long
    Except upon his knees.
Yet this was but a simple bird,
    Alone, among the trees.

William Alexander Percy — Overtones

Wonders

The miracles of nature do not seem miracles because they are so common. If no one had ever seen a flower, even a dandelion would be the most startling event in the world.

Anonymous

Nature is painting for us, day after day, pictures of infinite beauty if only we have the eyes to see them.

John Ruskin

I shall keep some cool green memory in my
        heart
    To draw upon should days be bleak and
        cold.
I shall hold it like a cherished thing apart
    To turn to now or when I shall be old.
Perhaps a sweeping meadow, brightly green,
    Where grasses bend and the winds of heaven
        blow
Straight from the hand of God, as cool and
    clean
    As anything the heart of man can know.

Or it may be this green remembered tree
    That I shall turn to if the nights be long,
High on a hill, its cool boughs lifting free,
    And from its tip, a wild bird's joyous song.
A weary city dweller to survive
    Must keep some cool green memory alive.

Grace Noll Crowell —
Keep Some Green Memory Alive

But beauty seen is never lost,
God's colors all are fast;
The glory of this sunset heaven
Into my soul has passed.

John Greenleaf Whittier

Join the whole creation of animate things in a deep, heartfelt joy that you are alive, that you see the sun, that you are in this glorious earth which nature has made so beautiful, and which is yours to conquer and enjoy.

Sir William Osler

The student and lover of nature has only to stay at home and see the procession pass. The great globe swings around to him like a revolving showcase; the change of the seasons is like the passage of strange and new countries; the zones of the earth, with all their beauties and marvels, pass one's door and linger in the passing.

John Burroughs

Doth not all nature around me praise God?
If I were silent, I should be an exception to
the universe. Doth not the thunder praise Him
as it rolls like drums in the march of the
God of armies? Do not the mountains praise
Him when the woods upon their summits
wave in adoration? Does not the lightning write
His name in letters of fire? Hath not the whole
earth a voice? And shall I, can I, silent be?

Charles Haddon Spurgeon

To look at any thing,
If you would know that thing,
You must look at it long:
To look at this green and say
'I have seen spring in these
Woods,' will not do — you must
Be the thing you see:
You must be the dark snakes of
Stems and ferny plumes of leaves,
You must enter in
To the small silences between
The leaves,
You must take your time
And touch the very peace
They issue from.

John Moffitt — To Look at Any Thing

O God, we thank Thee for this universe, our
  great home; for its vastness and its riches,
  and for the manifoldness of the life which
  teems upon it and of which we are part.
We praise Thee for the arching sky and the
  blessed winds, for the driving clouds and
  the constellations on high.
We praise Thee for the salt sea and the
  running water, for the everlasting hills, for
  the trees, and for the grass under our feet.
We thank Thee for our senses by which we
  can see the splendor of the morning, and
  hear the jubilant songs of love, and smell
  the breath of the springtime.
Grant us, we pray Thee, a heart wide open to
  all this joy and beauty, and save our souls
  from being so steeped in care or so darkened
  by passion that we pass heedless and un-
  seeing when even the thorn-bush by the
  wayside is aflame with the glory of God.

Walter Rauschenbusch — Prayer

We are but the ephemera of the moment,
the brief custodians of redwoods, which were
ancient when Christ was born, and of the
birds of the air and animals of the forest which
have been evolving for countless millenniums.
We do not own the land we abuse, or the
lakes and streams we pollute or the raccoons
and the otters which we persecute. Those who
play God in destroying any form of life are
tampering with a master plan too intricate for
any of us to understand.

Sterling North

Nature is man's religious book, with lessons
for every day.

Theodore Parker

Swift things are beautiful:
Swallows and deer,
And lightning that falls
Bright-veined and clear,
Rivers and meteors,
Wind in the wheat,
The strong-withered horse,
The runners' sure feet.

And slow things are beautiful:
The closing of day,
The pause of the wave
That curves downward to spray
The ember that crumbles,
The opening flower,
And the ox that moves on
In the quiet of power.

Elizabeth Coatsworth — Swift Things Are Beautiful

Some skeptics say, "Oh, the miracles, I can't
accept miracles." One may drop a brown seed
in the black soil and up comes a green shoot.
You let it grow and by and by you pull up
its roots and you find it red. You cut the red
root and find it has a white heart. Can any one
tell how this comes about — how brown cast
into black results in green and then in red
and white? Yet you eat your radish without
troubling your mind over miracles. Men are not
distressed by miracles in the dining room;
they reserve them all for religion!

Williams Jennings Bryan

If I were to name the three most precious resources of life, I should say books, friends, and nature; and the greatest of these, at least the most constant and always at hand, is nature. Nature we have always with us, an inexhaustible storehouse of that which moves the heart, appeals to the mind, and fires the imagination — health to the body, a stimulus to the intellect, and joy to the soul. To the scientist, nature is a storehouse of facts, laws, processes; to the artist she is a storehouse of pictures; to the poet she is a storehouse of images, fancies, a source of inspiration; to the moralist she is a storehouse of precepts and parables; to all she may be a source of knowledge and joy.

John Burroughs

Flower in the crannied wall,
I pluck you out of the crannies,
I hold you, root and all, in my hand,
Little flower — but *if* I could understand
What you are, root and all, and all in all,
I should know what God and man is.

Alfred, Lord Tennyson

The longer I live the more my mind dwells upon the beauty and the wonder of the world. I hardly know which feeling leads, wonderment or admiration.

John Burroughs

God is attracting our regard in and through all things. Every flower is a hint of His beauty; every grain of wheat is a token of His beneficence; every atom of dust is a revelation of His power.

W. H. Furness

A thing cannot be completely wonderful so long as it remains sensible. So long as we regard a tree as an obvious thing, naturally and reasonably created for a giraffe to eat, we cannot properly wonder at it. It is when we consider it as a prodigious wave of the living soil sprawling up to the skies for no reason in particular that we take off our hats, to the astonishment of the park-keeper.

Gilbert Keith Chesterton

O God, we thank Thee for everything!
For the sea and its waves, blue, green, and
     gray and always wonderful;
For the beach and the breakers and the spray
     and the white foam on the rocks;
For the blue arch of heaven; for the clouds in
     the sky, white and gray and purple;
For the green of the grass; for the forests in
     their spring beauty; for the wheat and corn
     and rye and barley;
For the brown earth turned up by the plow;
     for the sun by day and the dews by night.
We thank Thee for all Thou hast made and
     that Thou hast called it good.
For all the glory and beauty and wonder of
     the world;
For the glory of springtime, the tints of the
     flowers and their fragrance;
For the glory of summer flowers, the roses
     and cardinals and clethra;
For the glory of the autumn, the scarlet and
     crimson and gold of the forest;
For the glory of winter, the pure snow on the
     shrubs and trees.
We thank Thee that Thou hast placed us in
     the world to subdue all things to Thy glory,
And to use all things for the good of Thy
     children.
We thank Thee! We enter into Thy work and
     go about Thy business.

Edward Everett Hale — The One Thousandth Psalm

The mountains are God's majestic thoughts.
The stars are God's brilliant thoughts.
The flowers are God's beautiful thoughts.

Robert Stuart MacArthur

I took a day to search for God,
And found Him not. But as I trod
     By rocky ledge, through woods untamed,
     Just where one scarlet lily flamed,
I saw His footprint in the sod.

Then suddenly, all unaware,
Far off in the deep shadows, where
     A solitary hermit thrush
     Sung through the holy twilight hush—
I heard His voice upon the air.

Bliss Carman

Everywhere I find the signature, the autograph of God, and he will never deny his own handwriting. God hath set his tabernacle in the dewdrop as surely as in the sun. No man can any more create the smallest flower than he could create the greatest world.

Joseph Parker

Be not afraid because the sun goes down;
It brings the sunset and the plover's cry.
Before the colors of the evening drown,
The stars will make new colors in the sky.
Night is no enemy. She passes by,
And shows us silence for our own heart's good;
For while we sleep, the roses multiply,
The little tree grows taller in the wood.
Fear not the night; the morning follows soon.
Each has his task to make the earth more fair.
It is by these, by midnight and by noon,
That she grows riper and her orchards bear.
Her fields would wither in a sun too bright;
They need the darkness too. Fear not the night.

Robert Nathan — Be Not Afraid

Were it not for the exertions of some few inquiring minds who have looked into these things, and ascertained the very beautiful laws and conditions by which we do live and stand upon the earth, we should hardly be aware that there was anything wonderful about it.

Michael Faraday

Look at Nature. She never wearies of saying over her floral pater-noster. In the crevices of Cyclopian walls, on the mounds that bury huge cities, in the dust where men lie, dust also — still that same sweet prayer and benediction. The amen of Nature is always a flower.

Oliver Wendell Holmes

Earth's crammed with heaven, and every common bush afire with God.

Elizabeth Barrett Browning

The sun, with all its planets moving around it, can ripen the smallest bunch of grapes as if it had nothing else to do. Why then should I doubt His power?

Galileo

O most high, almighty, good Lord God, to thee
    belong praise, glory, honor, and all blessing!
Praised be my Lord God with all his creatures;
    and specially our brother the sun, who
    brings us the day, and who brings us the
    light; fair is he, and shining with a very great
    splendor: O Lord, to us he signifies thee!
Praised be my Lord for our sister the moon,
    and for the stars, the which he has set clear
    and lovely in heaven.
Praised be my Lord for our brother the wind,
    and for air and cloud, calms and all weather,
    by the which thou upholdest in life all
    creatures.
Praised be my Lord for our sister water, who
    is very serviceable unto us, and humble, and
    precious, and clean.
Praised be my Lord for our brother fire,
    through whom thou givest us light in the
    darkness; and he is bright, and pleasant, and
    very mighty, and strong.
Praised be my Lord for our mother the earth,
    the which doth sustain us and keep us, and
    bringeth forth divers fruits, and flowers of
    many colors, and grass.

St. Francis of Assisi — The Canticle of The Sun

Thank you very much indeed,
River, for your waving reed;
Hollyhocks, for budding knobs;
Foxgloves, for your velvet fobs;
Pansies, for your silky cheeks;
Chaffinches, for singing beaks;
Spring, for wood anemones
Near the mossy toes of trees;
Summer, for the fruited pear,
Yellowing crab, and cherry fare;
Autumn, for the bearded load,
Hazelnuts along the road;
Winter, for the fairy-tale,
Spitting log and bouncing hail.

But, blest Father, high above,
All these joys are from Thy love;
And Your children everywhere,
Born in palace, lane, or square,
Cry with voices all agreed,
"Thank you very much indeed."

Norman Gale — Thanks

129

Inspiration and Creativity

Literature

All that mankind has done, thought, gained or been: it is lying as in magic preservation in the pages of books.

Thomas Carlyle

God be thanked for books. They are the voices of the distant and the dead, and make us heirs of the spiritual life of past ages.

William Ellery Channing

But the images of men's wits and knowledges remain in books, exempted from the wrong of time, and capable of perpetual renovation. Neither are they fitly to be called images, because they generate still, and cast their seeds in the minds of others, provoking and causing infinite actions and opinions in succeeding ages.

Francis Bacon

Make me respect my mind so much that I dare not read what has no meaning or moral. Help me to choose with equal care my friends and my books, because they are both for life. Show me that as in a river, so in reading, the depths hold more of strength and beauty than the shallows. Teach me to value art without being blind to thought. Keep me from caring more for much reading than for careful reading; for books than the Bible. Give me an ideal that will let me read only the best, and when that is done, stop me. Repay me with power to teach others, and then help me to say from a disciplined mind a grateful amen.

Charles Lamb — Prayer

A good book is a wonder-thing
That sets the spirit traveling
Down strange exciting ways, and through
New doors undreamed of hitherto.
It opens vistas to the eyes
Where the happy, far-off distance lies;
It lifts the cares of every day
When one is off and on his way.
For oh, indeed, a heart can roam
Through a good book, yet stay at home.
A table, lamp, a chair, and he
Absorbed in rhyme or mystery,
Absorbed in words upon a page—
O questioning Youth, O seeking Age,
Read books, good books, and you will find
Adventure, and new worlds outlined.

Grace Noll Crowell — Good Books

The books which help you most are those which make you think the most.

Theodore Parker

There must be surprise in the books that I keep in the worn case at my elbow, the surprise of a new personality perceiving for the first time the beauty, the wonder, the humor, the tragedy, the greatness of truth. It doesn't matter at all whether the writer is a poet, a scientist, a traveller, an essayist, or a mere daily space-maker, if he have the God-given grace of wonder.

David Grayson

England has two books, one which she has made and one which has made her: Shakespeare and the Bible.

Victor Hugo

A house is not home unless it contains food and fire for the mind as well as the body.

Margaret Fuller

Books must be read as deliberately and reservedly as they were written.

Henry David Thoreau

To produce a mighty book, you must choose a mighty theme. No great and enduring volume can ever be written on the flea, though many there be that have tried it.

Herman Melville

I would rather be a poor man in a garret with plenty of books than a king who did not love reading.

Thomas Babington Macauley

I cannot live without books.

Thomas Jefferson

The world of books is the most remarkable creation of man. Nothing else he builds lasts. Monuments fall, nations perish, civilizations grow old and die out and after an era of darkness new races build others.
But in the world of books are volumes that have seen this happen again and again and yet live on, still young, still as fresh as the day they were written, still telling men's hearts of the hearts of men centuries dead.

Clarence Day

The worth of a book is to be measured by what you can carry away from it.

James Bryce

Society is a strong solution of books. It draws its virtue out of what is best worth reading, as hot water draws the strength of tea-leaves.

Oliver Wendell Holmes

For books are more than books, they are the life, the very heart and core of ages past; the reason why men lived, and worked, and died, the essence and quintessence of their lives.

James Russell Lowell

If you'd move to a bygone measure,
    Or shape your heart to an ancient mould,
Maroons and schooners and buried treasure
    Wrought on a page of gold—

Then take the book in the dingy binding,
    Still the magic comes, bearded, great,
And swaggering files of sea-thieves winding
    Back, with their ruffling cut-throat gait,
Reclaim an hour when we first went finding
    Pieces of Eight—of Eight.

Patrick Reginald Chalmers — Treasure Island

Some books are to be tasted, others to be swallowed, and some few to be chewed and digested: that is, some books are to be read only in parts, others to be read, but not curiously, and some few to be read wholly, and with diligence and attention.

Francis Bacon

Except a living man there is nothing more wonderful than a book! A message to us from the dead — from human souls we never saw, who lived, perhaps, thousands of miles away. And yet these, in those little sheets of paper, speak to us, arouse us, terrify us, teach us, comfort us, open their hearts to us as brothers.

Charles Kingsley

'Tis the good reader that makes the good book; in every book he finds passages which seem confidences or asides hidden from all else and unmistakably meant for his ear; the profit of books is according to the sensibility of the reader; the profoundest thought or passion sleeps as in a mine, until it is discovered by an equal mind and heart.

Ralph Waldo Emerson

A man ought to read just as inclination leads him; for what he reads as a task will do him little good.

Samuel Johnson

All that wearies profoundly is to be condemned for reading. The mind profits little by what is termed heavy reading.

Lafcadio Hearn

132

A good book is the precious life-blood of a
master-spirit, embalmed and treasured up on
purpose to a life beyond life.

John Milton

There is no frigate like a book
To take us lands away,
Nor any coursers like a page
Of prancing poetry.

This traverse may the poorest take
Without oppress of toll;
How frugal is the chariot
That bears a human soul.

Emily Dickinson

Then I thought of reading—the nice and
subtle happiness of reading . . . this joy not
dulled by Age, this polite and unpunishable
vice, this selfish, serene, life-long intoxication.

Logan Pearsall Smith

Whosoever therefore acknowledges himself
to be a zealous follower of truth, of happiness,
of wisdom, of science, or even of the faith,
must of necessity make himself a lover of books.

Richard de Bury

Books are the true levellers. They give to all
who will faithfully use them, the society, the
spiritual presence, of the best and greatest of
our race.

William Ellery Channing

There is no book so bad but there is something
good in it.

Miguel de Cervantes

If I read a book and it makes my whole body
so cold no fire can ever warm me, I know that
is poetry. If I feel physically as if the top of
my head were taken off, I know that is poetry.
These are the only ways I know it. Is there
any other way?

Emily Dickinson

Poetry is the record of the best and happiest
moments of the happiest and best minds.

Percy Bysshe Shelley

Ever I must sing
As poets have;
The old tradition keep,
To laugh or weep
In some forgotten attic
As they have done
Rousing the world from sleep
To laugh or weep.

Ever must I bring
As poets have
The passions of life and truth
From the bosom of youth
That never rouses itself in me
But leaves in its wake
A verse; an ache.

Lillian Arline Walbert — The Poet

Poetry is not the proper antithesis to prose,
but to science. Poetry is opposed to science,
and prose to metre. The proper and immediate
object of science is the acquirement, or communication, of truth; the proper and immediate
object of poetry is the communication of
immediate pleasure.

Samuel Taylor Coleridge

Who reads the verse I write
Shall know the falcon's flight,
The vision single and sure, the conquest of
    air and sun!
Is there aught else worthy to weave within
    your banners' folds?
Is there aught else worthy to grave on the
    blade of your naked swords?

Padraic Colum

What is poetry? Is it a mosaic
    Of colored stones which curiously are
        wrought
    Into a pattern? Rather glass that's taught
By patient labor any hue to take
And glowing with a sumptuous splendor, make
    Beauty a thing of awe where sunbeams
        caught,
    Transmitted fall in sheafs of rainbows
        fraught
With storied meaning for religion's sake.

Amy Lowell — Fragments

133

In spite of difference of soil and climate, of language and manners, of laws and customs — in spite of things silently gone out of mind, and things violently destroyed, the Poet binds together by passion and knowledge the vast empire of human society, as it is spread over the whole earth, and over all time.

William Wordsworth

Whatever your occupation may be and however crowded your hours with affairs, do not fail to secure at least a few minutes every day for refreshment of your inner life with a bit of poetry.

Charles Eliot Norton

Art

It is art that *makes* life, makes interest, makes importance, for our consideration and application of these things, and I know of no substitute whatever for the force and beauty of its process.

Henry James

Art is a human activity having for its purpose the transmission to others of the highest and best feelings to which men have risen.

Count Leo Tolstoy

Art is the place of the soul's freedom; there it forgets its dream unhampered; there, age after age, race after race, it gives its dream to the world that is.

G. E. Woodberry

Artistic growth is, more than it is anything else, a refining of the sense of truthfulness. The stupid believe that to be truthful is easy; only the artist, the great artist, knows how difficult it is.

Willa Cather

It is through art, and through art only, that we can realize our perfection; through art and art only that we can shield ourselves from the sordid perils of actual existence.

Oscar Wilde

Goethe wrote of "The Americas of the mind." In the artist's life of the imagination there is vision and adventure and the discovery of new worlds. An artist's masterpiece is such an America of the mind: a new world of meaning expressed in terms of abiding beauty, be it in marble or paint or words or musical tone. And in this great vision we are privileged to share. To see eye to eye with a great artist is to expand and enrich the world in which we live.

Radoslav A. Tsanoff

We adore Thee, God, because Thou hast empowered man to create beauty. Our every sense is conscious of beauty in
    the graceful column,
    the sound of a tuneful violin,
    the touch of soft linen,
    the odor of choice perfume,
    the flavor of good food.
All show beauty to the sensitive soul.

Marie Welles Clapp

A man that has a taste of music, painting or architecture, is like one that has another sense, when compared with such as have no relish of those arts.

Joseph Addison

I think the artist is a specially privileged person, because always he sees the world spread out like a stage before him, a play being enacted for his own special benefit. He approaches it objectively, with all his senses sharpened, filled with "a great awareness"— a sensitivity like that of a human camera, to make a record of it. He looks not for those things which are the same or similar to his own past experiences, but for differences; he forgets himself and identifies himself with the new scene and its activities.

Lois Lenski

Painting isn't an aesthetic operation; it's a form of magic designed as a mediator between this strange hostile world and us, a way of seizing power by giving form to our terrors as well as our desires.

Pablo Picasso

134

Art should be independent of all claptrap — should stand alone, and appeal to the artistic sense of eye and ear, without confounding this with emotions entirely foreign to it, as devotion, pity, love, patriotism and the like. All these have no concern with it.

James McNeill Whistler

But the artist appeals to that part of our being which is not dependent on wisdom; to that in us which is a gift and not an acquisition — and, therefore, more permanently enduring. He speaks to our capacity for delight and wonder, to the sense of mystery surrounding our lives: to our sense of pity, and beauty, and pain.

Joseph Conrad

Only through art can we get outside of ourselves and know another's view of the universe which is not the same as ours and see landscapes which would otherwise have remained unknown to us like the landscapes of the moon. Thanks to art, instead of seeing a single world, our own, we see it multiply until we have before us as many worlds as there are original artists . . . And many centuries after their core, whether we call it Rembrandt or Vermeer, is extinguished, they continue to send us their special rays.

Marcel Proust

Painting is only a bridge linking the painter's mind with that of the viewer.

Eugène Delacroix

Resemblance reproduces the formal aspect of objects, but neglects their spirit; truth shows the spirit and the substance in like perfection. He who tries to transmit the spirit by means of the formal aspect and ends by merely obtaining the outward appearance, will produce a dead thing.

Ching Hao

One is never tired of painting, because you have to set down, not what you knew already, but what you have just discovered. There is a continual creation out of nothing going on.

William Hazlitt

There's a minute of life passing! Paint it in its reality and forget everything to do that! Become it itself . . . give the image of what we actually see, forgetting everything that has appeared before us.

Paul Cezanne

The first virtue of a painting is to be a feast for the eyes.

Eugène Delacroix

I want to reach that state of condensation of sensations which constitutes a picture.

Henri Matisse

A youth who likes to study will in the end succeed. To begin with he should know that there are Six Essentials in painting. The first is called *spirit*; the second, *rhythm*; the third, *thought*; the fourth, *scenery*; the fifth, the *brush*, and the last is the *ink*.

Ching Hao

[Concerning the Six Principles of painting] The first is, that through a vitalizing spirit, a painting should possess the movement of life. The second is, that by means of the brush, the structural basis should be established. The third is, that the representation should so conform with the objects as to give their likenesses. The fourth is, that the coloring should be applied according to their characteristics. The fifth is, that through organization, place and position should be determined. The sixth is, that by copying the ancient models should be perpetuated.

Hsieh Ho

The imitator is a poor kind of creature. If the man who paints only the tree, or flower, or other surface he sees before him were an artist, the king of artists would be the photographer. It is for the artist to do something beyond this: in portrait painting to put on canvas something more than the face the model wears for that one day; to paint the man, in short, as well as his features.

James McNeill Whistler

135

The masterpiece should appear as the flower to the painter — perfect in its bud as in its bloom — with no reason to explain its presence — no mission to fulfill — a joy to the artist, a delusion to the philanthropist — a puzzle to the botanist — an accident of sentiment and alliteration to the literary man.

James McNeill Whistler

I have a predilection for painting that lends joyousness to a wall.

Pierre Auguste Renoir

For me, a painting is a dramatic action in the course of which reality finds itself split apart. For me, that dramatic action takes precedence over all other considerations. The pure plastic act is only secondary as far as I'm concerned. What counts is the drama of that plastic act, the moment at which the universe comes out of itself and meets its own destruction.

Pablo Picasso

O young artist, you search for a subject — everything is a subject. Your subject is yourself, your impressions, your emotions in the presence of nature.

Eugène Delacroix

Of all kinds of painting, figure painting is the most difficult; then comes landscape painting, and next dogs and horses. High towers and pavilions are definite things; they are difficult to execute, but easy to handle since they do not demand insight.

Ku K'ai-Chih

What interests me most is neither still life nor landscape, but the human figure. It is through it that I best succeed in expressing the almost religious feeling I have towards life.

Henri Matisse

Music

Music is a revelation; a revelation loftier than all wisdom and all philosophy.

Ludwig van Beethoven

Many love music but for music's sake,
Many because her touches can awake
Thoughts that repose within the breast
  half-dead,
And rise to follow where she loves to lead.
What various feelings come from days gone by!
What tears from far-off sources dim the eye!
Few, when light fingers with sweet voices play,
And melodies swell, pause, and melt away,
Mind how at every touch, at every tone,
A spark of life hath glistened and hath gone.

Walter Savage Landor — Many Love Music

The meaning of song goes deep. Who in logical words can explain the effect music has on us? A kind of inarticulate, unfathomable speech, which leads us to the edge of the infinite, and lets us for a moment gaze into that!

Thomas Carlyle

Music is the harmonious voice of creation; an echo of the invisible world; one note of the divine concord which the entire universe is destined one day to sound.

Giuseppe Mazzini

You ask me where I get my ideas. That I cannot tell you with certainty. They come unsummoned, directly, indirectly — I could seize them with my hands — out in the open air, in the woods, while walking, in the silence of the nights, at dawn, excited by moods which are translated by the poet into words, by me into tones that sound and roar and storm about me till I have set them down in notes.

Ludwig van Beethoven

Music has been called the speech of the angels; I will go farther and call it the speech of God Himself.

Charles Kingsley

Music's the cordial of a troubled breast
The softest remedy that grief can find;
The gentle spell that charms our care to rest
And calms the ruffled passions of the mind.
  Music does all our joys refine,
  And gives the relish to our wine.

John Oldham

136

There is in souls a sympathy with sounds;
   And as the mind is pitch'd, the ear is pleased
With melting airs or martial, brisk, or grave;
   Some chord in unison with what we hear
Is touch'd within us, and the heart replies.

William Cowper

We are the music-makers,
And we are the dreamers of dreams,
Wandering by lone sea-breakers,
And sitting by desolate streams;
World-losers and world-forsakers,
On whom the pale moon gleams;
Yet we are the movers and shakers
Of the world forever, it seems.

With wonderful deathless ditties
We build up the world's great cities,
And out of a fabulous story
We fashion an empire's glory.
One man with a dream, at pleasure,
Shall go forth and conquer a crown
And three with a new song's measure
Can trample an empire down.

We, in the ages lying
In the buried past of the earth,
Built Nineveh with our sighing,
And Babel itself with our mirth;
And o'erthrew them with prophesying
To the old of the new world's worth;
For each age is a dream that is dying,
Or one that is coming to birth.

Arthur William Edgar O'Shaughnessy —
We Are The Music-Makers

When I hear music I fear no danger, I am
invulnerable, I see no foe. I am related to the
earliest times, and to the latest.

Henry David Thoreau

There's music in the sighing of a reed;
   There's music in the gushing of a rill;
There's music in all things, if we have ears;
   The earth is but the music of the spheres.

George Gordon, Lord Byron

Where words fail, music speaks.

Hans Christian Andersen

Some of the loftiest aspirations of the human
soul are reserved to those who have the great
gift of musical expression, for they thereby
lift themselves out of a material world and
enter a spiritual one. In holding communion
with the great composers, who were surely
instruments in the hands of a Divine Power,
we are enabled to express something of the
Infinite. Whether I play in public in the midst
of thousands or in the privacy of my own room,
I forget everything except my music. Whenever
I am lifted out of the material plane and come
in touch with another, a holier world, it is as
if some hand other than mine were directing
the bow over the strings.

Fritz Kreisler

When music sounds, gone is the earth I know,
   And all her lovely things even lovelier grow;
Her flowers in vision flame, her forest trees
   Lift burdened branches, stilled with ecstasies.

When music sounds, out of the water rise
   Naiads whose beauty dims my waking eyes,
Rapt in strange dreams burns each enchanted
      face,
   With solemn echoing stirs their dwelling-
         place.

When music sounds, all that I was I am
   Ere to this haunt of brooding dust I came;
And from Time's woods break into distant song
   The swift-winged hours, as I hasten along.

Walter de la Mare — Music

And music, too — dear music! that can touch
   Beyond all else the soul that loves it much—
Now heard far off, so far as but to seem
   Like the faint, exquisite music of a dream.

Thomas Moore

When natural music is sharpened and polished
by art, then one begins to see with amazement
the great and perfect wisdom of God in His
wonderful work of music. . . . He who does not
find this an inexpressible miracle of the Lord
is truly a clod, and is not worthy to be
considered a man.

Martin Luther

I wept at the beauty of your hymns and canticles, and was powerfully moved at the sweet sound of your Church singing. These sounds flowed into my ears, and the truth streamed into my heart.

St. Augustine

We love music for the buried hopes, the garnered memories, the tender feelings it can summon at a touch.

Samuel Rogers

When someone questioned Handel on his feelings when composing the Hallelujah Chorus of *The Messiah,* he replied: "I did think I did see all Heaven before me and the great God Himself."

James Beattie

Music is in all growing things;
And underneath the silky wings
    Of smaller insects there is stirred
    A pulse of air that must be heard;
Earth's silence lives, and throbs, and sings.

George Parsons Lathrop

What is to reach the heart must come from above, if it does not come thence, it will be nothing but notes — body without spirit.

Ludwig van Beethoven

Music is love in search of a word.

Sidney Lanier

Music is the only language in which you cannot say a mean or sarcastic thing.

John Erskine

The soul of music slumbers in the shell
    Till waked and kindled by the master's spell;
And feeling hearts, touch them but rightly, pour
    A thousand melodies unheard of before.

E. E. Landon

In holy music's golden speech
    Remotest notes to notes respond:
Each octave is a world; yet each
    Vibrates to worlds beyond its own.

Aubrey Thomas de Vere

God be praised,
Antonio Stradivari had an eye
That winces at false work and loves
    the true . . .
And for my fame — when any master holds
'Twixt chin and hand a violin of mine,
He will be glad that Stradivari lived,
Made violins, and made of the best . . .

I say not God Himself can make man's best
Without best men to help Him . . .
    'Tis God gives skill,
But not without men's hands: He could not
    make
Antonio Stradivari's violins
Without Antonio.

George Eliot

How sweet the moonlight sleeps upon this
    bank!
Here we will sit, and let the sounds of music
Creep in our ears; soft stillness and the night
Become the touches of sweet harmony.
Sit, Jessica: look, how the floor of heaven
Is thick inlaid with patines of bright gold;
There's not the smallest orb which thou
    behold'st
But in his motion like an angel sings,
Still quiring to the young-eyed cherubins.
Such harmony is in immortal souls;
But whilst this muddy vesture of decay
Doth grossly close it in, we cannot hear it.

William Shakespeare

Drama

The dramatist, like the poet, is born, not made.

William Winter

In other things the knowing artist may
Judge better than the people; but a play,
(Made for delight, and for no other use)
If you approve it not, has no excuse.

Edmund Waller

The most difficult character in comedy is that of the fool, and he must be no simpleton that plays that part.

Miguel de Cervantes

138

Soul of the age!
The applause, delight, the wonder of our stage!
My Shakespeare, rise; I will not lodge thee by
Chaucer or Spenser, or bid Beaumont lie
A little further, to make thee a room;
Thou art a monument, without a tomb,
And art alive still, while thy book doth live,
And we have wits to read, and praise to give.

Ben Jonson

To wake the soul by tender strokes of art,
To raise the genius, and to mend the heart;
To make mankind, in conscious virtue bold,
Live o'er each scene, and be what they behold:
For this the Tragic Muse first trod the stage.

Alexander Pope

Popular Stage-plays are sinful, heathenish,
lewd, ungodly Spectacles, and most pernicious
Corruptions; condemned in all ages, as intolerable Mischiefs to Churches, to Republics,
to the manners, minds and souls of men.

William Prynne, 1632

As in a theatre, the eyes of men,
After a well-grac'd actor leaves the stage,
Are idly bent on him that enters next,
Thinking his prattle to be tedious.

William Shakespeare

The business of the dramatist is to keep
himself out of sight, and to let nothing appear
but his characters. As soon as he attracts
notice to his personal feelings, the illusion is
broken.

Thomas Babington Macauley

There be players that I have seen play, and
heard others praise, and that highly, not to
speak it profanely, that neither have the accent
of Christian, pagan, nor man, have so strutted
and bellowed, that I have thought some of
nature's journeymen had made men, and not
made them well, they imitated humanity so
abominably.

William Shakespeare

The drama's laws the drama's patrons give,
For we that live to please, must please to live.

Samuel Johnson

Here lies David Garrick, describe me, who can,
An abridgment of all that was pleasant in man.
On the stage he was natural, simple, affecting;
'Twas only that when he was off he was acting.

Oliver Goldsmith

Of all imitators, dramatists are the most
perverse, the most unconscionable, or the most
unconscious, and have been so time out of
mind.

Edgar Allen Poe

I love a natural, simple and unaffected speech,
written as it is spoken and such upon the paper
as it is in the mouth, a pithy, sinewy, full,
strong, compendious and material speech.

Michel de Montaigne

Like a strutting player, whose conceit
Lies in his hamstring, and doth think it rich
To hear the wooden dialogue and sound
'Twixt his stretch'd footing and the scaffoldage.

William Shakespeare

Faith and Worship

Belief

Whoso draws nigh to God one step
   through doubtings dim,
God will advance a mile
   in blazing light to him.

Anonymous

Faith is the force of life.

Count Leo Tolstoy

I have had so many evidences of His direction,
so many instances when I have been controlled
by some other power than my own will that
I cannot doubt this power.

Abraham Lincoln

A heathen philosopher once asked a Christian,
"Where is God?" The Christian answered, "Let
me first ask you, Where is He not?"

Aaron Arrowsmith

The person who has a firm trust in the Supreme
Being is powerful in his power, wise by his
wisdom, happy by his happiness.

Joseph Addison

He who would valiant be
'Gainst all disaster,
Let him in constancy
Follow the Master.
There's no discouragement
Shall make him once relent
His first avowed intent
To be a pilgrim.

John Bunyan

No coward soul is mine,
No trembler in the world's storm-troubled
   sphere:
I see Heaven's glories shine,
And faith shines equal, arming me from fear.

Emily Brontë

Faith is to believe, on the word of God, what
we do not see, and its reward is to see and
enjoy what we believe.

St. Augustine

I do not want merely to possess a faith;
I want a faith that possesses me.

Charles Kingsley

The person who has a firm trust in the
Supreme Being is powerful in his power, wise
by his wisdom, happy by his happiness.

Joseph Addison

Thine, O Lord, are the times we measure off
by days and months, and though the years pass
and the generations come and go, Thy purposes
abide and Thy love fails not.

Joseph King

No man ever saw God and lived; and yet I
shall not live until I see God; and when I have
seen Him, I shall never die.

John Donne

Before us is a future all unknown, a path
   untrod;
Beside us a friend well loved and known—
   That friend is God.

Anonymous

141

Thou one all perfect light;
Our lamps are lit at Thine;
And into darkness, as of night,
We go, to prove they shine.

M. Elizabeth Crouse

The highest pinnacle of the spiritual life is not
happy joy in unbroken sunshine, but absolute
and undoubting trust in the love of God.

Anthony Wilson Thorold

I say, the acknowledgment of God in Christ
Accepted by thy reason, solves for thee
All questions in the earth and out of it.

Robert Browning

I have no fear that the candle lighted in
Palestine years ago will ever be put out.

William Ralph Inge

Every one knows how to be resigned amid
the joys and happiness of prosperity, but to be
so amid storms and tempests is peculiar to
the children of God.

St. Francis of Assisi

There is something in the nature of things
which the mind of man, which reason, which
human powers cannot effect, and certainly that
which produces this must be better than man.
What can this be but God.

Cicero

We shall be made truly wise if we be made
content; content, too, not only with what we
can understand, but content with what we do
not understand — the habit of mind which
theologians call, and rightly, faith in God.

Charles Kingsley

I know not where His islands lift
    Their fronded palms in air;
I only know I cannot drift
    Beyond His love and care.

John Greenleaf Whittier

Keep thou my feet; I do not ask to see
The distant scene; one step enough for me.

John Henry Newman

A few weeks before he died, Franklin wrote
to Ezra Stiles, president of Yale University:
You desire to know something of my religion.
It is the first time I have been questioned
upon it. But I cannot take your curiosity amiss,
and shall endeavor in a few words to gratify
it. Here is my creed. I believe in one God,
Creator of the Universe. That he governs it
by his Providence. That he ought to be wor-
shipped. That the most acceptable service we
render to him is doing good to his other
children. That the soul of man is immortal,
and will be treated with justice in another life
respecting its conduct in this.
I shall only add, respecting myself, that having
experienced the goodness of that Being in
conducting me prosperously through a long life,
I have no doubt of its continuance in the next,
though without the smallest conceit of meriting
such goodness.

Benjamin Franklin, March 9, 1790

There is no unbelief;
Whoever plants a seed beneath the sod
And waits to see it push away the clod,
    He trusts in God.

Whoever says when clouds are in the sky,
"Be patient, heart, light breaketh by and by,"
    Trusts the Most High.

Whoever sees, 'neath fields of winter snow,
The silent harvest of the future grow,
    God's power must know.

Whoever lies down on his couch to sleep,
Content to lock each sense in slumber deep,
    Knows God will keep.

Whoever says, "Tomorrow," "The
        Unknown,"
"The Future," trusts that power alone
    He dares disown.

There is no unbelief;
And day by day, and night, unconsciously,
The heart lives by that faith the lips deny,
    God knoweth why.

Edward Robert Bulwer-Lytton

O Lord of the vineyard, we beg Thy blessing upon all who truly desire to serve Thee by being diligent and faithful in their several callings, bearing their due share of the world's burden, and going about their daily tasks in all simplicity and uprightness of heart.

John Baillie

How often we look upon God as our last and feeblest resource! We go to Him because we have nowhere else to go. And then we learn that the storms of life have driven us, not upon the rocks, but into the desired havens.

George MacDonald

And I said to the man who stood at the gate
  of the year
"Give me a light that I may tread safely into
  the unknown:"
And he replied,
"Go out into the darkness and put thine hand
  into the hand of God. That
shall be to thee better than any light and
  safer than any known way."

M. L. Haskins

Those who attempt to search into the majesty of God will be overwhelmed with its glory.

Thomas à Kempis

"The Everlasting Arms." I think of that whenever rest is sweet. How the whole earth and the strength of it, that is almightiness, is beneath every tired creature to give it rest; *holding* us, always! No thought of God is closer than that. No human tenderness of patience is greater than that which gathers in its arms a little child, and holds it, heedless of weariness. And He fills the great earth, and all upon it, with this unseen force of His love, that never forgets or exhausts itself, so that everywhere we may lie down in His bosom, and be comforted.

Adeline D. T. Whitney

Our Creator would never have made such lovely days, and have given us the deep hearts to enjoy them above and beyond all that, unless we were meant to be immortal.

Nathaniel Hawthorne

There is no soul that does not respond to love, for the soul of man is a guest that has gone hungry these centuries back.

Maurice Maeterlinck

Mutual love the token be,
Lord, that we belong to Thee;
Love, Thine image, love impart;
Stamp it on our face and heart;
Only love to us be given;
Lord, we ask no other heaven.

Charles C. Wesley

All that is good, all that is true, all that is beautiful, all that is beneficent, be it great or small, be it perfect or fragmentary, natural as well as supernatural, moral as well as material, comes from God.

John Henry Newman

So I go not knowing
—I would not, if I might—
I would rather walk in the dark with God
  Than go alone in the light;
I would rather walk with Him by faith
  Than walk alone by sight.

Mary Gardner Brainard

Cast all your cares on God; that anchor holds.

Alfred, Lord Tennyson

God hath not promised
  Skies always blue,
Flower-strewn pathways
  All our lives through;
God hath not promised
  Sun without rain,
Joy without sorrow,
  Peace without pain.

But God hath promised
  Strength for the day,
Rest for the labor,
  Light for the way,
Grace for the trials,
  Help from above,
Unfailing sympathy,
  Undying love.

Annie Johnson Flint — What God Hath Promised

Let nothing disturb thee,
Nothing affright thee;
All things are passing:
God never changeth;
Patient endurance
Attaineth to all things;
Who God possesseth
In nothing is wanting;
Alone God sufficeth.

St. Theresa of Avila — Lines Written in Her Breviary

Teach me, Father, how to go
Softly as the grasses grow;
Hush my soul to meet the shock
Of the wild world as a rock;
But my spirit, propt with power,
Make as simple as a flower.
Let the dry heart fill its cup,
Like a poppy looking up;
Let life lightly wear her crown,
Like a poppy looking down,
When its heart is filled with dew,
And its life begins anew.

Teach me, Father, how to be
Kind and patient as a tree.
Joyfully the crickets croon
Under shady oak at noon;
Beetle, on his mission bent,
Tarries in that cooling tent.
Let me, also, cheer a spot,
Hidden field or garden grot—
Place where passing souls can rest
On the way and be their best.

Edwin Markham — A Prayer

I will frankly tell you that my experience in
prolonged scientific investigations convinces
me that a belief in God, a God who is behind
and within the chaos of vanishing points of
human knowledge, adds a wonderful stimulus
to the man who attempts to penetrate into the
regions of the unknown. I never make
preparations for penetrating into some small
province of nature hitherto undiscovered
without breathing a prayer to the Being who
hides his secrets from me only to allure me
graciously on to the unfolding of them.

Louis Agassiz

I cannot find my way: there is no star
In all the shrouded heavens anywhere:
And there is not a whisper in the air
Of any living voice but one so far
That I can hear it only as a bar
Of lost, imperial music, played when fair
And angel fingers wove, and unaware,
Dead leaves to garlands where no roses are.

No, there is not a glimmer, nor a call,
For one that welcomes, welcomes when he
    fears,
The black and awful chaos of the night;
For through it all — above, beyond it all —
I know the far-sent message of the years,
I feel the coming glory of the Light.

Edwin Arlington Robinson — Credo

Lord, make me an instrument of your peace,
    Where there is hatred, let me sow love;
Where there is injury, pardon;
    Where there is doubt, faith;
Where there is despair, hope;
    Where there is darkness, light;
And where there is sadness, joy.

O Divine Master, grant that I may not
    Seek to be consoled as to console;
To be understood as to understand;
    To be loved as to love;
For it is in giving that we receive,
    It is in pardoning that we are pardoned,
And it is in dying that we are born to eternal
    life.

St. Francis of Assisi

Without faith, we are as stained glass windows
in the dark.

Anonymous

Though my soul may set in darkness,
    It will rise in perfect light,
I have loved the stars too fondly
    To be fearful of the night.

Sarah Williams

All I have seen teaches me to trust the Creator
for all I have not seen.

Ralph Waldo Emerson

144

O Lord, Thou knowest what is best for us;
let this or that be done, as Thou shalt please.
Give what Thou wilt, and how much Thou
wilt, and when Thou wilt. Deal with me as
Thou thinkest good. Set me where Thou wilt,
and deal with me in all things just as Thou
wilt. Behold, I am Thy servant, prepared for
all things: for I desire not to live unto myself,
but unto Thee! and oh, that I could do it
worthily and perfectly!

Thomas á Kempis

Within Thy circling arms we lie,
  O God! in Thy infinity:
Our souls in quiet shall abide,
  Beset with love on every side.

Anonymous

God has sown His name on the heavens in
glittering stars; but upon earth He planteth
His name by tender flowers.

Jean Paul Richter

I never saw a moor,
I never saw the sea;
Yet know I how the heather looks,
And what a wave must be.

I never spoke with God,
Nor visited in heaven;
Yet certain am I of the spot
As if the chart were given.

Emily Dickinson — I Never Saw a Moor

The world answers back to our faith. . . . It
says to the farmer, "Sow your seed"; to the
aviator, "Spread your wings"; to the miner,
"Sink your shaft"; to the sailor, "Hoist your
sail"; to the engineer, "Swing your bridge"; to
the scientist, "Trust your hypothesis"; to the
financier, "Make your investment"; to the
explorer, "Follow the gleam." Faith is man's
highest venture. The poet Whittier puts it thus:
"The steps of faith fall on the seeming void
and find the rock beneath." It is the "seeming
void" on which we set our faith; beneath us,
however, is the unseen reality, and faith gives
it substance.

Hugh Thompson Kerr

O Thou, Light of lights,
Keep us from inward darkness.
Grant us so to sleep in peace, that we may
arise to work according to Thy will.

Lancelot Andrewes 1555-1626, Bishop of Winchester

Back of the loaf is the snowy flour,
And back of the flour the mill;
And back of the mill is the wheat, and the
  shower,
And the sun, and the Father's will.

Maltbie Babcock

The little cares that fretted me
  I lost them yesterday,
Among the fields above the sea,
  Among the winds that play,
Among the lowing of the herds,
  The rustling of the trees,
Among the singing of the birds,
  The humming of the bees.

The foolish fears of what might happen,
  I cast them all away
Among the clover-scented grass,
  Among the new-mown hay,
Among the husking of the corn,
  Where drowsy poppies nod
Where ill thoughts die and good are born—
  Out in the fields with God.

Anonymous

Bestow Thy light upon us, O Lord, so that
being rid of the darkness of our hearts, we
may attain unto the true Light; through Jesus
Christ, who is the Light of the world.

Sarum Breviary

Teach me, my God and King,
In all things thee to see,
And what I do in any thing,
To do it as for thee.

George Herbert

Not what we give, but what we share,
For the gift without the giver is bare:
Who gives himself with his alms feeds three,
Himself, his hungering neighbor, and Me.

James Russell Lowell

Bad will be the day for every man when he becomes absolutely contented with the life that he is living, with the thoughts that he is thinking, with the deeds that he is doing, when there is not forever beating at the doors of his soul some great desire to do something larger, which he knows that he was meant and made to do because he is still, in spite of all, the child of God.

Phillips Brooks

Faith never yet outstripped the bounty of the Lord.

Anonymous

It cannot be that the earth is man's only abiding place. It cannot be that our life is a mere bubble cast up by eternity to float a moment on its waves and then sink into nothingness. Else why is it that glorious aspirations which leap like angels from the temple of our hearts are forever wandering unsatisfied? Why is it that all the stars that hold festival around the midnight throne are set above the grasp of our limited faculties, forever mocking us with their unapproachable glory? And, finally, why is it that bright forms of human beauty presented to our view are taken from us, leaving the thousand streams of our affections to flow back in Alpine torrents upon our hearts? There is a realm where the rainbow never fades; where the stars will be spread out before us like islands that slumber in the ocean, and where the beautiful beings that now pass before us like shadows will stay in our presence forever.

George D. Prentice

Close thine eyes, and sleep secure;
Thy soul is safe, thy body sure.
He that guards thee, he that keeps,
Never slumbers, never sleeps.
A quiet conscience in the breast
Has only peace, has only rest,
The wisest and the mirth of kings
Are out of tune unless she sings:
Then close thine eyes in peace and sleep secure,
No sleep so sweet as thine, no rest so sure.

Charles I of England

All the doors that lead inward to the secret place of the Most High, are doors outwards — out of self, out of smallness, out of wrong.

George MacDonald

I can see how it might be possible for a man to look down upon the earth and be an atheist, but I cannot conceive how he could look up into the heavens and say there is no God.

Abraham Lincoln

Even such is time, that takes in trust
Our youth, our joys, our all we have,
And pays us but with age and dust;
Who in the dark and silent grave,
When we have wandered all our ways,
Shuts up the story of our days.
And from which earth, and grave, and dust,
The Lord shall raise me up, I trust.

Sir Walter Ralegh (found at his death in his Bible)

O world, thou choosest not the better part;
It is not wisdom to be only wise,
And on the inward vision close the eyes,
But it is wisdom to believe the heart.
Columbus found a world, and had no chart,
Save one that faith deciphered in the skies;
To trust the soul's invincible surmise
Was all his science and his only art.
Our knowledge is a torch of smokey pine
That lights the pathway but one step ahead
Across the mystery and dread.
Bid, then, the tender light of faith to shine
By which alone the heart is led
Unto the thinking of the thought divine.

George Santayana

O Lord, support us all the day long, until the shadows lengthen and the evening comes, and the busy world is hushed, and the fever of life is over, and our work is done. Then in thy mercy grant us a safe lodging, and a holy rest, and peace at the last.

John Henry Newman

I have ever judged of the religion of others by their lives. For it is in our lives, and not from our words, that our religion must be read.

Thomas Jefferson

Thine, O Lord, are the times we measure off
by days and months, and though the years
pass and the generations come and go,
Thy purposes abide and Thy love fails not.

Joseph King

Thou hast made us for Thyself, O God,
and our hearts are restless until
they rest in Thee.

St. Augustine

To an open house in the evening
  Home shall men come,
To an older place than Eden
  And a taller town than Rome.
To the end of the way of the wandering star,
  To the things that cannot be and are,
To the place where God was homeless,
  And all men are at home.

Gilbert Keith Chesterton

Thou art the comfortable resting-place of the
righteous, and Thou enablest them to see
Thee. Thou art the Beginning and the End of
all things. Thou bearest up all things without
effort. Thou art the Way, and the Guide, and
the Bourne whither the way leadeth; And to
Thee all men are hastening.

Boethius

A religion that is small enough for our
understanding would not be large enough for
our needs.

Arthur Balfour

I have now disposed of all my property to my
family. There is one thing more I wish I could
give them, and that is the Christian religion.
If they had that, and I had not given them one
shilling, they would have been rich. And if
they had not that, and I had given them all the
world, they would be poor.

Patrick Henry

Lord,
  what I know not, teach me;
  what I have not, give me;
  what I am not, make me.
Amen.

To be of no church is dangerous. Religion, of
which the rewards are distant, and which is
animated only by faith and hope, will glide by
degrees out of the mind unless it be invigorated
and reimpressed by external ordinances, by
stated calls to worship, and the salutary
influence of example.

Samuel Johnson

Religion is nothing else but love to God and
man.

William Penn

During the past thirty years, people from all
civilized countries on the earth have consulted
me. Among all my patients in the second half
of life — that is to say, over thirty-five — there
has not been one whose problem in the last
resort was not that of finding a religious outlook
on life. It is safe to say that every one of them
fell ill because he had lost that which the living
religions of every age have given to their
followers, and none of them has been really
healed who did not regain his religious outlook.

Carl G. Jung

The object of preaching is, constantly to
remind mankind of what mankind are constantly forgetting: not to supply the defects of
human intelligence, but to fortify the feebleness
of human resolutions; to recall mankind from
the by-paths where they turn, into that broad
path of salvation which all know, but few tread.

Sydney Smith

Thou mayest anon drive away the Lord Jesus
and lose His grace, if thou apply thyself to
outward things; and if through negligence thou
lose Him, what friend shalt thou then have?
Without a friend thou mayest not long endure,
and if Jesus be not thy friend before all others,
thou shalt be very heavy and desolate . . .
Jesus only is to be beloved for Himself, for
He only is proved good and faithful before all
other friends. In Him and for Him both
enemies and friends are to be beloved.

Thomas à Kempis — The Friendship of Jesus

Religion is not a funeral announcement. There are religious leaders who seem to be always saying — "Let us cry." They have gotten the wrong phrase. "Let us rejoice!" When you begin to talk about faith and God, do not turn the corners of your mouth down. Face these matters as naturally, as joyously, as genuinely, as you would face any other interest in life.

Edmund Mead Mills

The more spiritual is a man's religion, the more expansive and broad it always is.

Phillips Brooks

I love thy kingdom, Lord,
    The house of thine abode,
The Church our blest Redeemer saved
    With his own precious blood.

For her my tears shall fall;
    For her my prayers ascend;
To her my cares and toils be given,
    Till toils and cares shall end.

Jesus, thou friend divine,
    Our Saviour and our King,
Thy hand from every snare and foe
    Shall great deliverance bring.

Timothy Dwight

How beautiful, how beautiful are spires;
    Black in rain, red in sunset fires;
Silvered in moonlight, tipped by a single star—
    How very, very beautiful they are!

It matters not what faith has lifted high
    These symbols of man's longing for the sky;
It matters not what creed, nor what name
    That raised them up, their beauty is the same.

Whether they reach their way with quiet grace
    Up to the blue above some leafy place,
Or pierce the city's snarl of bricks and wires,
    Nothing is more beautiful than spires!

They are man's emblem, lifting from the sod,
    Climbing their straight and certain way to
        God.

Grace Noll Crowell — Spires

It is common for those that are farthest from God to boast themselves most of their being near to the Church.

Mathew Henry

The Reverend Sydney Smith, who was famous for his wit, once said of a preacher known for his dull sermons, "He evidently thought sin was to be taken from man, as Eve was from Adam, by casting him into a deep sleep."

Sydney Smith

If we work upon marble, it will perish; if upon brass, time will efface it; if we rear temples, they will crumble into dust; but if we work upon our immortal minds — if we imbue them with principles, with the just fear of God and love of fellow men — we engrave on those tablets something which will brighten through all eternity.

Daniel Webster

Whatsoever
The form of building or of creed professed,
The Cross, bold type of shame to homage
    turned,
Of any unfinished life that sways the world
Shall tower as sovereign emblem over all.

James Russell Lowell

Everything in the world is done from hope. No farmer would sow one grain if he did not hope it would grow to seed. No young man would take a wife if he didn't hope to have children by her. No merchant or working man would work if he didn't hope for profit or wages. Then how much more hope calls us to eternal life.

Martin Luther

Faith goes up the stairs that love has made and looks out of the windows which hope has opened.

Charles Haddon Spurgeon

Hope, like a gleaming taper's light,
    Adorns and cheers the way;
And still, as darker grows the night,
    Emits a brighter ray.

Oliver Goldsmith

148

If but one message I may leave behind,
One single word of courage for my kind,
It would be this—Oh, brother, sister, friend,
Whatever life may bring—what God may send,
No matter whether clouds lift soon or late—
Take heart and wait!

Despair may tangle darkly at your feet,
Your faith be dimmed, and hope, once cool
   and sweet
Be lost—but suddenly, above a hill
A heavenly lamp, set on a heavenly sill
Will shine for you and point the way to go,
How *well* I know!

For I have waited through the dark, and I
Have seen a star rise in the blackest sky
Repeatedly,—it has not failed me yet
And I have learned God never will forget
To light the lamp—If we but wait for it
It *will* be lit!

Grace Noll Crowell — Wait

Now we must praise the Ruler of Heaven,
The might of the Lord and His purpose of mind,
The work of the Glorious Father; for He
God Eternal, established each wonder,
He, Holy Creator, first fashioned the heavens
As a roof for the children of earth.
And then our Guardian, the Everlasting Lord,
Adorned this middle-earth for men.
Praise the Almighty King of Heaven.

Caedmon's Hymn

We thank Thee for this place in which we
dwell, for the love that unites us, for the peace
accorded us this day, for hope with which
we expect the morrow, for the health, the work,
the food and the bright skies that make our
life delightful; for our friends in all parts of the
earth. Spare to us our friends, soften to us our
enemies. Bless us if it may be in all our
innocent endeavors. If it may not, give us
strength to encounter that which is to come
that we may be brave in peril, constant in
tribulation, temperate in wrath and in all
changes of fortune, and down to the gates of
death, loyal and loving one to another . . .

Robert Louis Stevenson

O, it is not for the rude breath of man to blow
out the lamp of hope.

Instead, let us hold it high, a guide by day,
a pillar of fire by night, to cheer each pilgrim
on his way.

For have there not been times, O God, when
we peered into the gloom, and the heavens
were hung with black, and then when life was
well-nigh gone, we saw a light.

It was the Star of Hope.

Elbert Hubbard

New every morning is the love
Our waking and uprising prove;
From sleep and darkness safely brought
Restored to life and power and thought.

John Keble

For the sweet sleep which comes with night,
For the returning morning's light,
For the bright sun that shines on high,
For the stars glittering in the sky,—
For these and everything we see,
O Lord! our hearts we lift to Thee.

E. I. Tupper

We cannot form a true conception of life when
the tide is out, any more than we can obtain a
true picture of the shore under the same
conditions. When all things seem at low ebb,
we must not give in to despondency, but must
wait—hopefully, prayerfully, confidently—for
the turn of the tide.

Walter J. Sidney

God's ways seem dark, but, soon or late,
They touch the shining hills of day.

John Greenleaf Whittier

Lord, when I look upon mine own life it seems
Thou hast led me so carefully, so tenderly,
Thou canst have attended to no one else; but
when I see how wonderfully Thou hast led
the world and art leading it, I am amazed that
Thou hast time to attend to such as I.

St. Augustine

O never a star
Was lost; here
We all aspire to heaven and there is heaven
Above us.
If I stoop
Into a dark tremendous sea of cloud,
It is but for a time; I press God's lamp
Close to my breast; its splendor soon or late
Will pierce the gloom. I shall emerge some day.

Robert Browning

Bible

The Bible teaches us to see, feel, grasp, and comprehend faith, hope, and charity far otherwise than mere human reason can; and when evil oppresses us it teaches how these virtues throw light upon the darkness, and how, after this poor, miserable existence of ours on earth, there is another and eternal life.

Martin Luther

A bit of the Book in the morning,
   To order my onward way,
A bit of the Book in the evening,
   To hallow the end of the day.

Margaret Sangster

Hold fast to the Bible as the sheet-anchor of your liberties. Write its precepts in your hearts, and practise them in your lives.

Ulysses S. Grant

A friend once asked the great composer Haydn why his church music was always so full of gladness. He answered: "I cannot make it otherwise. I write according to the thoughts I feel. When I think upon my God, my heart is so full of joy that the notes dance and leap from my pen; and since God has given me a cheerful heart, it will be pardoned me that I serve Him with a cheerful spirit."

Henry van Dyke

To what greater inspiration and counsel can we turn than to the imperishable truth to be found in this treasure house, the Bible?

Queen Elizabeth II

There is a very large part of the Bible which can be received by us only when we come into the places for which the words were given. There are promises for weakness which we can never get while we are strong. There are words for times of danger which we can never know while we need no protection. There are consolations for sickness whose comfort we can never get while we are in robust health. There are promises for times of loneliness, when men walk in solitary ways, which never can come with real meaning to us while loving companions are by our side. There are words for old age which we never can appropriate for ourselves along the years of youth, when the arm is strong, the blood warm, the heart brave. God cannot show us the stars while the sun shines in the heavens.

J. R. Miller

The Bible is not only many books. It is a literature. History, poetry, prophecy, philosophy, theology, oratory, humor, sarcasm, irony, music, drama, tragedy, strategy, love tales, war tales, travelogues, laws, jurisprudence, songs, sermons, warnings, prayers, all are here. Was there ever such a literature? The Bible begins with a garden and ends with a city. It starts with a morning followed by a night and ends with a day that shall know no night. It breaks the silence with "In the beginning" and it hushes the universe to sleep with "The grace of our Lord Jesus Christ be with you all."

John Snider

The Bible is a book in comparison with which all others are of minor importance, and which in all my perplexities and distresses has never failed to give me light and strength.

Robert E. Lee

The Bible is like a telescope. If a man looks *through* his telescope, then he sees worlds beyond; but if he looks *at* his telescope, then he does not see anything but that. The Bible is a thing to be looked through, to see that which is beyond; but most people only look at it; and so they see only the dead letter.

Phillips Brooks

What you bring away from the Bible depends to some extent on what you carry to it.

Oliver Wendell Holmes

The Bible is the book of all others to be read at all ages and in all conditions of human life. . . . I speak as a man of the world to men of the world, and I say to you, "Search the Scriptures."

John Quincy Adams

The foundations of our society and our government rest so much on the teachings of the Bible that it would be difficult to support them if faith in these teachings should cease to be practically universal in our country.

Calvin Coolidge

To me the greatest thing that has happened on this earth of ours is the rise of the human race to the vision of God. That story of the human rise to what I call the vision of God is the story which is told in the Bible.

Jan Christian Smuts

The Bible is a window in this prison-world, through which we may look into eternity.

Timothy Dwight

If there is anything in this life which sustains a wise man and induces him to maintain his serenity amidst the tribulations and adversities of the world, it is in the first place, I consider, the meditation and knowledge of the Scriptures.

St. Jerome

Prayer

No voice of prayer to Thee can rise,
But swift as light Thy Love replies;
Not always what we ask, indeed,
But, O most Kind! what most we need.

Harriet M. Kimball

Between the humble and contrite heart and the majesty of heaven there are no barriers; the only password is prayer.

Hosea Ballou

Prayer is a force as real as terrestrial gravity. As a physician, I have seen men, after all other therapy has failed, lifted out of disease and melancholy by the serene effort of prayer. It is the only power in the world that seems to overcome the so-called "laws of nature"; the occasions on which prayer has dramatically done this have been termed "miracles." But a constant, quieter miracle takes place hourly in the hearts of men and women who have discovered that prayer supplies them with a steady flow of sustaining power in their daily lives.

Too many people regard prayer as a formalized routine of words, a refuge for weaklings, or a childish petition for material things. We sadly undervalue prayer when we conceive it in these terms, just as we should underestimate rain by describing it as something that fills a birdbath in our garden. Properly understood, prayer is a mature activity indispensable to the fullest development of personality — the ultimate integration of man's highest faculties. Only in prayer do we achieve that complete and harmonious assembly of body, mind, and spirit which gives the frail human need its unshakable strength.

Dr. Alexis Carrel

Prayer, as the first, second, and third element of the Christian life, should open, prolong, and conclude each day. The first act of the soul in early morning should be a draught at the heavenly fountain. It will sweeten the taste for the day. A few moments with God at that calm and tranquil season, are of more value than much fine gold. And if you tarry long so sweetly at the throne, you will come out of the closet as the high priest of Israel came from the awful ministry at the altar of incense, suffused all over with the heavenly fragrance of that communion.

Henry Ward Beecher

More things are wrought by prayer
    Than this world dreams of. Wherefore,
        let thy voice
Rise like a fountain for me night and day.

Alfred, Lord Tennyson

151

Lord, what a change within us one short hour
Spent in Thy presence will prevail to make!
What heavy burdens from our bosoms take,
What parched grounds refresh as with a
    shower!
We kneel, and all around us seems to lower;
We rise, and all, the distant and the near,
Stands forth in sunny outline, brave and clear;
We kneel, how weak! We rise, how full of
    power!
Why, therefore, should we do ourselves this
    wrong,
Or others, that we are not always strong,
That we are ever overborne with care,
That we should ever weak or heartless be,
Anxious or troubled, when with us is prayer,
And joy and strength and courage are with
    Thee.

Richard C. Trench — Prayer

I have lived, Sir, a long time, and the longer
I live, the more convincing proofs I see of this
truth—that God governs in the affairs of men.
And if a sparrow cannot fall to the ground
without his notice, is it probable that an
empire can rise without his aid? We have been
assured, Sir, in the sacred writings, that 'except
the Lord building the House they labour in
vain that build it.' I firmly believe this; and I
also believe that without his concurring aid
we shall succeed in this political building no
better than the Builders of Babel:
I therefore beg leave to move — that henceforth prayers imploring the assistance of
Heaven, and its blessings on our deliberations
be held in this Assembly every morning before
we proceed to business. . . .

Benjamin Franklin,
Second Continental Congress (1775)

For what are men better than sheep or goats
That nourish a blind life within the brain,
If, knowing God, they lift not hands of prayer
Both for themselves and those who call them
    friends?
For so the whole round earth is every way
Bound by gold chains about the feet of God.

Alfred, Lord Tennyson

Prayer is the soul's sincere desire,
    Uttered or unexpressed —
The motion of a hidden fire,
    That kindles in the breast.

Prayer is the burthen of a sigh,
    The falling of a tear —
The upward glancing of an eye,
    When none but God is near.

Prayer is the simplest form of speech
    That infant lips can try —
Prayer the sublimest strains that reach
    The majesty on high.

O Thou by whom we come to God —
    The Life, the Truth, the Way!
The path of prayer Thyself hast trod;
    Lord, teach us how to pray.

James Montgomery — What Is Prayer?

Prayer is the application of want to Him who
alone can relieve it, the voice of sin to Him
who alone can pardon it. It is the urgency of
poverty, the prostration of humility, the fer-
vency of penitence, the confidence of trust. It
is not eloquence, but earnestness; not figures of
speech, but compunction of soul. It is the
"Lord, save, I perish" of drowning Peter. . . .
It is not a mere conception of the mind nor an
effort of the intellect, nor an act of the memory,
but an elevation of the soul towards its Maker.
It is the devout breathing of a creature struck
with a sense of its own misery and of the
infinite holiness of Him whom it is addressing,
experimentally convinced of its own emptiness
and of the abundant fullness of God, of His
readiness to hear, of His power to help, of His
willingness to save . . . Prayer is right in itself
as the most powerful means of resisting sin and
advancing in holiness. It is above all might,
as everything is, which has the authority
of Scripture, the command of God, and the
example of Christ.

Hannah More

Grant us grace, Almighty Father, so to pray
as to deserve to be heard.

Jane Austen

I know not by what methods rare,
But this I know, God answers prayer.
I know that He has given His Word,
Which tells me prayer is always heard,
And will be answered, soon or late.
And so I pray and calmly wait.

I know not if the blessing sought
Will come in just the way I thought;
But leave my prayers with Him alone,
Whose will is wiser than my own,
Assured that He will grant my quest,
Or send some answer far more blest.

Eliza M. Hickok — This I Know

He prayeth well, who loveth well
Both man and bird and beast.

He prayeth best who loveth best
All things both great and small;
For the dear God who loveth us,
He made and loveth all.

Samuel Taylor Coleridge

Praise

Love bade me welcome; yet my soul drew
  back,
  Guilty of dust and sin.
But quick-eyed Love, observing me grow slack
  From my first entrance in,
Drew nearer to me, sweetly questioning
  If I lacked anything.
A guest, I answered, worthy to be here.
  Love said, You shall be he.
I, the unkind, ungrateful? Ah, my dear,
  I cannot look on Thee.
Love took my hand, and smiling, did reply,
  Who made the eyes but I?
Truth, Lord, but I have marred them: let
  my shame
  Go where it doth deserve.
And know you not, says Love, who bore
  the blame?
  My dear, then I will serve.
You must sit down, says Love, and taste
  my meat.
  So I did sit and eat.

George Herbert — Love

Day by day,
Dear Lord, of thee three things I pray:
To see thee more clearly,
Love thee more dearly,
Follow thee more nearly,
  Day by day. Amen.

St. Richard of Chichester

We may not climb the heavenly steeps
  To bring the Lord Christ down;
In vain we search the lowest deeps,
  For Him no depths can drown.

But warm, sweet tender, even yet
  A present help is He;
And faith has still its Olivet,
  And love is Galilee.

O Lord and Master of us all,
  Whate'er our name or sign,
We own Thy sway, we hear Thy call,
  We test our lives by Thine!

John Greenleaf Whittier

All in the April evening,
April airs were abroad,
The sheep with their little lambs
Passed me by on the road.

The sheep with their little lambs
Passed me by on the road;
All in the April evening
I thought on the Lamb of God.

Up in the blue, blue mountains
Dewy pastures are sweet,
Rest for the little bodies,
Rest for the little feet.

But for the Lamb of God,
Up on the hill-top green,
Only a cross of shame,
Two stark crosses between.

All in the April evening,
April airs were abroad,
I saw the sheep with their lambs
And thought on the Lamb of God.

Katharine Tynan — Sheep and Lambs

153

I bind unto myself to-day
    The strong Name of the Trinity,
By invocation of the same,
    The Three in One, and One in Three.
Christ be with me, Christ within me,
    Christ behind me, Christ before me,
Christ beside me, Christ to win me,
    Christ to comfort and restore me,
Christ beneath me, Christ above me,
    Christ in quiet, Christ in danger,
Christ in hearts of all that love me,
    Christ in mouth of friend and stranger.
I bind unto myself the Name,
    The strong Name of the Trinity;
By invocation of the same,
    The Three in One, and One in Three.
Of whom all nature hath creation;
    Eternal Father, Spirit, Word:
Praise to the Lord of my salvation,
    Salvation is of Christ the Lord. Amen.

St. Patrick

O Christ who holds the open gate,
O Christ who drives the furrow straight,
O Christ, the plough, O Christ, the laughter
Of holy white birds, flying after.
Lo, all my heart's field red and torn,
And Thou wilt bring the young green corn
The young green corn divinely springing
The young green corn for ever singing;
The corn that makes the holy bread
By which the soul of man is fed,
The holy bread, the food unpriced,
Thy everlasting mercy, Christ

John Masefield — The Everlasting Mercy

He came all so still
    Where his mother lay
As dew in April
    That falleth on the grass.
He came all so still
    To his mother's bower
As dew in April
    That falleth on the flower.
He came all so still
    Where his mother lay
As dew in April
    That falleth on the spray.

Anonymous

In the cool of the evening, when the low
    sweet whispers waken,
    When the labourers turn them homeward,
        and the weary have their will,
When the censers of the roses o'er the
    forest-aisles are shaken,
    Is it but the wind that cometh o'er the
        far green hill?

For they say 'tis but the sunset winds that
    wander through the heather,
    Rustle all the meadow-grass and bend
        the dewy fern;
They say 'tis but the winds that bow the
    reeds in prayer together,
    And fill the shaken pools with fire along
        the shadowy burn.

In the beauty of the twilight, in the Garden
    that He loveth,
    They have veiled His lovely vesture with
        the darkness of a name!
Thro' His Garden, thro' His Garden it is
    but the wind that moveth,
    No more; but O, the miracle, the miracle
        is the same!

In the cool of the evening, when the sky is
    an old story
    Slowly dying, but remembered, ay, and
        loved with passion still,
Hush! . . . the fringes of His garment, in the
    fading golden glory,
    Softly rustling as He cometh o'er the far
        green hill.

Alfred Noyes — In The Cool of The Evening

Christ took our nature on Him, not that He
'Bove all else loved it for its purity;
No — He dressed Him in our human trim
    because
Our flesh stood most in need of Him.

Robert Herrick

Our Little Lord, we give Thee praise
That Thou hast deigned to take our ways,
Born of a maid, a man to be,
And all the angels sing to Thee.

Martin Luther

Master, they say that when I seem
  To be in speech with you,
Since you make no replies, it's all a dream
  — One talker, aping two.

They are half right, but not as they
  Imagine; rather I
Seek in myself the things I meant to say,
  And lo; the wells are dry.

Then, seeing me empty, you forsake
  The listener's role, and through
My dead lips breathe and into utterance wake
  The thoughts I never knew.

And thus you neither need reply
  Nor can; thus, while we seem
Two talking, Thou art One forever, and I
  No dreamer, but thy dream.

                        C. S. Lewis

What can I give him,
Poor as I am?
If I were a shepherd
I would bring a lamb,

If I were a Wise Man
I would do my part, —
Yet what I can I give Him,
Give Him my heart.

             Christina Rossetti

Little Lamb, who made thee?
Dost thou know who made thee?
Little Lamb, I'll tell thee;
Little Lamb, I'll tell thee;

He is calléd by thy name,
For he calls himself a Lamb.
He is meek and He is mild;
He came a little child.

I a child, and thou a lamb,
We are calléd by His name.
Little Lamb, God bless thee!
Little Lamb, God bless thee!

          William Blake — The Lamb

Jesus, meek and gentle,
  Son of God most high,
Gracious, loving Saviour,
  Hear thy children's cry.

              G. R. Prynne

First friend He was; best friend He is; all
times will try Him true.

           Robert Southwell

Strong Son of God, immortal Love,
Whom we, that have not seen thy face,
By faith, and faith alone, embrace,
Believing where we cannot prove.

         Alfred, Lord Tennyson

Go on your way in peace.
Be of good courage.
Hold fast that which is good.
Render to no man evil for evil.
Strengthen the fainthearted.
Support the weak.
Help and cheer the sick.
Honor all men.
Love and serve the Lord.
May the blessing of God be upon you
  and remain with you forever.

  Gloucester Cathedral — Benediction

155

Index of Authors

157

Topic Index

Acknowledgments

The editor and the publisher have made every effort to trace the ownership of all copyrighted material and to secure permission from copyright holders of such material. In the event of any question arising as to the use of any material the publisher and editor, while expressing regret for inadvertent error, will be pleased to make the necessary corrections in future printings. Thanks are due to the following authors, publishers, publications and agents for permission to use the material indicated.

ABINGDON PRESS, for extracts from *Lift Up Your Hearts* by Walter Russell Bowie, copyright © 1939, 1956 by Pierce and Washabaugh; for "November" from *Too Busy Not To Pray* by Jo Carr and Imogene Sorley, copyright © 1966 by Abingdon Press.

GEORGE ALLEN & UNWIN LTD., for excerpts from *Memoirs of Childhood and Youth* by Albert Schweitzer.

ANGUS & ROBERTSON (UK) LTD., for "Egrets" from *Birds* by Judith Wright.

ASSOCIATION PRESS, for excerpt from *Every Occupation a Christian Calling* by John Oliver Nelson.

BARNES & NOBLE BOOKS, for "To His Wife" by Ausonius from *Medieval Latin Lyrics* translated by Helen Waddell.

BARRIE & JENKINS PUBLISHERS for selection from *Green Fingers* by Reginald Arkell.

ADAM AND CHARLES BLACK, for extracts from *Philosophy of Civilization* by Albert Schweitzer.

BLACKIE & SON LTD., for "Swift Things Are Beautiful" from *Away Goes Sally* by Elizabeth Coatsworth.

THE BODLEY HEAD LTD., for selections from *Collected Poems of A. C. Benson.*

ELLA LYMAN CABOT TRUST, for excerpts from *The Meaning of Right and Wrong* by Richard C. Cabot.

CHATTO & WINDUS LTD., for extract from *Remembrance of Things Past* by Marcel Proust, translated by C. K. Scott Moncrieff.

THE CHURCH HYMNAL CORPORATION for verses from hymns by F. B. Tucker and E. I. Tupper.

CONSTABLE & COMPANY LTD., for "To His Wife" by Ausonius, from *Medieval Latin Lyrics* translated by Helen Waddell.

COWARD, McCANN & GEOGHEGAN, INC., for excerpts from *The White Cliffs* by Alice Duer Miller, copyright 1940 by Alice Duer Miller, renewed; for excerpts from "Caedmon's Hymn" from *A Diary of Prayer* by Elizabeth Goudge, copyright © 1966 by Elizabeth Goudge.

CRESCENDO PUBLISHING CO., for "Perfect House", from *Of Bitter Grapes* by Emery Petho.

REID CROWELL for "Good Books" by Grace Noll Crowell.

EDWARD J. DIETRICH for "A Little Song of Life" by Lizette Woodworth Reese, published by Holt, Rinehart and Winston, Inc.

DODD, MEAD & COMPANY, INC., for "A Vagabond Song" and excerpt from "Vestigia" from *Bliss Carman's Poems,* copyright 1931 by Dodd, Mead & Company, Inc.; for excerpt from "The House of Christmas" from *The Collected Poems of G. K. Chesterton,* copyright 1932 by Dodd, Mead & Company, Inc., renewed 1960 by Oliver Chesterton; for "Two Sewing" from *Curtains* by Hazel Hall, copyright 1921 by Dodd, Mead & Company, Inc., renewed 1949 by Ruth Hall; for "I Meant to Do My Work Today" from *The Lonely Dancer* by Richard LeGallienne, copyright 1913 by Dodd, Mead & Company, Inc., renewed 1941 by Richard LeGallienne.

DOUBLEDAY & COMPANY INC., for "October" from *Gay Go Up* by Rose Fyleman; for excerpts from *Great Possessions* by David Grayson; for selections from *Midstream* and *The Story of My Life* by Helen Keller; for "The Bridge" by Leopold Staff from *Postwar Polish Poetry* selected and translated by Czeslaw Milosz, copyright © by Czeslaw Milosz.

CONSTANCE GARLAND DOYLE and ISABEL GARLAND LORD, for "Do You Fear the Wind" and "My Prairies" by Hamlin Garland.

THEODORA DUNKERLEY, for selections from *Selected Poems* of John Oxenham, and "The Little Poem of Life" from *Bees in Amber* by John Oxenham.

E. P. DUTTON & CO., INC., for excerpt from *Raccoons Are the Brightest People* by Sterling North, copyright © 1966 by Sterling North; for excerpt from *The Temple* by W. E. Orchard. Copyright 1918 by E. P. Dutton & Co., renewed 1946 by W. E. Orchard.

WM. B. EERMANS PUBLISHING Co., for selection by Harold Kohn.

NORMA MILLAY ELLIS, for "God's World" from *Collected Poems* of Edna St. Vincent Millay, copyright 1917, 1945 by Edna St. Vincent Millay.

FIRST PENNSYLVANIA BANK for "Per Aspera", and "Narrow Window", by Florence Earl Coates.

BERNICE WILLIAMS FOLEY, for "The Friend Who Just Stands By" and "House of Happiness", by B. Y. Williams.

GIBSON GREETING CARDS, INC., for "In The Words of That Beautiful Vow" and "True Love" by Helen Farries.

MICHAEL GIBSON for "Marriage" by Wilfred Wilson Gibson.

MRS. NICOLETE GRAY and THE SOCIETY OF AUTHORS, on behalf of the Laurence Binyon Estate, for extract from "Little Hands" by Laurence Binyon.

MRS. ARTHUR GUITERMAN, for "The Coming of the Trees" from *Song and Laughter;* "Contentment" from *Brave Laughter,* and "Hills" from *Death and General Putnam,* all by Arthur Guiterman, originally published by E. P. Dutton & Co., Inc., copyrights renewed by Vida Lindo Guiterman.

HARCOURT BRACE JOVANOVICH, INC., for "Courage" from *Last Flight* by Amelia Earhart, copyright 1937 by George Palmer Putnam, copyright 1965 by Mrs. George Palmer Putnam; for excerpts from *Modern Man In Search of a Soul* by Carl G. Jung; for "Prayer" from *Poems* by C. S. Lewis, edited by Walter Hooper, copyright © 1964 by the Estate of C. S. Lewis; for selection from *Bring Me a Unicorn* by Anne Morrow Lindbergh, copyright © 1972 by Harcourt Brace Jovanovich, Inc.; for excerpt from *The Living Seed* by John Moffitt, copyright © 1961 by John Moffitt; for excerpts from *Wind, Sand and Stars* by Antoine de Saint-Exupery.

HARPER & ROW, PUBLISHERS, INC., for "A Blackbird Suddenly" from *Sunrise Trumpets* by Joseph Auslander, copyright 1924 by Harper & Row, Publishers, Inc., renewed 1952 by Joseph Auslander; for "Because of Thy Great Bounty" and "Wait" by Grace Noll Crowell, copyright 1936 by Harper & Row, Publishers, Inc., renewed 1964 by Grace Noll Crowell; "The Day" by Grace Noll Crowell, copyright 1928, 1934 by Harper & Row, Publishers, Inc., renewed 1956, 1962 by Grace Noll Crowell; "Silver Poplars" by Grace Noll Crowell, copyright 1934 by Grace Noll Crowell; "Keep Some Green Memory Alive" by Grace Noll Crowell, copyright 1950 by Harper & Row, Publishers, Inc., all from *Poems of Inspiration and Courage* by Grace Noll Crowell; "I Have Found Such Joy" by Grace Noll Crowell, copyright 1936 by Harper & Row, Publishers, Inc., renewed 1964 by Grace Noll Crowell, from *Light of the Years* by Grace Noll Crowell; for "Spires" from *This Golden Summit* by Grace Noll Crowell, copyright 1937 by Harper & Row, Publishers, Inc.; "Crab Apple Tree in Blossom" from *Bright Harvest* by Grace Noll Crowell, copyright 1952 by Harper & Row, Publishers, Inc.; for extract from *Ethics* (Revised Edition) by Radoslav A. Tsanoff (1955); for extract from *Religious Perplexities* by L. P. Jacks (1951); extracts from *You Can't Go Home Again* by Thomas Wolfe (1934); for "I Have A Rendezvous with Life" from *Caroling Dusk:* An Anthology of Verse by Negro Poets edited by Countee Cullen, copyright 1927 by Harper & Row, Publishers, Inc., renewed 1955 by Ida M. Cullen; for extract from *The Sense of Wonder* by Rachel Carson, copyright © 1956 by Rachel Carson.

A. M. HEATH & COMPANY LTD. on behalf of the Estate of the late A. E., for extracts from the *Selected Works of George William Russell (A. E.).*

WILLIAM HEINEMANN LTD., for excerpts from *The Brothers Karamazov* by Fyodor Dostoevsky, translated by Constance Garnett.

DR. KENNETH L. HOLLENBECK for "Hold Fast Your Dreams" by Louise Driscoll.

HOLT, RINEHART AND WINSTON, for excerpt from *The Decline and Fall of Practically Everybody* by Will Cuppy. Edited by Fred Feldkamp. Copyright 1950 by Fred Feldkamp; for excerpt from "Two Tramps in Mud Time", "The Road Not Taken", "Stopping by Woods on a Snowy Evening", "A Prayer in Spring", and "The Gift Outright" from *The Poetry* of *Robert Frost,* edited by Edward Connery Lathem, copyright 1916, 1923, 1934, © 1969 by Holt, Rinehart and Winston; copyright 1936, 1942, 1944, 1951, © 1962 by Robert Frost; copyright © 1964, 1970 by Lesley Frost Ballantine; for excerpt from *How To Be Happy Though Human* by W. Beran Wolfe, copyright 1931 by W. Beran Wolfe. Copyright © 1959 by Florence Wolfe; for "Loveliest of trees, the cherry now" from "A Shropshire Lad" (Authorised Edition) from The Collected Poems of A. E. Housman, copyright 1939, 1940 © 1965 by Holt, Rinehart and Winston, Inc., copyright 1967, 1968 by Robert E. Symons.

THE HORN BOOK, INC., for excerpt by Lois Lenski, from *Newbery and Caldecott Books, 1922-1955.*

HOUGHTON MIFFLIN COMPANY for extracts from the works of John Burroughs; for "The Sandpiper" by Celia Thaxter, and for extracts from the works of Ralph Waldo Emerson, Oliver Wendell Holmes, Henry Wadsworth Longfellow, James Russell Lowell, Henry David Thoreau, and John Greenleaf Whittier.

I. H. T. CORPORATION for "High Flight" by John Gillespie Magee, Jr. © New York Herald Tribune.

ALFRED A. KNOPF, INC., for "Dreams" and "Youth" from *The Dream Keeper and Other Poems* by Langston Hughes, copyright 1932 by Alfred A. Knopf, Inc.; renewed 1960 by Langston Hughes; for "Autumn Sonnets" #7, by Robert Nathan, copyright 1950 by Robert Nathan, and "Watch, America" by Robert Nathan, copyright 1945, 1950 by Robert Nathan, both from *The Green Leaf: The Collected Poems of Robert Nathan;* for "Old Friendship" and excerpt from "From the Mountains" from *Leaves in Windy Weather* by Eunice Tietjens, copyright 1929 by Alfred A. Knopf, Inc., renewed 1957 by Cloyd Head; for excerpt from *The Prophet* by Kahlil Gibran, copyright 1923 by Kahlil Gibran, renewal copyright 1951 by Administrators C.T.A. of Kahlil Gibran Estate and Mary G. Gibran.

LIN YUTANG for excerpt from *My Country and My People.*

J. B. LIPPINCOTT COMPANY, for "A Kitten" from *Poems for Children* by Eleanor Farjeon, copyright 1933, © renewed 1961 by Eleanor Farjeon, from *Poems for Children* copyright 1951 by Eleanor Farjeon; for excerpt from *Mince Pie,* by Christopher Morley, copyright 1919, renewed 1947 by Christopher Morley; for selections from *Songs for a Little House* by Christopher Morley, copyright 1917, renewed 1947 by Christopher Morley; for selections from *Collected Poems In One Volume* by Alfred Noyes, copyright 1906, renewed 1934 by Alfred Noyes.

THE LITERARY TRUSTEES OF WALTER DE LA MARE, and THE SOCIETY OF AUTHORS as their representative, for "Music" by Walter de la Mare.

LITTLE, BROWN AND COMPANY, for selections from *The Complete Poems of Emily Dickinson.*

LIVERIGHT, for excerpt from *The Story of Mankind* by Hendrik Willem van Loon, copyright 1921, 1926 by Boni & Liveright, Inc., copyright renewed 1948 by Helen C. van Loon, copyright renewed 1954 by Liveright Publishing Corporation, copyright © by Henry B. van Loon and Gerard W. van Loon.

MACMILLAN PUBLISHING COMPANY, INC., for "Spray" and "The Coin" from *Collected Poems* by Sara Teasdale, copyright 1920 by Macmillan Publishing Co., Inc., renewed 1948 by Mamie T. Wheless; for "Night" from *Collected Poems* by Sara Teasdale, copyright 1930 by Sara Teasdale, renewed 1958 by Guaranty Trust Company of New York, Executor; for "Grace Before Sleep" from *Collected Poems* by Sara Teasdale, copyright 1933 by Macmillan Publishing Co., Inc., renewed 1961 by Guaranty Trust Company of New York, Executor; for "Joy" from *Collected Poems* by Sara Teasdale, copyright 1915 by Macmillan Publishing Co., Inc., renewed 1943 by Mamie T. Wheless; for "Barter" from *Collected Poems* by Sara Teasdale, copyright 1917 by Macmillan Publishing Co., Inc., renewed 1945 by Mamie T. Wheless; for "The Secret Heart" from *Collected Poems* by Robert P. Tristram Coffin, copyright 1935 by Macmillan Publishing Co., Inc., renewed 1963 by Margaret Coffin Halvosa; for song from "Fruit-Gathering" from *Collected Poems and Plays* by Rabindranath Tagore, copyright 1916 by Macmillan Publishing Co., Inc., renewed 1944 by Rabindranath Tagore; for "White Fields" from *Collected Poems* by James Stephens, copyright 1915 by Macmillan Publishing Co., Inc., renewed 1943 by James Stephens; for excerpt from "The Everlasting Mercy", "Sea Fever" and "Laugh and Be Merry" from *Poems* by John Masefield, copyright 1912 by Macmillan Publishing Co., Inc., renewed 1940 by John Masefield; for "Swift Things Are Beautiful" from *Away Goes Sally* by Elizabeth Coatsworth, copyright 1934 by Macmillan Publishing Co., Inc., renewed 1962 by Elizabeth Coatsworth Beston; for excerpts from *Memoirs of Childhood and Youth* and *Philosophy of Civilization,* both by Albert Schweitzer; for excerpt from *Art of Worldly Wisdom* by Baltasar Gracián, translated by Joseph Jacobs; for excerpt from *Rufus Jones Speaks To Our Time,* edited by Harry Emerson Fosdick, copyright 1951 by Macmillan Publishing Co., Inc.; excerpt from *Power To Become* by Lewis L. Dunnington, copyright © 1956 by Macmillan Publishing Co., Inc.

THE MACMILLAN COMPANY OF CANADA LIMITED, for "White Fields" from *Collected Poems* by James Stephens, reprinted by permission of Mrs. Iris Wise.

MACMILLAN LONDON & BASINGSTOKE for "White Fields" from *Collected Poems* by James Stephens, reprinted by permission of Mrs. Iris Wise; and Trustees of the Tagore Estate for "Fruit Gathering" by Rabindranath Tagore.

McCALL's for "The Borrowers" by Elaine V. Emans (November 1962 issue) and "Thought for Thanksgiving" by Barbara Parsons Hildreth (November 1963 issue).

McGRAW-HILL BOOK COMPANY for excerpt from *The Arts of Leisure* by Marjorie Bristow Greenbie, copyright 1935 by Marjorie Bristow Greenbie; for excerpts from *The Power of Positive Living* by Douglas Ellsworth Lurton, copyright © 1950 by McGraw-Hill Book Company.

MRS. VIRGIL MARKHAM for "A Prayer", "Imperious Love", "Preparedness", "Victory in Defeat", "Earth Is Enough", "The Task That Is Given You", "Imbrothered", and "Golden Rule" all by Edwin Markham.

MRS. GEORGE JEAN NATHAN for excerpt from *Testament of a Critic* by George Jean Nathan.

THE NEW YORK TIMES for "A Prayer for Thanksgiving" by Joseph Auslander, copyright © 1947 by The New York Times Company.

NRTA JOURNAL AND NELL CRAVENS, for "Triumph" by Nell Cravens, copyright 1968 by the National Retired Teachers Association.

HAROLD OBER ASSOCIATES, INC., for "I Dream a World" by Langston Hughes, copyright 1945 by Langston Hughes, from *American Negro Poetry;* for "A Kitten" from *Over the Garden Wall* by Eleanor Farjeon, copyright 1933 by Eleanor Farjeon, renewed 1961.

PHILOSOPHICAL LIBRARY for excerpt from *The World as I See It* by Albert Einstein; for excerpt from *A Dictionary of Thoughts* by Dagobert D. Runes.

G. P. PUTNAM'S SONS, for excerpts from *Alone* by Richard E. Byrd, copyright 1938 by Richard E. Byrd, renewed.

RANDOM HOUSE, INC., for excerpt from *Remembrance of Things Past* by Marcel Proust, translated by C. K. Scott Moncrieff, copyright 1928 and renewed 1956 by Modern Library Inc.

THE READER'S DIGEST, for excerpt from *Prayer Is Power* by Alexis Carrel, M.D., The Reader's Digest, March 1941, copyright 1941 by The Reader's Digest Assn., Inc.

HENRY REGNERY COMPANY, for poems from *Collected Verse of Edgar Guest,* copyright 1934 by the Reilly & Lee Co., Chicago.

REVIEW AND HERALD PUBLISHING ASSOCIATION, for excerpt from *I Love Books* by John D. Snider.

CHARLES SCRIBNER'S SONS, for excerpts from *Thoughts for Everyday Living* by Maltbie D. Babcock; for selection from *Diary of Private Prayer* by John Baillie; for selection from *Wind in the Willows* by Kenneth Grahame; for excerpt from *Human Nature in the Bible* by William Lyons Phelps; for "Credo" from *Children of the Night* by Edwin Arlington Robinson; for "O World" from *Poems of George Santayana;* for selections from *Music and Other Poems* by Henry Van Dyke and from *Collected Poems of Henry Van Dyke.*

THE SOCIETY OF AUTHORS as the literary representative of the Estate of A. E. Housman, and Jonathan Cape Ltd., as publishers of A. E. Housman's *Complete Poems* for "Loveliest of Trees, the cherry now"; The Society of Authors on behalf of the Bernard Shaw Estate; The Society of Authors as the literary representative of the Estate of John Masefield for "Laugh and Be Merry", "Sea Fever", and extracts from "The Everlasting Mercy", all by John Masefield; The Society of Authors and MISS PAMELA HINKSON for "Sheep and Lambs" by Katharine Tynan.

A. M. SULLIVAN, for "Measurement" from *Selected Lyrics and Sonnets* by A. M. Sullivan, © copyright by A. M. Sullivan.

GILBERT THOMAS for "The Cup of Happiness".

THE UNITED METHODIST PUBLISHING HOUSE, for "Discovery" by Elaine V. Emans, reprinted from *Together* magazine, May, 1968, copyright © 1968 by The United Methodist Publishing House; for "The Long Remembered" by Annabelle Stewart Altwater, reprinted from *Mature Years,* Fall, 1967, copyright © by Graded Press.

THE VIKING PRESS, INC., for "Prayer of the Ox" from *Prayers from the Ark* by Carmen Bernos de Gasztold, translated by Rumer Godden, copyright © 1962 by Rumer Godden.

FREDERICK WARNE & CO., for excerpt from *The Journal of Beatrix Potter,* transcribed by Leslie Linder, copyright © Frederick Warne & Co., Ltd. 1966.

A. P. WATT & SON, for excerpts from the prose writings by G. K. Chesterton.

G. R. WELCH COMPANY LIMITED, for excerpt from *Meditation for Teachers and Parents* by Minton Johnston.

WESLEYAN UNIVERSITY PRESS, for "Early Supper" from *Light and Dark* by Barbara Howes, copyright © 1959 by Barbara Howes. "Early Supper" first appeared in the New Yorker.

YALE UNIVERSITY PRESS for "Courage" from *Burning Bush* by Karle Wilson Baker; for "Good Company" from *Blue Smoke* by Karle Wilson Baker; for "Comparison" from *Songs for Parents* by John Farrar.